M000289988

Challenging the Secular State

Published with the support of the
School of Pacific and Asian Studies,
University of Hawai'i

CHALLENGING
the Secular State

The Islamization of Law in Modern Indonesia

Arskal Salim

University of Hawai'i Press

Honolulu

13 12 11 10 09 08   6 5 4 3 2 1

Library of Congress Cataloging-in-Publication Data

Salim, Arskal.
    Challenging the secular state : the Islamization of law
in modern Indonesia / Arskal Salim.
        p. cm.
    Includes bibliographical references and index.
    ISBN 978-0-8248-3237-7 (hardcover : alk. paper)
    1. Law—Indonesia. 2. Constitutional law—Indonesia.
3. Islamic law—Indonesia. 4. Islam and state—Indonesia.
I. Title.
    KNW469.S25 2009
    340.5'909598—dc22

                                        2008014910

Designed by University of Hawai'i Press Production Staff

Printed by The Maple-Vail Book Manufacturing Group

To my wife and children

Maya

Akmal

Maykal

Contents

V: The Localization of *Shari'a* in Aceh

Acknowledgments

Working simultaneously on three different sociolegal case studies (constitutional amendment, *zakat* legislation, and religious law autonomy in Aceh) was rarely an easy task. Many people have helped me in many different ways during this mission and I would like here to express my gratitude to them. Of course, it is impossible to mention them all in the limited space available. So if your name does not appear, be assured that my gratitude is no less than for those who are listed below.

This work could not have been accomplished without assistance I received from Tim Lindsey (Faculty of Law, the University of Melbourne, Australia), whose help, stimulating suggestions, and encouragement helped me in writing the earlier draft. I would also like to gratefully acknowledge the persistent support I received from Merle C. Ricklefs, who provided me with useful suggestions on how to deal with the complexities of the early process of publication, and for his constructive comments on a particular part of the final version of the manuscript.

The fieldwork that led to this book was funded by various institutions including AusAID/ADS; Melbourne Abroad Travel Scholarship; MIALS Fieldwork/ Travel Grants; Asian Muslim Action Network (AMAN) Research Fellowship; and Faculty of Law Research Support Funds. I thank them all for their generous support. I also extend my gratitude to my home institution, Syarif Hidayatullah State Islamic University (UIN), Jakarta, Indonesia, for encouragement and invaluable support over the past few years during my PhD study.

I am very grateful for a research fellowship from the Max Planck Institute for Social Anthropology at Halle, Germany, which enabled me to revise the manuscript and for financial support to publish this work. A number of editors at the University of Hawai'i Press—Pamela Kelley, Ann Ludeman, and Drew Bryan— have helped me in the preparation of this book. Their professional assistance is deeply appreciated and gladly acknowledged.

My very special thanks are due to my wife, Maya, whose love, patience, and encouragement enabled me to complete this project. My children, Akmal and Maykal, also deserve my very special thanks. They both have endured and accepted the fact that their father had to leave them frequently. I hope one day they will understand and write a book as well. The chain of my gratitude would be certainly incomplete if I did not include my thanks to the Causer of this chain, the Prime Mover, in Aristotle's words. My sincere praise *(alhamdulillah al-rabb al-'alamin)* is due to Him for guiding this humble being.

Abbreviations

BAZ	Badan Amil Zakat (government-sponsored agency for *zakat* management)
BAZIS	Badan Amil Zakat, Infak dan Sedekah (government-sponsored agency for *zakat,* alms, and donation management)
BAZNAS	Badan Amil Zakat Nasional (National Zakat Agency)
BPUPKI	Badan Penyelidik Usaha Persiapan Kemerdekaan Indonesia (Investigatory Committee for Independence of Indonesia)
BRR	Badan Rehabilitasi dan Rekonstruksi (Board for Rehabilitation and Reconstruction)
DDII	Dewan Dakwah Islamiyah Indonesia (Council of Islamic Propagation of Indonesia)
DIRJEN	Direktorat Jenderal (General Directorate)
DKI Jakarta	Daerah Khusus Istimewa Jakarta (Special Region of Jakarta)
DOM	Daerah Operasi Militer (Military Operation Zone)
DPA	Dewan Pertimbangan Agung (Supreme Advisory Council)
DPR	Dewan Perwakilan Rakyat (House of People's Representatives or National Legislature)
DPRD	Dewan Perwakilan Rakyat Daerah (legislature at provincial or district level)
DPRGR	Dewan Perwakilan Rakyat Gotong Royong (National Legislature in early years of the New Order regime)
DPU	Dewan Paripurna Ulama (Plenary Board of Ulama)
DSI	Dinas Syariat Islam (Office of Shari'a in Aceh)
F-ABRI	Fraksi Angkatan Bersenjata Republik Indonesia (faction that represents armed forces)
F-KKI	Fraksi Kesatuan dan Keadilan Indonesia (faction of several tiny nationalist parties)
F-KP	Fraksi Karya Pembangunan (faction of Golkar Party during the New Order period)
FOZ	Forum Zakat (association of *zakat* agencies)
FPI	Front Pembela Islam (Defender Front of Islam)
F-PBB	Fraksi Partai Bulan Bintang (faction of Crescent Moon Star Party)

F-PDKB	Fraksi Partai Demokrasi Kasih Bangsa (faction of a Christian party)
F-PDU	Fraksi Perserikatan Daulatul Ummat (faction of several tiny Islamic parties)
F-PG	Fraksi Partai Golkar (faction of Golkar party in the post–New Order era)
F-PKB	Fraksi Partai Kebangkitan Bangsa (faction of National Awakening Party)
F-PP	Fraksi Persatuan Pembangunan (faction of United Development Party during the New Order regime)
F-PPP	Fraksi Partai Persatuan Pembangunan (faction of United Development Party in the post–New Order era)
F-Reformasi	Fraksi Reformasi (faction that consisted of PAN (National Mandate Party) and PK (Justice Party))
F-TNI/POLRI	Fraksi Tentara Nasional Indonesia/Polisi Republik Indonesia (faction of armed and police forces)
F-UD	Fraksi Utusan Daerah (faction of representatives of regions)
F-UG	Fraksi Utusan Golongan (faction of interest groups representatives)
GAM	Gerakan Aceh Merdeka (Free Aceh Movement)
GBHN	Garis Besar Haluan Negara (Broad Outlines of National Policy). During the New Order period, it was always a part of MPR's decrees, which placed it third in the rank of Indonesian legal hierarchy after Pancasila and the 1945 constitution.
GOLKAR	Golongan Karya (Functional Groups)
HUDA	Himpunan *Ulama Dayah* Aceh (Association of Dayah Ulama of Aceh)
IAIN	Institut Agama Islam Negeri (State Institute for Islamic Studies)
INPRES	Instruksi Presiden (presidential instruction)
KEPPRES	Keputusan Presiden (presidential decree)
KMA	Keputusan Menteri Agama (decree of minister of religious affairs)
KNIP	Komite Nasional Indonesia Pusat (Central National Committee of Indonesia)
KORPRI	Korps Pegawai Republik Indonesia (Corps of Indonesian State Employees)
LAZ	Lembaga Amil Zakat (non-state-sponsored *zakat* agency)
MMI	Majelis Mujahidin Indonesia (Indonesian Council of Muslim Fighters)
MORA	Ministry of Religious Affairs

MPR	Majelis Permusyawaratan Rakyat (People's Consultative Assembly)
MPRS	Majelis Permusyawaratan Rakyat Sementara (Provisional People's Consultative Assembly)
MPU	Majelis Permusyawaratan Ulama (Consultative Council of Ulama)
MUI	Majelis Ulama Indonesia (Council of Indonesian Ulama)
NAD	Nanggroe Aceh Darussalam
NGO	Non-government organization
NU	Nahdlatul Ulama
PAH I	Panitia Ad Hoc I (Ad Hoc Committee One)
PAN	Partai Amanat Nasional (National Mandate Party)
PARMUSI	Partai Muslimin Indonesia (Indonesian Muslims Party)
PDI-P	Partai Demokrasi Indonesia Perjuangan (Indonesia's Struggle Democratic Party)
PDR	Partai Daulat Rakyat (People Sovereignty Party)
Perda	Peraturan Daerah (regional regulation)
Persis	Persatuan Islam (Union of Islam)
PERTI	Persatuan Tarbiyah Islamiyah (United Islamic Education)
Pilkada	Pemilihan Kepala Daerah (election of regional leaders)
PIRAC	Public Interest Research and Advocacy Center
PK	Partai Keadilan (Justice Party)
PK(S)	Partai Keadilan Sejahtera (Prosperous Justice Party)
PKI	Partai Komunis Indonesia (Indonesian Communist Party)
PKPU	Pos Keadilan Peduli Ummat (Justice Post of Muslim Care)
PKU	Partai Kebangkitan Umat (Muslim Community Awakening Party)
PNI	Partai Nasional Indonesia (Indonesian National Party)
PNU	Partai Nahdlatul Umma (Muslim Community Revival Party)
PP	Peraturan Pemerintah (government regulation)
PPKI	Panitia Persiapan Kemerdekaan Indonesia (Preparatory Committee for Independence of Indonesia)
PPP	Partai Persatuan Pembangunan (United Development Party)
PSI	Partai Sosialis Indonesia (Indonesia Socialist Party)
PSII	Partai Sarekat Islam Indonesia (Indonesian Islamic Union Party)
PUSA	Persatuan Ulama Seluruh Aceh (All-Aceh Association of Ulama)
RUU	Rancangan Undang-Undang (bill of statute)
Sekjen	Sekretaris Jenderal (general secretary)

Sekneg	Sekretariat Negara (State Secretariat)
SIRA	Sentral Informasi Referendum Aceh (Information Center for Referendum of Aceh)
UIN	Universitas Islam Negeri (State Islamic University)
UPZ	Unit Pengumpulan Zakat (Zakat Collection Unit)
UDHR	Universal Declaration of Human Rights
UIDHR	Universal Islamic Declaration of Human Rights
UU	Undang-Undang (statute)
UUD	Undang-Undang Dasar (constitution)
YABMP	Yayasan Amal Bakti Muslim Pancasila (Pancasila Muslim Charity Services Foundation)
ZIS	Zakat Infak Shadaqah (*zakat,* alms, and donation)

Introduction

The relationship between religion and law has been a recurring theme in the history of the major monotheistic faiths. Judaism and Islam, in particular, have always considered law inseparable from religion and hold God to be the one and the only legitimate lawmaker. Since the rise of the modern nation-state in the nineteenth century, however, the supremacy of holy laws has been endlessly challenged. There has been a growing debate about whether the law of a state should remain closely related to religion or be wholly detached from it. In many Muslim countries and in the Jewish state of Israel, religious leaders are attempting to realize the former option; that is, to give religious law status as the law of the land.[1]

In Indonesia, home to more Muslims than any other nation in the world, attempts to give religious law (*shari'a*) a constitutional status have been undertaken several times since the nation's independence on 17 August 1945. Questions of the formal implementation of *shari'a* first appeared in the early days of Indonesian independence when some Muslim leaders (in June–August 1945) struggled to introduce the so-called *Piagam Jakarta* into the 1945 constitution. The *Piagam Jakarta*, or the Jakarta Charter, was actually the first draft of the preamble to that constitution and it contained what has since become a well-known seven-word phrase in Indonesia: *dengan kewajiban menjalankan syariat Islam bagi pemeluknya* [with the obligation of carrying out Islamic *shari'a* for its adherents]. This phrase, famous today simply as the 'seven words,' was eventually withdrawn from the final draft of the preamble on 18 August 1945.[2] Since then, however, the status of the seven words has been a constantly controversial issue.

One example of how the Jakarta Charter has remained an ongoing issue in Indonesian politics is the struggle that arose during the debates over the most appropriate ideology for the Indonesian state during sessions of the Constituent Assembly from 1957 to 1959. However, for those expecting a profound role for Islam in the modern nation-state, the struggle ended in failure. A decade later, the call for *shari'a* re-emerged in the Provisional People's Consultative Assembly (MPRS) sessions in 1966–1968, only to fail again. Although calls for implementation of *shari'a* rules were unsuccessful on both these occasions, they certainly did not end in the late 1960s. There have been four discernible Muslim constituencies demanding it in the aftermath of the New Order regime (1966–1998), namely Islamic political parties, certain regions with a majority of Muslim inhabitants, Muslim militant groups, and sections of the Islamic print media. Even though the People's Consultative Assembly (MPR) in its annual session in 2002 decided not to amend the 1945 constitution to give *shari'a* constitutional status, calls for the formal recognition of *shari'a* continue.

This book examines the interaction between *shari'a* and the nation-state and the profound and ongoing legal political dissonances that characterize this interaction. These dissonances can be traced back to the fact that the character of *shari'a* in the history of Islam has changed over the centuries and that the understanding of the role of the state is now fundamentally different from what it was at the time *shari'a* law developed in the seventh and eighth centuries.

This study of 'Islamization' focuses on the *shari'a* and the state laws of contemporary Indonesia and looks at the constitutionalization of *shari'a*, the nationalization of *shari'a*, and the localization of *shari'a* in Aceh. It argues that attempts to formally implement *shari'a* in Indonesia have always been marked by a tension between political aspirations of the proponents and the opponents of *shari'a* and by resistance from the secular state. The result has been that *shari'a* rules remains tightly confined in Indonesia.

Approach of the Study

As far as calls for the implementation of religious law in a modern nation-state are concerned, there are at least five perspectives.

First, judicial discourses related to the application of religious law can be seen as political expressions linked to the legitimization of either incumbent regimes or the religious opposition.[3] In the latter case, it is often suggested that calls for the implementation of religious law serve as a means of politicization and are often used as an ideological weapon to criticize the government (which, of course, has different political interests and religious goals).[4] In my view, to claim that calls for religious law result solely from the political activism of religious groups is superficial, as there is a whole range of motives (religious, psychological, and economic) that should also be taken into account. One must go beyond this purely political approach to examine what religious law really means for the individuals involved.

A second view is that religious revivalism,[5] or, more precisely, religious radicalism,[6] is the impetus behind the movement toward the application of religious law.[7] It has been observed that the emphasis upon morality and legal obedience is the main objective of religious revivalist movements. These movements strongly believe that a return to religious law is the panacea for all modern evils. Moreover, through the application of religious law, the religious revivalists seek to transform the present reality of the religious community (which is deemed to have deviated or gone astray) into something that aligns better with the original teachings of the religion. However, to explain the growing aspirations for the implementation of religious law solely through a framework of religious revivalism is, again, unsatisfactory, as the term 'revivalism' is a concept that has almost no boundaries. Indeed, movements of religious revivalism in the contemporary world may include either attempts to purify religious beliefs (*tawhid*)[8] or, as in Sufi movements, attempts to escape from the worldly non-transcendent state.[9]

The third explanation is that the current resurgence of support for religious law is a symptom of the emergence of so-called fundamentalist movements, observable especially in religions such as Judaism, Christianity, Islam, and Hinduism.[10] These fundamentalist movements often support the restoration of elements of the past to contemporary reality, including the reintroduction of religious law. In order to legally transform religious law from the sacred texts into the law of the state, these movements disavow any distinction between public and private life. Therefore the state's lack of concern for the implementation of religious law has been a rhetorical device of the fundamentalist opposition.[11] Additionally, governments' attempts to incorporate religious law into national legal systems have been regarded as a symptom of fundamentalism.[12] The problem with this argument is that it often fails to distinguish between government campaigns and popular demands for the official implementation of religious law. The latter cannot be easily explained within the framework of a fundamentalist movement as it is often motivated either by emotional or practical reasons.

The fourth view is that the implementation of religious law can be seen as part of the reassertion of the religious identity of the state or society. As several states define themselves religiously, for example the Jewish state of Israel or the Islamic states of Pakistan and Iran, some nationals of these states see the implementation of religious law in these countries as a logical consequence, even a necessity.[13] Likewise, it has been observed that the implementation of religious law is an essential expression of religious people.[14] Therefore, the call for the implementation of religious law has often been claimed as the legitimate collective right of religious people to self-determination in terms of their religious identity.[15] The difficulty with this approach is that it mainly focuses on the reactions of religious people to a potential threat to their religious identity and does not adequately consider the fact that religious law itself is not identical to state law. Indeed, for religious law to function as state law and to be applied by judicial bodies, intricate preconditions are required, and political or demographic identity alone is not sufficient.

The fifth perspective considers that implementation of religious law is not a goal in itself, but simply a means to religionize (Islamize or Judaize) the modern nation-state.[16] A more or less similar approach is the argument that the hallmark of an authentically religious state system is the implementation of religious law, and not any particular political order.[17]

My theoretical position in this book shares much with this last approach in that I will mainly focus on the recent attempts of either Indonesian Muslim groups or the government apparatus to make the modern state of Indonesia more Islamized. These Islamization attempts, as further theoretically elaborated in chapters 2, 3, and 5, are viewed as the continuation of an ongoing process of Islamization that has been in progress since the coming of Islam to Indonesia in the thirteenth century.[18]

This book seeks to explore legal and political dissonances that occur in the attempts at Islamization of the Indonesian legal system. What I mean here by the term 'dissonance' is a spectrum between mild tension in meanings on the one hand and a direct contradiction in terms on the other hand. It becomes an umbrella term to cover a large range of meanings such as 'inconsistency,' 'incongruity,' 'ambivalence,' 'ambiguity,' 'conflict,' 'contradiction,' 'disagreement,' 'tension,' and 'inappropriateness.' Instead of using one of these words, I choose the term 'dissonance' because it relates to the profound inconsistencies of both theoretical and practical nature in Indonesia's pluralistic society.

I propose in this book that there are at least two types of dissonance that would take place in the formal implementation of *shari'a*. First is dissonant constitutionality, which would take place if the constitution required the state to standardize a number of Islamic practices by prioritizing a particular interpretation over other various religious interpretations. This situation would create an ambiguity since an individual Muslim would not be permitted to subscribe to an interpretation that does not comply with the state's standard. The individual Muslim would no longer be free to exercise his or her religious liberty based on his or her own conviction, as guaranteed by the constitution. In addition, since the Indonesian constitution, for instance, grants religious rights to individuals, the official implementation of *shari'a* would lead to an inconsistent application of the constitution as it deals with citizens as different religious groups. The way Islamic parties struggled for amending Article 29 on Religion of the constitution, as will be seen in chapters 10 and 11, demonstrates this dissonance.

Second is dissonant legislation in the sense that the formal implementation of *shari'a* in a nation-state often produces tensions between different legal sovereignties, causes contradiction in its enactment, creates disagreement between national laws, raises conflict with higher laws, results in inappropriate legal drafting, leads to ambivalences in practice, and brings inequality between citizens. The discussion of complexities relating to the legislation of *zakat* in part IV and the formal imple-mentation of *shari'a* in Aceh, discussed in part V, clearly show this.

The latter type of dissonance emerges because of a dislocation in the minds of the proponents of the formal implementation of *shari'a* about the role of the state and the meaning of law in the era of the modern nation-state. There is a mistaken perception that the modern nation-state is similar to the premodern nation-state, where the religious law as well as the religious elite played a major role. This leads to the mistaken view that the religious elite would have legitimate power to enact the law of the land in accordance with religious injunctions.[19] These two types of states are different. Unlike the traditional state, the modern nation-state is com-plex, with constitutions, parliaments, supreme courts, and legislatures that act as rival institutions to the position of religious law and religious elite in a traditional state.

There is also confusion over the term 'religious law,' which indicates either the divine meaning given by God's revelation on the one hand and the worldly mean-ing expanded by human interpretation on the other hand. Therefore, when propo-nents of religious law raise their demand, it is actually a call for the implementation of the acquired meaning of the term in human religious thought. This has further raised the issue of whether God alone imposes obligations for Muslims through divine revelation, or if human beings also have an authority to create obligations that have divine character.

Organization of the Book

After describing various explanations for calls for the implementation of religious law (*shari'a*) in this introduction, part I will develop the theoretical framework of this book. By explaining various conceptions of *shari'a* and its relation with the state, chapters 1, 2, and 3 will largely discuss why the implementation of *shari'a* rules in a modern nation-state often result in dissonances. Different approaches in different Muslim countries (Saudi Arabia, Iran, and Pakistan) toward the problem of dissonance will be considered as well. Yet, as chapter 3 argues, legal and politi-cal dissonance in the formal implementation of *shari'a* in a nation-state remains, in the end, inevitable. Chapter 4 will present a discussion of the millet system and its transformation to the nation-state. It is particularly important to demonstrate how many religious leaders were not aware of the implication of this shift and con-tinued to seek privileges for their positions, which were no longer justifiable as the transition took place.

Part II consists of four chapters. It aims not only to describe early aspirations for the formal implementation of *shari'a* in Indonesia, but also how the conception of religious law has since pre-independence Indonesia been perceived to be in conflict with the idea of the modern nation-state. Chapter 5 will look at the Islamization in Indonesia from both historical and theoretical points of view. Chapter 6 will present debates over the idea of nationalism and Islam-state relations in pre-independence Indonesia (from the 1920s to the early 1940s). Chapter 7 will trace the discourse between the nationalist groups and the Islamic groups on the formation of the Indonesian state in the important meetings of the Investigatory Committee for the Independence of Indonesia (BPUPKI) and the Preparatory Committee for the Independence of Indonesia (PPKI) in the early days of the new Republic of Indonesia in 1945. Focusing on the Ministry of Religious Affairs in Indonesia, chapter 8 will point out how the Ottoman millet system was reintroduced in an Indonesian context.

Part III has four chapters that focus on the efforts to have *shari'a* constitutionally acknowledged. Chapter 9 explores what Islamic constitutionalism means and its implications for Muslim countries. This chapter will look at the variety of Islamic constitutionalism available in the Muslim world and will demonstrate a basic dissonance in Islamic constitutionalism across the globe. Chapter 10 will present the historical facts of constitution making or reform in the Indonesian context, with particular reference to the position of *shari'a* in Article 29 on Religion. Chapter 11 will undertake a closer look at the stance of Islamic parties on amending Article 29 on Religion during consecutive Annual Sessions of the People's Consultative Assembly (MPR) from 2000 to 2002. Chapter 12 will be a comparative reference of the positions of Islamic parties on the amendment of Article 28 on Human Rights and an investigation of their maneuvers to put *shari'a* over warranties of religious freedom in the Indonesian constitution. Additionally, this last chapter of part III contains short remarks on the still vague nature of constitutional guarantees of religious freedom in Indonesia.

Part IV will explore the nationalization of *shari'a* in a modern nation-state by presenting a case study of the Zakat Administration Law (UU 38/1999). Rather than the Marriage Law (UU 1/1974), Religious Court Law (UU 7/1989), or the *Wakaf* or Religious Endowment Law (UU 41/2004), I prefer to focus on the Zakat Administration Law because it represents a test case of the complicated relationship between the religious duties of Muslim citizens and the non-religious character of the modern nation-state. There are three chapters in part IV that will not only look at how Islamization has been deepened with the enactment of *zakat* law, but also seek to demonstrate that incongruities have emerged from its implementation. To this end, by making a comparative reference to the experience of Pakistan in legislating *zakat,* chapter 13 explains how the institutionalization of *zakat* turns out to be a means of Islamization in Indonesia. Chapter 14 will briefly trace the historical background of the practice of *zakat* in Indonesia before independence, and the rest of the chapter will discuss *zakat* administration under the New Order regime. Chapter 15 will present some issues of legislation that have emerged in the aftermath of the Soeharto government. And, focusing on the double burden of *zakat* and tax for Muslims living in a modern nation-state, chapter 16 shows a natural dilemma between dual circumstances as both an almsgiving adherent to religion and as a taxpaying citizen of the state.

Part V will discuss the efforts of certain Muslim local inhabitants to apply *shari'a* in their regions, such as in Aceh, Banten, West Java, and South Sulawesi. But it is Aceh that will receive particular attention in this book. Attempts at the Islamization of laws in Aceh are the most significant because Aceh is the only province in Indonesia that has been officially granted the opportunity to move toward a *shari'a*-based system. In order to examine the formal implementation of *shari'a*, one has to understand the position of *ulama* (religious scholars) in a political sphere of Muslim community. As the position of *ulama* becomes significant, the Islamization process in Aceh increases. Two chapters in this part (17 and 18), therefore, will focus on the reawakened role of the Acehnese *ulama* (represented by the MPU or the Ulama Consultative Assembly) in the formation of regional regulations (*peraturan daerah* or *perda*), known locally as *qanun,* in the post–New Order era. In fact, the MPU has almost created an Islamic territory within the secular state of Indonesia. Chapter 18, in particular, will show dissonant legislation in Aceh where some *qanun* of *shari'a* rules have already begun to restrict constitutional rights, not only by ruling out ideological freedoms but also by defining rights according to the *ulama*'s understanding of tolerable conduct and their view of Acehnese communal identity. Chapter 19 will close with some observations on how the tsunami generally affected the formal implementation of *shari'a* in Aceh.

Finally, in the conclusion, I will review the dissonances found in these motivations behind the process of Islamization. This last part will demonstrate how religious practices and sociopolitical life in Indonesia have been reconfigured by attempts to Islamize laws, and how this has meant as much an Indonesianization of *shari'a* as an Islamization of Indonesia.

PART I

Shari'a and the Nation-State

The Notion of *Shari'a*

Many proponents of the formal implementation of *shari'a* characterize Islam as essentially a legal phenomenon.[1] This has much to do with the fact that many modern Muslim scholars emphasize only the legal subject matter in defining the *shari'a*.[2] No wonder then that the term *shari'a* is used interchangeably with 'Islamic law.' Yet this is not really accurate.

There is a variety in the degree of emphasis as to how much, and what kinds of, *shari'a* is legal. Many Muslim scholars have, on the one hand, held that *shari'a* means 'law' in its Western conception, though they are aware that the respective sources of *shari'a* and Western laws are different.[3] As they see *shari'a* as identical to the Western concept of law, the formal application of *shari'a* in a modern nation-state, for them, is reasonable. However, there are also those who hold that the application of *shari'a* requires a state that is distinctly structured to be a legitimate working operative of Islamic law.[4]

On the other hand, there are other Western scholars and a few reformist Muslims who are of the view that only certain parts of *shari'a* can appropriately be classified as law because *shari'a* is mixed with non-legal elements. This point of view asserts that in *shari'a* there exists all of religion, morality, and law, and that early Muslim scholars never distinguished between these.[5]

Legal subject matter actually constitutes only a moderate part of the Qur'an, the primary source of *shari'a*. Of the more than six thousand verses of the Qur'an, there are only about five hundred that are definitely legal subject matter. They can be classified into five areas: (1) worship and rituals; (2) family matters; (3) trade and commerce; (4) crimes and punishments; and (5) government and international relations.[6] However, according to Tahir Mahmood, these verses do not necessarily correspond with what in modern times is termed law. They "were supplemented, explained, interpreted and used as the basis for induction and deduction of legal rules" along the course of Islamic history. The Prophet, his companions, and the early Muslim jurists, one after the other, gradually developed the original law of the Qur'an into a wider legal fabric.[7]

Between *Shari'a* and *Fiqh*

One has seen that there is a gap between God as lawgiver and human beings as law-makers. Coulson shows this clearly when he points out that there are six principal tensions and conflicts within the concept of Islamic jurisprudence itself: between revelation and reason; between unity and diversity; between authoritarianism and liberalism; between idealism and realism; between morality and law; and between stability and change.[8] In my view, this gap is inevitable if one has the perception that religious law in Islam is a monolithic concept. One has to accurately distinguish between *shari'a* and *fiqh* (Islamic jurisprudence) since the latter is not equivalent to *shari'a*. In fact, not all of *fiqh* is *shari'a*. They are distinctly different concepts.

The six categories illustrated by Coulson are not a set of dichotomies within the religious law of Islam, but they accurately reflect the distinctions between *shari'a* and *fiqh*. As many have explained, while *shari'a* comes from God through those verses of the Qur'an which do not need further clarification, *fiqh* (which literally means understanding) on the other hand is the interpretations of human beings of those Qur'anic legal verses that have imprecise or multiple meanings. Likewise, because *shari'a* is revealed, it takes only one form, while *fiqh* varies according to different individuals' reasoning. In addition, while it is imperative that *shari'a* be implemented, one can choose any legal understanding (*fiqh*) available and suitable to one's situation. Finally, *shari'a* is unchangeable and applicable to any time and any place, while *fiqh* is subject to change according to its local circumstances.[9] These distinctions help to clarify that there are two distinct concepts of religious law in Islam, the immutable, transcendent *shari'a* and the mutable, temporal *fiqh*. In this sense, although it is still a much broader concept since it also deals with ritual worship, it is *fiqh* that is more comparable to what is currently called 'law,' and hence, when the term 'Islamic law' is used in this study it will refer mainly to *fiqh*, except when it is quoted from the work of another author.

Two Kinds of *Shari'a*

Despite the differences between *shari'a* and law and between *shari'a* and *fiqh*, exactly to what extent a rule or law can be identified as *shari'a* remains unresolved. However, it is important to emphasize here that *shari'a* in legal rules is not only seen in legal texts, but is being found more in the substantive content of the legal rules. Here we have at least two kinds of *shari'a*. First it is mostly a set of legal rules, and second it is substantially a collection of principal values.

I propose here that the question of whether a rule contains *shari'a* values is twofold. First, the distinction between *shari'a* and secular law is not a decisive criterion for what *shari'a* is. What is a determining factor, as pointed out by Ibn Qayyim al-Jawziyya (d. 1373), a disciple of Ibn Taymiyya (1263–1328), is *justice*. As he asserted, "If the indications of justice or its expressions are evident through any means, then the *shari'a* of God (Islam) must be there. . . . Any means that can produce justice and fairness is certainly part of the religion." [10] Thus, any provision that reflects the close affinity of Islam and justice could be identified as part of *shari'a*.

The second criterion is *legitimization,* that is, making a valid reference to the *shari'a* or at least taking inspiration from it. This means that a legal code is identified as *shari'a* by so-called incorporation by valid reference. The reason behind this is that not everything in this world is necessarily divine and to deny the existence of secular matters is impractical. Thus secular aspects might be religiously justified if there is legitimization or a valid reference is made to (the sources of) *shari'a*.[11] One example of this is the secular provisions in the marriage law of many Muslim countries. According to *al-fiqh al-munakahat* (Islamic rules of marriage), a husband can divorce his wife wherever and whenever he wishes. But the Indonesian marriage law, for instance, states that in order to be valid and lawfully enforceable, a divorce must be examined and executed only before the court.[12] Although not considered in line with the jurisprudence of Islamic marriage, this provision is religiously acceptable since its objective is to prevent the overly frequent occurrence of divorce. In fact, this provision was closer to the implied meaning of the *hadith: Abghad ul-halali ila-llahi al-talaq* [Of permitted matters the most loathsome before Allah is divorce].[13] From this example, it can be argued that such a secular provision (that is, divorce is considered valid only before the court) should be seen as *shari'a,* since it substantially refers to the source of *shari'a,* namely *hadith.*

We can justify this division of *shari'a* into two categories by relying on the analysis of Nathan J. Brown and Muhammad Sa`id al-Ashmawi. They claim there has been a major shift in the meaning of *shari'a* in the history of Islam over the centuries. They argue that the original broad meaning of *shari'a*, which included principal values, codes, institutions, practices, and legal rules, has been restricted to denote only fixed legal rules.[14] Ashmawi views evolution of the meaning of *shari'a* as taking place in four phases. First, the original meaning of *shari'a* in the Arabic language in the Qur'an "refers not to legal rules but rather to the path of Islam consisting of three streams (1) worship, (2) ethical code, (3) social intercourse." This proper meaning of *shari'a* was initially applied by the first generation of Muslims. Second, over time the meaning of *shari'a* extended to refer to the legal rules found in the Qur'an. Third, after some time, the meaning of *shari'a* expanded to incorporate more legal rules, both in the Qur'an and in the Prophetic traditions. Finally, the concept of *shari'a* came to include the whole body of legal rules developed in Islamic history, with all the interpretations and opinions of the legal scholars. These four phases indicate that the way the term *shari'a* is applied today is not the way the word was used in the Qur'an and no longer corresponds to its original meaning in the Arabic language.[15] As a result, the concept of *shari'a* consisted of both its principal values and its legal subject matter, and it is this latter portion that has become widespread through the Muslim countries. It is no wonder then that this understanding of *shari'a* as meaning legal rules has inevitably had an impact on the current growing political demand for the implementation of *shari'a*.

The two kinds of *shari'a* above are important in this study. Both help determine what kind of *shari'a* is relevant or irrelevant to the concept of the modern nation-state. Given that the main concern of what is called law, in the modern sense, as it pertains to religion, is merely the right to worship and perform rituals,[16] I will argue that dissonance would be more likely to occur in response to the perception that sees *shari'a* mostly as legal rules, rather than the view that considers *shari'a* as a natural way of life or a collection of principal values. In present-day Indonesia, it appears that the notion of *shari'a* as legal subject matter has more support among the proponents of the formal application of *shari'a*.

As I put an emphasis on the notion of *shari'a* as a collection of principal values rather than as a set of legal rules, Figure 1.1 may clarify its position among the terms *fiqh* and Islamic legal codes in the modern sense.

Based on Figure 1.1, one can argue that:

1. Seen from top to bottom, the figure shows the historical development of the meaning of *shari'a* as propounded by Brown and Ashmawi.

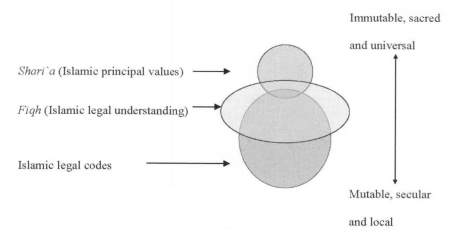

FIGURE 1.1. *Shari'a, fiqh,* and Islamic legal codes

2. *Shari'a* is not identical to *fiqh*, but some *fiqh* may be considered *shari'a*, as several classical legal understandings have successfully reached the status of acceptance by consensus (*ijma'*) of the majority of *ulama*.

3. Few Islamic legal codes may come under *shari'a* given that *shari'a* provides, or at least inspires, their basic forms and methods.

4. There are several areas of *fiqh* that are neither dependent on *shari'a* nor attached to Islamic legal codes, since such areas of *fiqh* are particular to a certain time and place.

5. Some areas of Islamic codes are *fiqh* because the state has codified a number of Islamic legal understandings and Islamic courts have applied certain *fiqh* doctrines to settle disputes between Muslims.

6. Many parts of Islamic legal codes are outside both *shari'a* and *fiqh*. These are the domains of contemporary *ijtihad* or legal improvisation based on, or inspired by, the Islamic principal values (*shari'a*) to meet new worldly situations and the challenges of modern civilization.

7. The vertical line on the right indicates that the higher the area along the line the more it becomes immutable, sacred, and universal, and conversely the lower the area the more it is mutable, secular, and local.

8. The secularization of law in Islam has nothing to do with the notion of separation of religion and politics, but mostly refers to the penetration of non-divine aspects (local customs and parliamentary human legislation) into the formation and the implementation of Islamic legal codes.[17]

The description above reflects both an understanding of *shari'a* as principally substantial values and a simplistic equalization of *shari'a* to legal subject matter, namely *fiqh* and Islamic legal codes. Both will be employed simultaneously as the working operational definition throughout this book.

2

Is There Unity of Islam and the State?

Neither of the primary sources of *shari'a,* the Qur'an and the *hadith* (Prophet's saying), have explicit or specific instructions regarding the establishment of a state. Although there are several Qur'anic verses that contain terms relevant to political concepts, such *khalifa* (leadership), *shura* (consultation), *umma* (community), *ulu al-amr* (commander), *sultan* (ruler), *mulk* (kingdom), and *hukm* (law), the interpretation of those terms has never reached the consensus that the Qur'an clearly commands the foundation of a state. It is agreed, however, that the Qur'an provides ad hoc concepts that relate to the principles of social life, such as *mushawara* (consultation), justice, equity, mutual assistance, and religious tolerance, which can be interpreted as guidance for government.[1] In addition, despite the *hadith* saying, "If three people are on a journey, they should choose one of them as a leader,"[2] it is only through inferences drawn from this *hadith* that we can arrive at the understanding that the foundation of a state is required in Islam. However, it is clear that *hadith* like this are more concerned with leadership rather than state administration.

It is, therefore, difficult to draw a precise picture of so-called Islamic political theory, since Islamic political thought mostly concentrates on non-state unit analysis such as the community (*umma* or *jama'a*), justice (*'adl* or *shari'a*), and leadership (*khilafa, imama,* and *sultan*), rather than on "the state as a generic category or [on] the body politic as a social reality and a legal abstraction."[3] In the political thought of the medieval Muslim thinkers, ideas about the state, such as the origin of the state, mostly stemmed from the influence of the Greek philosophers, albeit with varying degrees of strength. The adoption of Greek philosophy by Muslim thinkers did not necessarily mean the abandonment of Islamic teachings. In fact, Greek philosophy on the origin of the state was Islamized by emphasizing that man is a social (or political) being created by God. The concept of a state that might link all those Islamic terms became important political tools only in the twentieth century, though such a discourse did appear for the first time in Jamaluddin al-Afghani's writing in the nineteenth century.[4]

One basic important idea about Islamic political doctrine is the unity of religion and politics. The principle of *tawhid* (God's oneness) underpins this idea. In the context of Muslim political theory, *tawhid* implies that the community (*umma*) itself must reflect this unity. Interpreted in this way, no social divisions should be allowed to threaten the unity of the *umma*. Political Islam, accordingly, should make no distinction between religious and political orders. This led to the understanding that political Islam basically seeks to establish an Islamic political system (the Islamic state) with a single religious function, that is, to enable Muslims to live as good Muslims by implementing *shari'a*.[5]

Conceptualizing Unity

Through the course of Islamic history, three interrelated concepts, *umma, khalifa,* and *shari'a,* have represented and preserved the religious and political unity of Islam (*al-Islam din wa dawla*). Currently, these three concepts have become a vehicle for any individual or group with a political agenda of Islamizing the state to advance their political goals.[6] The notion of religious and political unity reveals that Islam does not recognize any separation of religion and politics, that Islam does not differentiate between public and private domains, that the state and the religious community (*umma*) are one and the same, and that political authority (*khalifa*) and religious authority (*shari'a*) are delegated to the same person. As a result, the Islamic community must be seen as unique and distinguished from non-Muslim society. This point of view is still dominant among many Western and Muslim scholars.[7] The following paragraphs will undertake an investigation of the historical application of the terms *umma, khalifa,* and *shari'a.*

Umma

The *umma* may have been the first religiopolitical concept to emerge in Islam, though it was originally a sociohistorical one. The term *umma* appears sixty-four times in the Qur'an[8] and twice in the Constitution of Medina,[9] with multiple and diverse meanings including followers of a prophet, followers of a divine plan of salvation, a religious group, a small group within a larger community of believers, a misguided people, and an order of beings.[10] Given the ambiguity of the meaning of *umma,* there have been different interpretations among scholars as to whether it originally had an inclusive sense (applicable to all human beings) or an exclusive sense (applicable only to Muslim believers) in the early Islamic period.[11]

In spite of this, most scholars share the opinion that over time the term *umma* has narrowed to denote exclusively a human group that is united by a prophet on the basis of divine guidance. This shift of meaning can be traced to the Constitution of Medina or to the first months of Prophet Muhammad's residence in Medina (ca. 622 CE). As Hassan writes:

> The term umma retained a universal application (while it only had a small fol-
> lowing in Mecca) until, at least, the time of the *hijra* [Muhammad's emigration
> from Mecca to Medina]. . . . The Constitution of Medina was drawn up in order
> to incorporate the diaspora community of Medina into the already established
> geographical community of Mecca. . . . The result was that the religious term of
> umma . . . began to carry a more a specific connotation of a Muslim umma. Thus
> began the evolution of the term from a universal monotheistic religious term to a
> socio-religious one that would become even more specific with further political
> and sociological developments.[12]

Khalifa

Like the term *umma,* which not only became a framework for accommodating the cultural diversity of the believers but also a concept to maintain the unity
of believers, the term caliph (*khalifa*)[13] turned out to be the symbol of Islam's
religious and political unity throughout the Islamic empire.[14] In political practice,
the term *khalifa* refers to the successor of the Prophet Muhammad, whose main
duty was to provide non-divine guidance on the right path (Islam) for the *umma.*
According to many Muslim legal scholars of the medieval period, it was the *khalifa* that sustained the Prophetic mission, formulating such concepts as *hifz al-din*
(preserving the religion) and *siyasa al-dunya* (administering the world).[15] So the
caliphs inherited the Prophet's executive authority to implement and defend the
truth, along with the authority to 'announce' the truth or make public policy in
matters not explicitly provided for in the Qur'an or the Sunna. The caliphs' authority applied to everything from individual piety to ritual, family, business, political,
and military matters.[16]

This authority of the caliphs in legal and doctrinal matters was later considered to be the foundation of the concept of *al-siyasa al-shar'iyya,* which includes
all measures undertaken by the Muslim leader to bring the people closer to benefi-
cence and further away from harm, even if such measures were not approved by the
Prophet nor regulated by divine revelation.[17] Thus, the caliph provided a unity of
religious and political authority, enabling Muslims all over the world (one *umma*)
to integrate in one community, bound by one law and governed ultimately by one
ruler.[18]

The picture of Islamic political thought, which reflects the historical development of early Islam, is one in which the unity of the people as one *umma* under a single caliphate with both religious and political authority is "accorded supreme value. [And for this reason], any subversion of this unity by heresy or rebellion is considered great evil." [19] This unity, however, was no longer tenable following the decline of the religious authority of the caliphate itself.

Shariʻa

There are two explanations as to the precise date the caliphate lost its status as symbol of the unity of the community. The first explanation was put forward by Rosenthal and Ayubi. They mention that it was Ibn Taymiyya (d. 1328) who shifted the center of interest and importance from the caliphate to *shariʻa*. [20] Ibn Taymiyya did so because of the fall of the caliphate in Baghdad (1258) under the Mongol invasion and the fragmentation of the Muslim world into several different caliphates and kingdoms. In fact, it was Ibn Taymiyya who emphasized the corresponding goals of *shariʻa* and state. For Ibn Taymiyya, the form of caliphate or leadership was not his main concern. Rather, he focused mostly on the function and goals of the leadership (state), which was to realize all God's commands (*shariʻa*), promote the good, and prohibit the evil (*amr maʻruf nahy munkar*). Both the goals of *shariʻa* and state were similar. Ibn Taymiyya therefore sought to create a new united religiopolitical symbol (i.e. *shariʻa*) for the survival of the *umma*. As Rosenthal explained,

> The reforming zeal of Ibn Taymiyya was aimed at full restoration of the *shariʻa* to secure the survival of Islam. . . . [He] even went so far as to deny the necessity of the *imama* [caliphate] by concentrating on the rule of the divine law. By going back to the Sunna and also by administrative reform, he tried to restore the *shariʻa* to its full authority and efficacy. . . . He insisted that the welfare of the community [*umma*] depended on a Muslim's obedience to God and His *shariʻa*. [21]

Henceforth, given that the integration of the *umma* could not be achieved politically, it had to be achieved religiously. So instead of *khalifa*, the emphasis of unity was shifted to the *shariʻa* as the basis for ideological unity since political and human unity were no longer obtainable. [22]

Another explanation regarding the shift is supplied by Ira M. Lapidus, a renowned historian of Islamic societies. He argues that unity had begun to slip from the caliphs' control in the early centuries of Islam, specifically in the period of the four immediate successors of the Prophet Muhammad (*khulafa al-rashidun*), that is, from 661 CE onwards. [23] He mentions that there are three phases in which the unity of religion and state within the hands of the caliph gradually disappeared and the differentiation between religion and state started to manifest. [24]

The differentiation began first when the Umayyad dynasty (661–750) gained power. Following the Byzantine and Sassanian traditions, the Umayyads preferred the political authority of the caliphate to its religious authority.[25] Second, the emergence of the Muslim schools of law (*madhhabs*)[26] in the eighth and ninth centuries was important in the development of a religious life independent from the caliphate. In the post–*khulafa al-rashidun* era, many *madhhabs* came to oppose the authority of the caliphs in the elaboration of law. The *ulama* greatly influenced the Muslim people, who turned directly to them rather than to the caliphs for moral instruction and religious guidance as Muslims. This situation, from a religious and a communal point of view, reflected the fact that the caliphate (state) and religion were no longer wholly integrated.[27]

Third, the establishment of the Hanbali *madhhab* marked the next development of the termination of the union of religion and state in Islam. In the face of the inquisition (*mihna*) undertaken by the Abbasid caliph, al-Ma'mun in particular, who forced government officials and religious leaders to accept religious views (such as the 'createdness' of the Qur'an) and the caliph's authority in matters of religious ritual and doctrine, Ahmad ibn Hanbal (780–855), the founder of the Hanbali *madhhab,* not only confronted theological problems, but, more importantly, dealt with the problem of the nature of the religious authority of the caliphate and the limits of the obligation to obedience. He held that Islamic religious obligations stemmed not from caliphal declarations, but from the Qur'an and the Sunna (way or practice of the Prophet) as interpreted and explained by the *ulama*. The caliph might be requested to uphold the law, but not to define its content, because that was beyond his authority. For Ibn Hanbal, religious authority no longer belonged to the caliph, but was now under the direct command of the *ulama*. Although Ibn Hanbal himself did not articulate it as such, his views implied a practical distinction between secular and religious authority.[28] And so, from this time onwards, there was no need to look to the caliphate as the symbol of united religious and political authority.

It is worth considering here Vikør's analysis of the reason behind the shift of the hub of unity to *shari'a*. According to him, it was due to the *ulama*'s reluctance to attach the *shari'a* they developed to the authority of any specific ruler, as so doing would validate *shari'a* only where that particular ruler held power. Thus, *shari'a* would split into regional variants for the dynasties and political entities changed in rapid succession, which would be an unimaginable situation for such a divine law. Therefore, the *ulama* had to retain the *shari'a* since they were independent and international scholars moving from city to city without regard for political boundaries.[29]

Lapidus' explanation appears more historically inclusive, but his explanation cannot easily be reconciled with Rosenthal's and Ayubi's interpretation. Given that

Ibn Taymiyya was an adherent of the Hanbali *madhhab*, perhaps it is fair to say that it was he who later clearly formulated what his predecessor in the same *madhhab* had experienced regarding the crisis in the unity of caliphal authority. While Rosenthal and Ayubi interpret Ibn Taymiyya's emphasis on the *shari'a* as showing a shift of unity from the caliphate to the *shari'a*, Lapidus holds the view that the upshot of Ibn Taymiyya's theorizing was that "the state [caliphate] was not a direct expression of Islam, but a secular institution whose duty it was to uphold Islam." [30] This interpretation seems closer to what Ibn Taymiyya had said regarding the state and justice (i.e., Islam): "Verily God supports a just government even if it is infidel, but does not endorse a despotic government though it is Muslim," and "Justice even if combined with infidelity may sustain life, but unfairness though it comes with Islam will not do so." [31]

Seen through such a lens, Ibn Taymiyya did not actually argue about the union of religion and state in the light of *shari'a*. Indeed, he contended that religion and the state were discrete institutions and the relationship between them was merely mutual or functional, not organic. [32] The state or caliphate is thus not the ends of religion, but simply a means to realize the principal values of the religion (*shari'a*). This implies that the caliphate, including its ruler, is not only unequal to the religion itself, but is also not sacred and has no religious merit per se. Therefore, obedience to the caliphate is only given so long as the caliphate's commands do not contradict core Islamic teachings. [33] Although Ibn Taymiyya proposed a differentiated relationship, he maintained that obedience must be given first to religion and only then to the state. Hence, Ibn Taymiyya's ideal was actually for an unequal relationship between religion and the state, with religion having the ascendant position.

The distinction between religion and state (between sacred and secular) described above has led us to presume that the lack of differentiation between state and religious institutions in the history of Islamic societies is not a static phenomenon. In fact, the supposed integration of the state and religious authority accurately represents only a small segment of Islamic regions and Muslim populations. As pointed out by Lapidus,

> [I]n the 'Abbasid, Saljuq, Ottoman and Safavid empires the central fact is the differentiation of state and religious institutions. . . . The state-religion relations vary across a wide spectrum from a high degree of state control over a centrally managed religious establishment, to a more independent but co-operative relationship, to full autonomy and even open opposition to state policies. [34]

All the foregoing discussions show that there is no single relationship between religion and state in Islam. In fact, a historical review of religion-state relations in Muslim societies reveals that the permanently unitary relationship in Islam is more likely to be theoretical than factual. Unity was an ideal that actually existed only in the period of the Prophet Muhammad at Medina, for about ten years (622–632). But that ideal was limited in a community in which state and society were not distinguished and in which government was identical with leadership. As Zubaida pointed out, when the state later acquired institutional and military forms distinct from the community, that ideal relationship collapsed.[35]

The ideal unitary relationship in Islam described above, though it was only practiced for a short time in the early history of Islam, has been a motivating force that has perpetually stimulated individuals as well as Islamic groups to struggle for achieving that ideal. As the next chapter illustrates, a number of Muslim leaders and their movements in different countries (Saudi Arabia, Iran, and Pakistan) sought to revive this imaginative model of the integration of political and religious authorities into one hand.

Categorizations of Islam-State Relations

Given that there is no single relationship pattern between religion and state in the historical record of Islam, it is plausible to have various categorizations of Islam-state relations. One categorization divides the relationship into two patterns. The first is an indissoluble relationship between state and religion under the unified leadership of the caliph, whose authority extends to all realms of personal and public concern. The second is a tacit separateness between the structures of state and religion that isolates the religious sphere as being only for personal and communal fulfillment.[36] This categorization of two types of relationship between religion and the state, however, makes a sweeping generalization and fails to recognize the dynamics between the two poles.

The other important categorization creates three types of relationships. The first type proposes *an integration* of Islam and state in which the state is both a religious and political institution at once. The second form *differentiates* between religion and state institutions and views them as being in mutual symbiosis. The state needs religion to progress, while religion needs the state because religion will not develop without the support of the state. The third outlook envisages *a separation* between religion and state. This last view rejects any efforts of religion to influence the state, since both religion and state have their own authority within their respective domains.[37]

Although this tripartite classification may more accurately reflect reality than the simpler dichotomous version of the relationship between religion and the state, there is still a problem with it. There is ambiguity regarding differentiation. Theoretically, the second form (differentiation) must be easily distinguishable from the third form (separation), but that is difficult in practice due to their subtle frontiers. Additionally, the first (integration) and the second form (differentiation) above are often indistinguishable and, in fact, many Muslims often subscribe to both at the same time depending on their own political circumstances. Further observation of the dynamics within this latter classification is therefore needed.

3

Dissonant Implementation
of *Shari'a*

As Theda Skocpol points out, "various sorts of states give rise to various conceptions of the meaning and method of politics itself." [1] In a situation of differentiated
religion-state relations (that is, where religion and state occupy different spaces),
the goal of the state is to advance the interests of citizens regardless of their religious backgrounds. In a situation of undifferentiated religion-state relations (that
is, where the spaces of religion and state are integrated), the state merely functions
to achieve security and order in ways that are conducive to its people attending to
their religious duties. As noted by England,

> The modern [nation-]state's purpose is to serve as a framework or instrument for
> the furthering of human welfare, [while] within the religious view, [the] state's
> function is to implement . . . divinely ordained precepts in order to achieve . . .
> super-human ends as defined by religion. [2]

Consequently, while the legitimacy of a modern nation-state lies in its ability to
provide welfare, the premodern state bases its legitimacy on its capacity to implement religious law.

State legitimacy resulting from the formal implementation of *shari'a* often
generates a conflict of interests between the theory underlying the nation-state and
the view of an indissoluble domain. The conflicts exist and are significant given
that the Islamic world is divided into a number of nation-states. The Western concept of the modern nation-state, which is thought to have emerged in Europe in the
seventeenth century through the 1648 Treaty of Westphalia, [3] spread throughout
the world via colonialism. Colonialism, in fact, had partitioned Muslim regions
into numerous territories, and by the twentieth century, these territories were
transformed into newly born different countries, which took the nation-state as
their form of political organization. [4]

Legal and Political Dissonances

The idea of the nation-state is perhaps the most challenging theme and 'ism' that confronts the modern Muslim world. A great number of political and religious discourses have arisen among modern Muslim thinkers as to whether Islam can legitimately tolerate such concepts of territorial boundaries, state sovereignty, or even citizenship. According to Piscatori, there have been three responses among Muslims to the reality of the nation-state in modern era. The first argues that the nation-state is unavoidable. It is a fact of life, which can only be accepted. The second claims that the nation-state is a natural institution and only to be expected in the order of things. The third calls for a new synthesis between Islamic and modern nation-states.[5] It is clear that the nation-state was picked partly due to the lack of any other respectable model of statehood[6] or simply because it is a *fait accompli*.[7] This new development further devastated the myth of a non-fragmented *umma*.

The combination of a concept of *shari'a* that places emphasis mostly on legal codes with a concept of the state that makes no distinction between religion and politics has generated a double legal-political dissonance in the contemporary nation-state era. This is because of a conflict of authority between the different sources of legal sovereignty that lies between the exclusive preserve of the state and the legal authority of religious elites (*ulama*).[8] In such an interpretation of Islam, divine revelation is the foundation of all law, whereas the nation-state claims a monopoly over lawmaking, carried out by the legislative organs of the state. Thus, the nation-state as "a legally arranged set of organs for the framing, application, and enforcement of laws" has inevitably yielded tensions and conflicts with such a mode of interpretation of Islam and *shari'a*.[9] Tensions and conflicts result partly because there is one thing they have in common, that is, a greater emphasis on law.[10]

As Cammack argues, it is the doctrine of state positivism—the doctrine that only the legislative organs of the state possess an absolute monopoly over lawmaking within the territorial boundaries of the state—that contradicts the version of Islam that claims unitary sovereign authority. This doctrine allows the ruler to produce law and secure its effective enforcement since it is naturally conceived as an aspect of the state's sovereign power, which was understood to be supreme and indivisible. The identification of law with unitary state sovereignty impelled the conclusion that only that which has been recognized by the state shall have the status of law.[11] On the one hand, this principle of state positivism, as further argued by Cammack, rejects the authority of any law with a source outside the state unless it has been expressly adopted and given the force of law by the state. On the other hand, this dogma of state positivism denies legal force to laws produced by non-

TABLE 3.1 Views on Islam-state relations and perceptions of *shari'a*

Views on Islam-state relationships	Legal Codes	Principal Values
Integration	Dissonance	N/a
Unequal Differentiation	Dissonance	N/a
Equal Differentiation	N/a	Consonance
Separation	N/a	Consonance

state entities, such as local courts or merchant groups. This kind of legal product can only acquire the status of state law through state enactment.[12]

Given that the modern nation-state acknowledges no rivals to its legal authority and asserts that no law claiming authority from any other source is entitled to recognition, how then does a non-unitary relationship of religion and state in Islam fit with this particular circumstance? As can be seen from the table above (Table 3.1), a non-unitary view of religion-state relations will generate legal and political consonance only if it conceives of *shari'a* mainly as Islamic *principal values* rather than merely as a set of Islamic *legal codes*. The view that makes no distinction between religion and politics and holds that Islam is indistinguishably and simultaneously religion and state is most likely to lead to dissonance in the implementation of *shari'a*.

However, 'differentiation' that has the position of religion and state as unequal will not lead to legal and political consonance. This is because such a differentiation, though it distinguishes between religious and political institutions, will certainly subordinate the state to religion due to its tendency to perceive the state as a vehicle for the interests of religion. As a result, a conflict of legal sovereignty between religion and the nation-state becomes more apparent. Table 3.1 emphasizes that in order for the implementation of *shari'a* to be consonant in a modern nation-state, the view of differentiation must distinguish between unequal differentiation and equal differentiation. As I have noted in the previous chapter, the vague border between integration and differentiation likely exists at this point.

Struggles to Resolve Dissonances

Wael B. Hallaq has pointed out that there exists an obvious dislocation in Muslims' minds between two perceptions of legal authority, one emanating from the state and the other from religion. The latter has been dominant for more than a millennium, while the former was introduced only during the last two centuries.[13] In light of this, there have been three key modern attempts to reconcile these two dissimilar sources of legal authority. While accepting the nation-state as a fact of life, these attempts have sought to give religious authority back to the state by defining in the constitution a special role for the *ulama* in which they would actively participate in governance, specifically with the right to maintain the supreme position of *shari'a*. In this case, instead of creating hostility between the *ulama* and the *umara* (a plural of *amir*, which means commander or ruler), a union or an alliance between the *ulama* and *umara* has been sought to govern and guide the country toward faith.

Saudi Arabia

The first example of a functionally integrated relationship between religion and state, or *ulama* and *umara*, is the kingdom of Saudi Arabia, which is often referred to as a basic model for Sunni Islam. The kingdom, established in 1932, has deep roots in the eighteenth century in the form of an alliance between the *'alim* Muhammad b. 'Abd al-Wahhab (1703–1791) and the *amir* Muhammad Ibn Sa'ud (reigned 1747–1765), who together ruled and shared power in Dar'iya, a town near the modern capital of Riyadh. While the alliance provided 'Abd al-Wahhab with needed support and protection, it offered Ibn Sa'ud the ideological platform of Wahhabism and the recruits needed to effect his designs. In short, both the religious and political spheres shared a complementarity of objectives. The existence of one was dependent on the survival and continued support of the other. Two hundred years of mutual support have created a strong political alliance between them, which has been continued by their respective successors in the twentieth century.[14]

The doctrine of Wahhabism has been influential and has become deeply anchored in the culture as well as in the constitution. The doctrine of Wahhabism stresses that obedience to the rulers is obligatory even if such rulers are oppressive. The people are advised to be patient with oppressive rulers and armed rebellion against them is denounced. The rulers, however, are warned to be just. The rulers' commands must be followed as long as they do not contradict the rules of religion. The ruler's main objective should be the application of *shari'a*, which may be accomplished through cooperation with the *ulama*. Because of their knowledge of *shari'a*, the *ulama* constitute the premier directive class in the community, and the rulers must govern with their advice and cooperation. The teachings of Ibn Taymiyya were believed to largely inspire this doctrine. Although Ibn Taymiyya differentiated between religion and state, his notion that the state was responsible for facilitating the performance of religious duties has been interpreted to mean that he was expecting a collaboration between the *ulama* and the *umara* in the implementation of *shari'a*. Muhammad Ibn 'Abd al-Wahhab seemed to have understood Ibn Taymiyya in this way.[16]

This sort of integrated relationship between religion and state in Saudi Arabia, however, has been altered due to the rapid development of complex administrative institutions in the era of modern nation-states. The expansion of the oil industry in the 1950s and the subsequent increase in government revenues ushered in an augmentation of the power of the *umara,* though the central position of the *ulama* within the regime is still secure. The increased role of the *umara* required an expansion of state jurisdiction, which has fed back to a deepening of the differentiation between the religious and political spheres. What is more, a broad range of areas that were formerly dominated by religion, under the control of the *ulama,* now come under the auspices of the *umara,* such as the administration of *waqf* (religious endowments) and religious schools and education. Indeed, the *ulama* are currently dependent on the state for their survival. They are appointed and their activities are regulated by state laws.[17]

Political-economic development is not the only factor to have caused the expansion of state jurisdiction in Saudi Arabia and the gradual decline of *ulama* authority. It is the doctrine of *siyasa shar'iyya,* welcomed by the *ulama,* that ironically has become a crucial means of enhancing the judicial authority of the *umara.*[18] This doctrine was derived from the works of Ibn Taymiyya (*al-Siyasa al-Shar'iyya fi Islah al-Ra'i wa al-Ra'iyya*) and Ibn al-Qayyim (*al-Turuq al-Hukmiyya fi al-Siyasa al-Shar'iyya*). These works revived the doctrine of *siyasa shar'iyya* from ancient precedents, especially those first four caliphs (Abu Bakr, 'Umar b. Khattab, Uthman b. 'Affan and 'Ali b. Abu Talib), who were regarded as being more rightly guided caliphs. This doctrine, according to Vogel, allows the ruler to "take any acts, including legislating to supplement the *shari'a* and creating new courts, that are needed for the public good (*maslahat 'amma*), provided that the *shari'a* is not infringed thereby, or, as long as the *shari'a* has no text (*la nass*) on the matter."[19]

The position of the *ulama* has been subordinated to the state in Saudi Arabia under the doctrine of *siyasa shar'iyya.* Although what the *umara* manage with *siyasa shar'iyya* has mainly to do with procedural matters rather than the content of *shari'a,* the procedural aspects appear to be more imperative because the successful implementation of *shari'a* rules largely depends on these aspects. This development seems to relocate the major part of religious authority, formerly in the hands of the *ulama,* to the domain of the *umara.* As observed by Al-Yassini, the rulers of Saudi Arabia extended their authority to the religious sphere because they could "not tolerate an autonomous religious domain that would compete with [them] for loyalty." Since its origin, the Saudi state needed Wahhabism precisely to strengthen its religious authority and legitimacy. As a result, although Wahhabism continues to be the state ideology, it is the ruler that is the source of all authority in the state, and the religious institutions act according to the political interests of the ruler. In sum, Saudi Arabia's political scene is a nation-state developed under the ideology of Wahhabism.[20]

Iran

The experience of Iran has been cited as the second modern example of a unitary relationship between religion and state. A fusion of religious and political functions performed by a unitary structure in contemporary Iran has been possible thanks to the doctrine of *wilaya al-faqih* (rule by Islamic jurists or 'Mandate of the Jurist'), which requires the religious elites to play a major role in governance.[21] Designed by Ayatollah Ruhollah Khomeini (1902–1989), this doctrine reinstated the notion of inseparability of the sacred and secular, and of Islam and politics, by combining the authority to rule with religious authority under the jurisdiction of the *ulama*. For Khomeini, "undertaking a government and laying the foundation of the Islamic state is a duty incumbent on just Jurists."[22]

This notion of *ulama* government had no real precedent in the history of political thought of Shi'i Islam.[23] In fact, it was an effort to apply more of what Muslim Sunni thinkers, such as Rashid Rida (1865–1935) and Abu al-'A'la al-Mawdudi (1903–1979), both twentieth-century theoreticians of a modern Islamic state, had envisaged about the role of the religious elites in an Islamic state.[24] Khomeini wanted to see the *ulama* not merely "as benign dispensers of advice and consent, but as real wielders of power."[25] Given that the Islamic state in Khomeini's view is based on the idea that those most knowledgeable in Islam should rule, the *ulama* government is the logical consequence of this view. In Arjomand's words, Iran's political experiment is "the synthesis of the theocratic idea of the Mandate of the Jurist with the principles and organization of the modern nation-state."[26]

Unlike Saudi Arabia, whose *ulama* have been co-opted by the regime, the Iranian *ulama* have turned out to *be* the regime itself. To justify the *ulama* government, the *shari'a* has been adopted as the judicial basis for the state and employed as the sole means for managing society. In addition, the position of the *ulama* is emphasized in the new constitution as the Guardians of Religion, thus giving them authority as the sole judge of what is and what is not compatible with the *shari'a*.[27] This judicial conception, according to Enayat, cancels all man-made laws, even if intelligently designed and appropriately passed by the parliament, and subordinates them to the authorization of the *ulama*. "Human regulation is allowed *only* as a practical contrivance for the enforcement of the divine law"[28] (emphasis added).

However, the regime, when confronted with the realities of modern government, "has had to gradually move away from traditional *shari'a* and rely on revisionist doctrines that enable the government to enact laws as it sees fit, no matter what the connection with the *shari'a*."[29] To validate this legal endeavor, the *ulama* reinvented and put forward the Islamic doctrines of *maslaha* (public interest) and *darura* (necessity), which allowed them to seclude the *shari'a* on public interest grounds. In Tamadonfar's analysis, this approach detracts from the unity of the state and religion since "the farther the regime moves away from the *shari'a* the more it erodes the fundamental philosophical foundation of its own legitimacy." [30]

Tamadonfar's analysis, in my view, is valid only if it regards *shari'a* merely as legal doctrine. Additionally, if it can be assumed that the notion of *siyasa shar'iyya* (the Sunni legal political view) is implicit in the doctrine of *wilaya al-faqih* (the Shi'i political theory), the use of *maslaha* and *darura* by the *ulama* regime at the expense of classical *shari'a* doctrine is religiously valid. For this reason, it is fair to conclude that instead of diminishing the unity of religious and political authority, the legal maneuvers of the Iranian *ulama* government to expand its jurisdiction beyond *shari'a* matters is, in reality, strengthening the fusion of religious and political authority.

However successful it has been, political experimentation that combines religious authority with political power has resulted in legal-political dissonance. The monopoly on power by the *ulama* in Iran has largely restricted individual rights by defining these rights in accordance with the *ulama*'s understanding of permissible rights and for the sake of communal unity as well as the regime's interests. As a result, many legal products in this Shi'i Muslim state have become more authoritarian and more detached from social reality than in a number of Sunni Muslim countries.[31]

The legal-political adventures regarding the institutionalization of unified religious and political authority in Islam that have occurred in Saudi Arabia (Sunni) and Iran (Shi'i) in the twentieth century may be summarized as the struggle of the religious authority holders (*ulama*), either Sunni or Shi'i, to become the principal agent in the definition of the legal-political situation in the modern nation-state era. In the past, both Sunni and Shi'i *ulama* in their respective regions "never had, nor sought the opportunity to seize, the power to use the levers of the state directly to further their religious program." [32] Although in Saudi Arabia the doctrine of Wahhabism was successful to a certain degree in securing broader legal political rights for the *ulama,* the *umara* or the monarchy is still the sole institution that has effective authority in both religious and political domains.[33] Quite the reverse is the case in Iran, where Khomeini's doctrine of *wilaya al-faqih* has exceeded even the ambitions of the Saudi *ulama* by introducing into the 1979 constitution the uncontested right to rule on behalf of God.[34]

Pakistan

The third variant within the category of integrative relationships between religion and state is the case of Pakistan. This case demonstrates the struggle of religious elites that have failed to transform themselves into the state, though they were able to secure some formal religious authority in the educational and legal systems. One important criterion by which to measure the successful incorporation of the religious elites in the organization of a modern nation-state is through constitutional acknowledgment of the rights of *ulama*. This may include an issuance of official religious commands, a review of all existing legislation to identify whether there is a conflict with the *shari'a*, and a right to give advice to bring legislation into conformity with *shari'a*. While in Saudi Arabia and Iran such rights of the religious elites are guaranteed in their respective constitutions,[35] in the Pakistani constitution the demands of the *ulama* for the exclusive right to settle issues of 'repugnancy' to Islam [36] were rejected.[37] Instead, this special right is granted to the Federal Sharia Court.[38]

Another attempt to create special rights for the Pakistani *ulama* that occurred during the Islamization program of President Zia ul-Haqq (r. 1977–1988) was once again fruitless. Following the alliance that had been established between President Zia and the *ulama* and Muslim fundamentalist groups, President Zia issued a decree (the Islamic Law Enforcement Ordinance) on 15 June 1988, in which, among other things, he proposed to establish authority for the *ulama* to supervise the formal implementation of *shari'a* in the country and to assume a major role in deciding whether any existing laws conflicted with *shari'a* rules. However, this decree never came into effect since it had not been formally ratified by the time Zia died on 17 August 1988 in an airplane crash.[39]

~

Given the key idea of the indissoluble relationship between religion and state in Islam, many proponents of Islamization remain committed to advance these ultimate goals. In this sense, the Islamization of the nation-state is an attempt to seek a way to establish an unbreakable nexus between religious and political authority. However, they propose different models of what an Islamic state should be (a universal caliphate state or a territorial nation-state), what form it should take (for example, monarchy or republic), and by whom it should be led (*ulama* or politicians).

The preceding discussions reveal that both integration of religious and political authority and the role of the religious elites are important factors, necessary for undertaking any plans to establish an Islamic state and launch the formal implementation of *shari'a*. The most successful example among the three models has been the Iranian religious elites. The experience of the Iranian *ulama* has been the most striking, as they retain various prerogatives and exercise decisive power. This was possible thanks to the concept of *wilaya al-faqih*, introduced by Ayatollah Ruhollah Khomeini in conjunction with the Iranian revolution in 1979. This Iranian model of the *ulama* government suggests that a creation of a polity of religious elites (*ulama*) constitutes an important stage of the Islamization of laws. This legal-political experience has certainly inspired many Muslims to think of Iran as a prototype for an Islamic state with a constitution that allows the implementation of God's rules on earth, within the framework of a modern nation-state.

The vital role of the Iranian *ulama* is, however, perhaps a peculiarity of the Shi'ite Muslim community, while for the Sunni who dominate the rest of the Muslim world a similarly important position of the *ulama* has rarely been accepted. Instead, the principal role of Sunni *ulama* in legal production has been subordinated under the authority of the Muslim rulers, be they sultan, king, president, or the national legislature. This is largely because the concept of *siyasa shari'iyya* remains popular among some Sunni *ulama* and may have discouraged them from competing against the legal authority of the state.

The Iranian model of the *ulama* government, however effective it may be, has failed to cope with the problem of legal and political dissonances in the formal implementation of *shari'a* in the modern nation-state era. Zubaida has aptly illustrated the challenge that the Iranian *ulama* have faced:

> The question of taxes in the early days of the Islamic Republic of Iran was a crucial issue: were they to be confined to the religiously specified dues of *zakat, khoms,* and *jizya?* Whilst Khomeni in his pre-revolutionary writing advocated the confinement of taxation to the religiously sanctioned dues, he very quickly changed his mind when faced with the fiscal considerations of a state. It remains another indication that the Islamic state, under the constraints and necessities of rule, is increasingly secularized, and the religious institutions continue to thrive alongside distinct boundaries from the state. State personnel at the higher levels are predominantly clerics, but increasingly they look like an entrenched interest group clinging onto state power, legitimizing their control in terms of religious formulae which increasingly seem to ring hollow.[40]

As will be shown later in part V, the experience of the Iranian *ulama* also challenged the Acehnese *ulama,* though not in the same manner.

4

Between Nation and Millet

It is my contention that the study of the dissonant implementation of religious law in the era of nation-states requires a close observation of the millet system of the Ottoman Empire. This is because, first, it shows a particular historical environment where religious law was applied for its adherents, and second, it shows that the dissonance of the secular idea of state with the religious concept of nation had its origin in the millet system. In light of this, it is important to differentiate between nationality and citizenship. As pointed out by Karpat, "[n]ationality drew its essence from the religious-communal experience in the millet, while citizenship was a secular concept determined by territory."[1] Thus, it may be fair to say that "the dual process of state and nation formations in many Muslim countries followed a dichotomous course and created nation-states in which secular citizenship and religious nationality remained dissonant and at times conflicting."[2]

Taking the Ottoman millet system as a case study, this chapter emphasizes the distinction between the traditional world order (millet) and the modern world order (nation). As suggested by Pollard, the history of the state takes place in three stages: the city-state of the classical ages, the universal religious state of the medieval ages, and the national state of the modern ages.[3] This chapter, therefore, will describe how the world political order has shifted since the late eighteenth century from being based on a distinct religious affiliation (for example, the *Dar al-Islam–Dar al-Harb* dichotomy) to a distinct state boundary. Likewise, global values have also dramatically changed from discriminative practices and social segregation to more fully embrace universal values of equality, pluralism, and non-discrimination.

Before going any further, it is useful at this stage to define some key concepts employed in this book: those of 'nationalism,' 'nation-state,' and 'millet.' The first two concepts need to be carefully distinguished as they are frequently confused. Both have already been subjected to extensive discussions, but it is not my aim here to review the literature on those subjects. Instead, I prefer to rely on Montserrat Guibernau's work.[4]

Nationalism

There are three major explanatory approaches to nationalism.[5] The first focuses on the immutable character of the nation as a natural, quasi-eternal entity created by God.[6] The second approach considers nationalism in terms of political modernization.[7] The third develops psychological theories associated with the need of individuals to be involved in a collective with which they can identify.[8]

Guibernau was not, however, satisfied solely with these approaches, as they did not include two fundamental attributes of nationalism: psychological and political characters. For this reason, she argues that nationalism was "the sentiment of belonging to a community whose members identify with a set of symbols, beliefs and ways of life, and have the will to decide upon their common political destiny."[9] This definition of nationalism has its roots in the term 'nation,' which refers to "a human group conscious of forming a community, sharing a common culture, attached to a clearly demarcated territory, having a common past and a common project for the future and claiming the right to rule itself."[10] This definition has both psychological and political features that will be employed in this chapter. However, it must be added here that nationalism in the context of nation-state building is not merely an inheritance, but, most importantly, is "a common project for the present and the future . . . fulfillment [of which] is never finally complete."[11]

As Giddens argues, nationalism is a condition for entry into a modern world political and economic system based on the building blocks of nation-states.[12] Nationalism is, therefore, something that must be struggled for. It is not present at birth, but it must be created and endlessly embedded in the people's minds. However, this seems to be difficult to comprehend, especially for religious leaders whose religion is mostly adhered to by the majority population in a region. For them, since religion has provided everything, nationalism is inherent in and identical to, if not subject to, religion.

Nation-State

The nation-state differs from nationalism. Unlike nationalism, which is a psychological and political phenomenon, the nation-state is more a political and institutional one.[13] Guibernau has aptly defined the nation-state as

> a modern phenomenon, characterized by the formation of a kind of state which has the monopoly of what it claims to be the legitimate use of force within a demarcated territory and seeks to unite the people subjected to its rule by means of

homogenization, creating a common culture, symbols, values, reviving traditions and myths of origin, and sometimes inventing them.[14]

Although this definition cannot be employed as a general rule, since it rules out multicultural countries like Canada, it is nonetheless useful to ascertain that the decisive character of nation-states is to enforce law and use violence to do so.[15] Based on this definition, there are three important features of the nation-state vis-à-vis religion that need to be underscored.

First, it is the nation-state, not religion, that has the monopoly on use of the means of violence. This implies that the formation of a police force, the establishment of courts, and the creation of law all belong to the sovereignty of the nation-state. Second, unlike religion, which could reach individuals across the boundaries of ethnic groups, languages, races, and skin colors, the ability of the nation-state to control its subjects is restricted to a particular territory with demarcated boundaries. While the surveillance of religion is maintained through the personal devoutness of each individual, the success of the nation-state in preserving its authority over the people is "mainly the result of 'action at a distance' made possible by the rapid movement by sea [and air transportation], and by the superiority of [armed] forces."[16] Third, although religious believers are free to observe various practices of rituals in different times and spaces, the nation-state attempts to homogenize its population. Using media and education, the nation-state modifies and reproduces a common culture, thus enhancing the cohesion of its citizens.[17]

Millet

The term 'millet' derives from *milla* in Arabic, which literally means religion. It is mentioned in the Qur'an four times to refer to "the religion of Abraham,"[18] which applies to Islam and the other two monotheistic faiths: Judaism and Christianity. The embryo of the practice of the millet system, though not closely parallel, can perhaps be traced back to the Medina Charter enacted during the first month of the Prophet Muhammad's life in Medina. The Medina Charter mainly concerns the rights and responsibilities of the Muslim, Jewish, and other tribal communities of Medina during the war between that city and its neighbors. This charter fully recognized the coexistence of religious, ethnic, linguistic, and tribal diversities within the society of Medina.[19]

The term millet has often been inaccurately defined simply as non-Muslim religious communities, popularly known as the *ahl al-dhimma* or *dhimmis,* that is, non-Muslims protected by a treaty of surrender who pay a poll tax. This particular understanding, which first appeared in the decrees issued by the Ottoman sultans in the nineteenth century, ignored a significant connotation of millet, namely sovereignty. Tracing back the use of the term millet to the early Ottoman Empire (1450s), Braude discovered that its most common usage before the formal establishment of the millet system (c. 1454) was to denote the community of Muslims in contradiction to *dhimmis*. Later, as Braude discovered, the Ottoman Empire used the term for international correspondence to address overseas Christians and Jews. Furthermore, the term was employed as well to refer to the Christians and Jews inside the empire, but it was restricted to those who were highly influential and wealthy.[20] All these usages of millet suggest that it has connotations of sovereignty, since the term addressed foreign and honored Christians and Jews, as opposed to other ordinary non-Muslim subjects of the empire, implicitly suggesting that the former led, or were above, the latter. Given this, it may be correct to state that through the establishment of the millet system, the Ottoman government sought to grant virtual sovereignty for each religious community in perpetuity without being subject to renewal, abolition, or limitation, at least until the *Tanzimat* reform in the nineteenth century.

The Millet System of the Ottoman Empire

The millet system of the Ottoman Empire lasted for more than four hundred years. It was initially established during the reign of Sultan Mohammed II (1451–1481) before being gradually abolished by the mid-nineteenth century. The millet system was driven by the external and internal political condition of the empire. Externally, Sultan Mohammed II sought to neutralize the influence of the Papacy and Venice (his main enemies) among the Christians living in the Balkans, the western parts of his territory. In addition, by establishing the Armenian patriarch in Istanbul, the Ottoman Empire attempted to disengage the Armenians in Anatolia from their spiritual capital and demographic center in Armenia, which was outside the eastern borders of the Ottoman Empire, in adjacent hostile territory.[21] Internally, the millet system was a response to the heterogeneous nature of society within the Ottoman Empire. Ruling over a population with a mosaic of religions, languages, and cultures, Mohammed II was aware of the dangerous implications of such a complex ethnic and religious social situation. The millet system was therefore introduced to enable the Ottoman Empire to cope with this ethnic and religious diversity and to secure a degree of harmony.[22] Above all, by allowing non-Muslim religious leaders, patriarchs or rabbis, to assume high positions in his government in Istanbul, Mohammed II sought to unify their followers under their respective millet leadership and build support and legitimacy for the Ottoman rule over people with diverse religious, ethnic, and linguistic backgrounds.[23]

The first major millet established was the Orthodox Christian millet in 1454, one year after the conquest of Constantinople. For the first time since the heyday of the Byzantine Empire, Christians were brought together under the single religious authority of a patriarch (mostly from a Greek background). This Greek patriarch, usually based in Istanbul, had jurisdiction over Greeks, Bulgarians, Serbians, Albanians, Wallachians, Moldavians, Ruthenians, Croatians, Caramanians, Syrians, Melkites, and Arabs.[24] The Jews were the second millet recognized by the Ottoman Empire after the Orthodox Christians. It is not clear exactly when the Jewish millet was established for the first time, since the existence of the institutional religious leadership had already been traditionally central to the Jewish communities. It was Elijah Capsali, whose previous role was as a judge for internal Jewish affairs, who became the first chief rabbi.[25] An Armenian millet was founded in 1461 with a central office in Istanbul. Although there is not enough evidence to say that the Armenian patriarch had patriarchal authority across the empire, he was certainly authorized to assume spiritual jurisdiction over all the Armenians, Syrians, Chaldaeans, Copts, Georgians, and Abyssinians.[26]

There was, of course, also the Muslim community as the dominant millet and the sole millet constituting the political community. Inside the Muslim millet, there were Turks, Arabs, Kurds, and Persians who lived together under the authority of the sacred law, with the sultan as the operator of the law.[27] The sultan's religious role, however, was in practice conducted by the office of *shaykh al-Islam,* an institution that antedated the millet system. This office, first established in 1424, was assigned to give *fatawa* (legal opinions) regarding both Ottoman administrative affairs and general public issues. Under Mohammed II, the *shaykh al-Islam* was given the title "the chief of the *ulama,*" which carried the idea of the unity of church-state interests along with the necessity for moral/legal guidance in imperial affairs. Nevertheless, throughout the history of the Ottoman Empire the office of *shaykh al-Islam* had rarely secured significant political powers, except under Abu al-Su'ud in the last quarter of the sixteenth century.[28]

Karpat argued that the millet system was the Ottoman administration's attempt to allow for the organization and culture of the various religious and ethnic groups it ruled in accordance with the commandments of Islam. Based on this framework, the Ottoman government dealt with non-Muslim subjects of all denominations as members of a community, not as individuals. The millet chief, be he patriarch or rabbi, was in effect the administrative officer responsible to the state for his community, and to his community for the state. Each millet chief had sovereign powers to maintain its own religious institutions and to undertake the functions not carried out by the Ottoman government, such as education, religion, justice, and social security.[29] The fiscal and judicial autonomy of each recognized religious community, Greek, Armenian, or Jewish, was thus preserved through this office.[30]

(In)equality under the Millet System

As far as the application of religious law under the millet system is concerned, each religious community had the right to preserve its own courts, to appoint judges, and to apply legal principles for the use of coreligionists.[31] The patriarch, for example, had the right to apply Orthodox law in secular and religious matters to his Orthodox followers.[32] The Ottoman millet system was not, however, always completely conducive to the internal plurality of the Muslim community itself. When the Ottomans captured and integrated Syria into its dominion in the sixteenth century, they began to change the former condition of total equality between the Hanafi and Shafi'i law courts and adopted a policy of bias toward the Hanafi, the official *madhhab* of the Ottomans.[33] In fact, although there was not any serious suppression, the Ottomans sought to persuade many elite families in Syria to change their affiliation from Shafi'ism to Hanafism.[34] This reveals a negative side of the Ottoman millet system: it could lead to the variety of religious interpretations becoming less tenable, and the condition of intrapluralism within a religion, even the dominant one, could be threatened.

The abolition of the millet system in the nineteenth century had much to do with the effort of the Ottomans to respond to external challenges and to western European threats in particular.[35] In a series of reforms, known as *Tanzimat*, undertaken from 1839 to 1876, the Ottoman Empire offered full equality for its subjects regardless of their particular faith and ethnic backgrounds, thus seeking to eliminate the system of capitulations.[36]

The capitulation system was initially a trade agreement consisting of concessions provided by the Ottomans to the non-Muslim merchant communities to enable them to live in the empire with a number of trade advantages. Later, the capitulations were not only limited to economic matters such as full exemption from Ottoman taxes and custom duties, but also extended to judicial issues. This implied that all subjects of western European states or Christians of the Ottoman Empire who had become protégés of those states remained under the foreign laws and were thus granted exemption from the jurisdiction of the Ottoman court and its legal system.[37]

Following the defeat of the Ottoman Empire in the Russo-Turkish Wars (1768–1774), the capitulation system was exploitatively taken out from its specific technical and legal context and given stronger political connotations by European powers in different treaties signed by the sultans. The capitulations finally came to mean the economic and judicial protection of Christians of the Ottoman Empire by the European states.[38] In this sense, the capitulation system became a virtual reproduction of the millet system, but to the advantage of one particular minority millet.[39]

This reveals that the doctrine of equality not only became a weapon for the Ottoman Empire to attack the capitulation system that undermined its power,[40] but also signified a transformation of the meaning of millet toward something much more like a nation-state. As a result, the concept of 'Ottomanism' emerged during the *Tanzimat* era (1839–1876). Ottomanism was the idea of regarding all individuals living in Ottoman territories as Ottoman subjects regardless of their faith and language. Equal treatment was the philosophical basis of Ottomanism.[41] This concept made a shift from the idea of a state that organized its subjects based on their respective loyalty to an autonomous religious institution to the idea of a state that sought to base itself on the concept of nation, which acknowledged the equal rights of each individual residing within a well-defined territory and which shared a common political culture and a similar ultimate goal. This shift required a reconfiguration of state, community, and freedom as it granted civil and political rights equally and directly to each individual within a nation-state.[42]

As far as the legal systems of the Ottoman Empire since the nineteenth century were concerned, equal treatment was a cornerstone. The old system of differentiation and of Muslim legal superiority formally disappeared. Equality before the law instead became a channel for the introduction of mixed tribunals and the reception of Western laws. Regarding the introduction of mixed tribunals, Quataert comments:

> [Although] religious courts remained, many of their functions vanished. [To replace them,] new courts appeared: so called mixed courts at first heard commercial, criminal, and then civil cases involving persons of different religious communities. Then, beginning in 1869, secular courts (*nizamiye*) presided over civil and criminal cases involving Muslim and non-Muslim.[43]

Additionally, with regard to the reception of Western laws, Coulson noted that during the period of *Tanzimat* a number of French codes (penal code, commercial code, code of commercial procedure, and code of maritime commerce) were translated and ratified for application in all territories under Ottoman jurisdiction.[44] All these developments are evidence that the decline of religious law, *shari'a* in particular, during the reform of the Ottoman legal system was because the millet system no longer fit well with a changing international political order.

However, the principle of equality adopted by the Ottoman Empire was by no means welcomed by the leading figures of each millet. While many Muslim leaders complained about the loss of their rights as the ruling millet and reproached the Christians and the European powers for their plight, the patriarchs and other spiritual chiefs were unhappy to find themselves trapped between accepting new equal treatment under Ottomanism and preserving their privileges under the millet system.[45] In fact, the resistance among religious leaders to Ottomanism was fierce, as Feroz Ahmad describes.

> The Greek Patriarch, Yuvakim Joachim Efendi, clearly perceived the threat [of the principle of equality] . . . to the privileges of his community. He attempted to meet this threat by issuing a proclamation urging the Ottoman government to make concessions that would undercut the program of Ottomanism. He urged the Porte [the ruling Ottoman government] to: guarantee the freedom of person and conscience and accept the traditionally acquired rights of the millets as fundamental principles; confirm ecclesiastical and educational privileges; restore completely the privileges accorded to the Ecumenical Patriarchate and the Greek community (*millet-i Rum*) in the past.[46]

The Ottoman government's attempt to take a step toward equality by deactivating the millet system had restricted the jurisdiction of the clergy of each millet. In addition, this reform had opened the gate for the government to directly handle the legal affairs of all Ottoman subjects regardless of their faith and ethnicity. The increasing authority of the Ottoman government over its subjects did not simply originate from its ambition to take over the influence of religious leaders, but it was an inevitable consequence of the concept of monopolized unitary characteristic of a nation-state.

Legacy of the Millet System

The unitary characteristic of the nation-state assigns to no institution but the state the prerogative of lawmaking and law enforcement within the boundaries of the nation-state. This notion had hardly ever been easy for many religious leaders in the former territories of the Ottoman Empire to accept, especially because the cultural legacy of the past millet system was still influential. As a result, they considered the nation-state a superstructure that organized religious communities similarly to the millet system and hence they felt entitled to maintain the implementation of their particular religious law. This misleading understanding of the nation-state came about because many religious leaders considered the nation to be a religious community. Accordingly, "nationality came to be determined first by religious affiliation . . . and most [religious people] remained faithful to this principle in their understanding of a nation." [47]

The decline of the millet system led to disenchantment, if not resentment, among religious leaders toward the ruling Ottoman government. It is immediately clear here that what was at the stake was the political role of shaping the social structure of society and even the future of the state. For the government, religious leaders were seen as a stumbling block on the path toward modernization, often resisting new technological inventions and social progress. For religious leaders, government officers were a new source of threat to religious power since they could more or less do anything they wanted, including ignoring religious norms, so long as their objectives could be achieved. This situation genuinely reflects a contest between religious leaders and government officers, most of whom had non-religious backgrounds, for the role of principal agent in defining present and future objectives.

What has been described above suggests an argument that the Muslim world did undergo a shift from the traditional world political order (before the nineteenth century) to the modern world political system (the nineteenth century onwards). The evidence derived from the experiences during the late Ottoman era shows that the dichotomous categories of *Dar al-Islam* and *Dar al-Harb* were no longer tenable given the rise of various nation-states in the Muslim lands. In the same way, social segregation under the old system had been transformed into a new structure that provided individuals with sovereign status and equal rights.

In light of the strong influence of millet system over many religious leaders in the late Ottoman era, it is possible to assume that a similar case, though in a different mode of expression, might also have affected some Indonesian Muslim leaders in the early years prior to and during the making of nation-state in 1945. It must be admitted that there is no evidence that the Ottoman millet system was referred to specifically by Muslim leaders in either their speeches or writings. Nevertheless, the way the millet system operated under the Ottoman Empire was quite similar to what some Indonesian Muslims saw as the model established by the Prophet Muhammad in early Medina. Indeed, many Muslim leaders pointed out that the Medina Charter was the first 'constitution' in the world to govern ethnic and religious diversity.[48] This is the part of the general understanding of Indonesian Muslim leaders regarding the doctrine and the history of Islam.

The discussion of the Indonesian context in chapter 6 reveals that some Muslim leaders in early years of independence wanted the new state to prioritize Muslim people over other nationals by granting them privileges in legal and political spaces within the state. These Muslim leaders, however, were not really aware of the implications of the shift from the millet system to the nation-state, and hence their responses seemed to be apologetic rather than assertive.

PART II

Islamization and Nationalism

5
Islamization in Indonesia

Defining 'Islamization'

Although what 'Islamization' means and what it implies is certainly debatable, this study prefers to understand the term 'Islamization,' particularly in the context of a modern nation-state, as a process of certain measures and campaigns, regardless of the identity of the advocates and the motives behind the actions, that call for the establishment of what are regarded as Islamic doctrines in Muslim legal, political, and social systems.[1] It is manifested by the rise of various Islamic movements as a proactive force for political change and social development. The aim of Islamization at this stage is no longer merely to convert people from their previous beliefs to Islam, but to replace a secular-based government with a government grounded in the doctrines of religion and to bring about a new society wholeheartedly committed to the teachings of Islamic *shari'a* in their totality, and striving to abide by those teachings in all aspects of life.[2]

It is clear that the proponents of the formal implementation of *shari'a* consider *shari'a* the foundation of Islamization. In this light, Islamization specifically refers to attempts to produce an Islamic constitution, to introduce *shari'a* rules into the national legal system, and to discard all existing laws that contradict *shari'a*. In sum, the assumption of the proponents of *shari'a*-based reform is that the more *shari'a* rules are incorporated into the state legal system, the deeper the Islamization of a country. Under this scheme, moves toward Islamization ultimately lead to attempts at founding an Islamic state.

According to Taji-Farouki, the meaning of 'Islamic state' is twofold. First, it refers to a state that serves as "a technique by which the *shari'a* can be implemented and its ultimate purposes actualized, regardless of its specific character and the details of its system, institutions, and offices."[3] Second, it refers to a state that "achieves not only the supreme values of the *shari'a,* but also adheres in its systems and institutions to forms precisely defined by the *shari'a* itself."[4] Both of these definitions generally acknowledge that the central ingredient of the concept of an Islamic state is the implementation of *shari'a*. Thus, the formal implementation of *shari'a* is perceived as the single most decisive criterion for determining an Islamic state. The more *shari'a* rules are officially implemented in a state, the more it theoretically becomes a perfect Islamic state.

It is important to mention here that the formal implementation of *shari'a* can be divided into five ranked areas.

1. Family issues, such as marriage, divorce, and inheritance;
2. Financial matters and institutions like *zakat, waqf,* and Islamic banking;
3. *Ta'zir* (discretionary) punishments for committing the prohibited acts, such as liquor consumption and gambling, or for omitting the required acts, for instance, the use of headscarf for women;
4. *Hudud* and *qisas* penalties. *Hudud* for those who commit adultery or fornication and theft, and *qisas* for those found guilty of murder;
5. Islam both as a basis of the state and as a system governing the country.

This hierarchy of the formal implementation of *shari'a* is set from the lowest step (no. 1) to the highest step (no. 5). Thus, demands for implementing the five areas of *shari'a* automatically lead to the calls for the foundation of an Islamic state. In other words, the higher the demand, the closer it is to a demand for the establishment of an Islamic state, and the lower the demand, the less commitment it has to initiate an Islamic state.[5]

Different Phases of Islamization

According to Ricklefs, there have been three phases of Islamization.[6] Throughout these three phases, the term Islamization has had a variety of meanings and different emphases from time to time. The first phase was from the fourteenth to the early nineteenth century. The meaning of Islamization during this period referred to the process of the coming of Islam to Indonesia or the conversion of the indigenous people to the religion of Islam.[7] The term does not simply denote the process of replacing old beliefs with new ones, but also includes the absorption or assimilation of Islam into the local culture, symbols, literature, political institutions, legal texts, traditions, and customs.[8] By and large, this permeation of Islam into Indonesian life was peaceful in the sense that there was no direct Arab conquest to spread Islam in the archipelago. Wars between locals for the purpose of Islamic conversion were, nevertheless, observable.[9]

As a result of this permeation, an acculturated Islam, rather than the orthodox or scriptural versions of Islam, appeared to be more established, in Java in particular. As Ricklefs argued, there were ongoing processes of both Islamization of

Javanese and Javanization of Muslims who had foreign origin by accommodating the cultural style of the Hindu-Buddhist Javanese aristocracy. Moreover, the use of Javanese rather than Arabic terms for crucial concepts in the teaching of orthodox Islamic mysticism, for example, indicated the accommodation of Islam within Javanese society as well as the assimilation of Javanese concepts within local Islam. Having examined various historical evidence, Ricklefs conclusively stated that mysticism (Sufism) was the dominant style of Islam from the sixteenth century until at least the early nineteenth century in Java. The emergence of this mode of religiosity in Java was possible thanks to Sultan Agung (d. 1646) and Ratu Pakubuwana (d. 1732). Ricklefs called this mode "mystic synthesis," which had three characteristic features: (1) commitment to Islamic identity; (2) observation of the five pillars of Islam (the confession of faith or *shahada,* the quintuple of daily prayers, fasting in Ramadan, paying *zakat,* and pilgrimage to Mecca if affordable); but, nevertheless, (3) acceptance of local spiritual forces, such as the Goddess of the Southern Ocean (*Ratu Kidul*). Given that there were conceptual continuities, this mystic synthesis enabled the transition from mystical Hindu-Buddhism to mystical Islam, though with some complexities. The description found in *Sĕrat Cĕnthini* (the monumental Javanese poem composed in 1815) and the religious life of prince Dipanagara (1785–1855) almost completely reflected and personified the Javanese mystic synthesis in one way or another, but the mystic synthesis had never constituted a formal orthodoxy that the courts were able, or concerned, to enforce.[10]

The second phase of Islamization took place from 1830 to 1930.[11] During this period, the reconciliation of Islamic and Javanese identity in the form of mystic synthesis in the previous period was now contested. It was in this period that some Javanese ordinary people began to be less religious and pious and abandon the five pillars of Islam, which marked the rise of the *abangan* (nominal Muslim) category in Javanese society. In fact, as Ricklefs noted, the small minority of Javanese that had converted to Christianity for the first time in history signified the end of the equivalence of Javanese and Islamic identities.[12]

Tensions and clashes among Muslims themselves often characterized this second phase.[13] This partly had to do with the establishment of colonial rules on the one hand and the influence of global Islamic reform on the other.[14] The return of Indonesian pilgrims from Mecca paved the way for the rise of *shari'a*-oriented reformers. In West Sumatra, the Padri movement, led by Muslim figures who had returned from the pilgrimage, wanted a comprehensive and radical reform of Islam. They attempted to purify Islamic teachings from *bid'a* (religious heresy), to fight against acculturated Islam, and to demonstrate a commitment to an untainted Islam.[15] This movement later triggered a civil war (1821–1838) between the reformers and the Minangkabau royal family with the support of Dutch colonial forces. The reformers were defeated.[16]

Given the description above, the term Islamization during the second phase referred to the purification of acculturated Islam, a meaning that lasted until the first half of the twentieth century. In fact, as the impact of religious reforms in the Middle East in the late nineteenth century filtered through to the archipelago, a number of Islamic reformist movements that held to a more strict commitment to Islam emerged by the early decades of the twentieth century.[17] The foundation of Indonesian Muslim modernist movements such as Muhammadiyah, Al-Irsyad, and Persatuan Islam (Persis) was thus intended to purify and rectify what was perceived to be a degeneration of religious belief and Islamic practice.[18] While the impetus behind this movement was the return to the Qur'an and Sunna and the introduction of modern Islamic education,[19] its target was, among other things, the elimination of the third element of mystic synthesis, the acceptance of multiple local spiritual forces. In the light of this purification, Islamization was meant to educate Muslim people who nominally already subscribed to the worldview of Islam, so that they would become true Muslims with a more precise and righteous orthodoxy.[20]

The third phase of Islamization has been from 1930 onwards.[21] The meaning of the term Islamization in this phase has implied several concepts and emphases at different times. Given that a more thorough Islamization of Indonesia has been undertaken in a purposeful and organized way only in this modern era, a new grouping of phases within this modern period of Indonesia is needed.

Islamization in the Modern Period

It is my contention that there have been three distinct modern periods within an ongoing process of Islamization since 1930. First, there was an effort to Islamize the state. This kind of Islamization, according to Muzaffar, is "a part of the reassertion of an identity, which was suppressed under Western colonial rule." Viewed through this lens, "Islamization is an endeavor to establish the uniqueness of a civilization which refuses to accept Western domination and control."[22] Thus, it is not surprising that some key Western political concepts, such as nationalism, the nation-state, presidential government, parliamentary democracy, constitutionalism, and the idea of a state political ideology, were the objects of this form of Islamization.

An attempt at Islamizing the state was initially observable in the early 1930s when some Muslim figures from the Persatuan Islam (Persis), such as Ahmad Hassan and M. Natsir, fiercely criticized the lack of Islamic elements within the movement for Indonesia's independence led by the nationalist leaders, such as Soekarno.[23] The criticism intensified prior to and during Indonesia's independence in 1945, as will be discussed in detail in chapter 7. This type of Islamization lasted until the political consolidation of the New Order regime in 1968. Political parties, parliamentary debates, armed struggle, and the 1955 elections were devices to Islamize the country during this period.[24] For a variety of reason, however, these efforts did not succeed, as will be explained in the next chapters.

Second, there was an attempt to Islamize social life by focusing on society rather than on the state. As described by Salleh, the Islamization of society usually refers to the process where Islamic culture and values become embedded in society, though it tends to refer more to the ceremonial and ritual habit of the individual Muslim, such as the observance of the main tenets of Islamic teaching in everyday life.[25] In fact, the Islamization of society in Indonesia has established among Muslims a stronger sense of identity,[26] including their exclusive economic activity.[27] This type of Islamization is usually able to produce a strong awareness of self-identity that often results in an individual becoming a more devout and practicing Muslim. However, it has not necessarily led to a stronger role for Islam in Indonesian public life.

Islamization of society took place from 1968 to the fall of the New Order regime in 1998. Significantly, it emerged when it appeared that all hopes and formal opportunities for the Islamization of the state were gone. Realizing that struggles related in particular to the proclamation of an official Islamic state had failed, many Islamic leaders looked at the problem from another angle and began to infuse society with Islamic precepts, thus working toward Islamization from below. Intensive *da'wa* (Islamic preaching) and the publication of great numbers of Islamic books during this period were seen as ways to accelerate the process of Islamization.[28] So, for example, having failed in 1968 to re-establish the Masyumi political party, banned by Soekarno in 1960, one of its prominent leaders, Mohammad Natsir, decided to devote himself to *da'wa* rather than politics by founding the DDII (Council of Islamic Propagation of Indonesia) in 1967. This council has since sought to transform Indonesian people into more pious Muslims.[29]

The Islamization of society gained its momentum only after the New Order government suspended all discussions regarding the Jakarta Charter at the end of the 1960s, forced all Islamic political parties to be fused into a single party (Partai Persatuan Pembangunan) in 1973, and imposed Pancasila to replace Islam as the sole ideological basis of all political parties by the early 1980s. Perhaps as an unintended consequence of the New Order's policy of depoliticizing Islam, the state apparatus, through the Ministry of Religious Affairs, had transformed itself into an official agent of Islamization by initiating the incorporation of some aspects of *shari'a* into the national legal system.[30] As there was limited accommodation of certain Islamic institutions within the state administration during the 1990s,[31] many felt that the formal depoliticization of Islam by the Soeharto regime was a blessing in disguise, as it encouraged a deepening Islamization of Indonesian society in non-political contexts.[32]

Third, in the post–New Order era (from 1998 onwards), there has been an increasing endeavor to concurrently Islamize both the state and society. Several Islamic radical groups saw the governmental campaign of Islamization during the Soeharto regime as a 'pseudo-Islamization,' since it merely accommodated certain Islamic elements in a partial or fragmentary manner while the government apparatus itself continued to be dominated by un-Islamic attributes, such as corruption, bribery, fraud, and blackmail. These Islamic groups insisted upon Islamizing both the outer form and the inner substance of political institutions, social relations, and Muslim individuals. Their efforts included establishing Islamic political parties, seeking to give *shari'a* a constitutional status, promulgating Islamic regulation in some regions and localities, demanding Islamic morality in public life, pushing for full recognition of Islamic holidays and events, showing solidarity with other Muslim countries, and expressing a commitment as devout Muslims who practice Islam in all aspects of human social relations through attempts, for instance, at the introduction of the Islamic penal law and the establishment of the caliphate.[33]

Why do such Islamic groups regard the Islamization of the state and society in post-Soeharto Indonesia as crucial? To these groups, everything that had seemingly been Islamized in Indonesia during the last decade remains in their eyes secular in form.[34] Furthermore, while this is not the underlying cause, the inability of the state legal apparatus to uphold the law and to reduce crime in present-day Indonesia has aggravated the situation and provided these groups with the grounds to launch a campaign for the Islamization of state and society by invoking the call for formal *shari'a* implementation.[35]

Given this account of Islamization in modern Indonesia, one can argue that each period has sought to generate a specific character of Muslims. If Islamization through purification tended to result in 'puritan Muslims,' then, by contrast, the Islamization of the state attempted to create 'partisan Muslims' since the involvement with and support of Islamic political institutions was the single accepted criterion for determining one's authentic attachment or commitment to Islam.[36] Meanwhile, if creating 'practicing Muslims' was the objective of the Islamization of society during the period from 1968 to 1998, the 'ideological Muslims' have been the target of the Islamization of state and society that exists in current times, as this is the only type that makes the ideologization of Islam possible. The 'ideologization' of Islam here means making Islam a religion that offers not only a spiritual belief or values, but also a set of rules by which to govern the state. This manifests itself, as Mir Zohair Husain points out, in the ceaseless efforts of Islamic parties and interest groups, as well as in the form of government-sponsored Islamic policies and programs in some states, to establish an Islamic political system.[37]

6

Different Conceptions
of Nationalism

The perception that Islam is compatible with nationalism stemmed not only from the Ottoman millet system, as discussed in chapter 4, but also from the experience of many Muslim countries that were colonized by non-Muslim powers. There was widespread conviction that nationalism in Muslim countries was a direct result of the foreign, non-Muslim colonialism of Islamic lands. Thus, in the light of colonialism, nationalism was often understood as a shared response of Muslim peoples to the foreign infidel power. As William C. Smith has already pointed out, this nationalism devoted to resisting Western imperialism was "compatible with Islam in its traditional, in its religion, and its social and every other aspect."[1] For this reason, it is no wonder that as early as the twentieth century some Muslim leaders in Indonesia were prone to perceive Islam automatically as nation.

Islamic Nationalism vs. Fatherland Nationalism

Of the four critical contributing factors to the Indonesian nationalist conscious-ness, the most important factor, according to Kahin, was the high degree of religious homogeneity (Islam) that prevailed in Indonesia.[2] Islam became not only a force to break down local patriotism, but also a carrier of the national (self)-con-sciousness of the Indonesian people. Islam in Indonesia, as argued by Muham-mad Natsir, had, indeed, been a unifier among its believers across the different remote islands of the archipelago. For many inhabitants of the archipelago, Islam had played an important role in mobilizing and strengthening the feeling of being united under the oppression of the non-Muslim colonialists, the Dutch.[3]

The foundation of Sarekat Islam in 1911 had initially established this Islamic nationalism. At its Sixth Congress in Surabaya (1921), Sarekat Islam under Tjokro-aminoto and Agus Salim restated the importance of Islam as both the foundation and aims of the party movement. They developed Islamic nationalism to mean not only the unity of the Indonesian Muslims but also solidarity with the struggle of Muslims elsewhere in the world.[4] Because of this approach, the National Indies Party, which promoted the concept of an East Indies nationalism (a concept of nationhood based on the territories in the archipelago occupied by the Netherlands), accused the leaders of Sarekat Islam of developing an Islamic nationalism as part of Pan-Islamism, which led to the deterioration of national unity.

Explaining that Islamic nationalism did not contradict the notion of East Indies nationalism, Tjokroaminoto fiercely contended that:

> Islam did not in the least hamper or obstruct the creation and the course of real nationalism, but in fact promotes it. Islamic nationalism was not narrow nationalism and was not dangerous [to others], but . . . that would lead to Islamic socialism, i.e. socialism, which creates mono-humanism (the unity of mankind) controlled by the Supreme Being, Allah, through the laws which had been revealed to His apostle, the last prophet of Muhammad.[5]

In addition, Tjokroaminoto argued that Islam contains the complete teachings that regulate all aspects of life including politics, society, and economy. There is therefore no legitimate reason to alter the Islamic concept of nationalism by introducing other notions. In fact, Islamic nationalism helped Indonesians avoid dividing into a great number of small ethnic group nationalisms. Thus, for him, it was Islamic nationalism that united Indonesians, regardless of their diverse ethnic cultural backgrounds.[6]

Some Muslim leaders, however, rejected Indonesian nationalism because it divided the international community of Muslims and because it originated from Europe and brought war and imperialism.[7] Agus Salim, another leader of Sarekat Islam, argued that the love for the country as in Europe encouraged the worshipping and idolizing of one's nationality, and he further pointed to other dangers dormant in nationalism that nationalists were prone to commit.[8] For Salim, this meant not that his party abandoned the love of one's country, but that it continued to regard it as an important principle. Love of country, according to him, should be in favor of justice as fixed by God, meaning that it should not exceed faith in God.[9]

In his response to these criticisms, Soekarno, a leader of the Indonesian Nationalist Party (PNI, established in 1927), sought to avoid contrasting Indonesian nationalism and Islamic nationalism. Instead he attempted to reconcile them by saying that both stemmed from a common basis, the fight against Western imperialism. In addition, he offered a particular understanding of Islamic nationalism. Soekarno wrote that the internationalism of Islam would strengthen the power of

Indonesian nationalism in the face of colonialism, because those Muslims who reside in any country of the Muslim world (*Dar al-Islam*) are required to struggle for the defense of the country where they live. Anywhere Muslims live, according to Soekarno, they must love and work for the victory of their abode, and so too must Muslims in Indonesia.[10]

It is obvious here that there was little difference between the leaders of Sarekat Islam and Soekarno in their conceptions of the psychological features of nationalism. There was much difference, however, in their political objectives for nationalism. What Soekarno and his party wanted was full independence with self-governance for Indonesia. Such independence, he believed, would come only as the result of the united efforts of all Indonesians, regardless of their religious backgrounds.[11] This point was stressed by Soekarno, who stated that "independence was as much the objective of Indonesian Christians as of Muslims [and it] was useless . . . to wait for help from an airplane from Moscow or a caliph from Istanbul." [12]

Meanwhile, with their conception of Islamic nationalism, the leaders of Sarekat Islam desired a solution to the international caliphate question. At its special meeting in Surabaya on 4–5 October 1924 (seven months after the abolition of the Ottoman caliphate), Sarekat Islam, through its leader, Tjokroaminoto, emphasized the need for Muslims to have a replacement caliph. As Muslims of the East Indies at that time still lived under another government, Tjokroaminoto explained the relevance of the caliphate as a religious one. He further reproached foreign non-Muslim powers who sought to interfere in the religious affairs of Muslims in the colonized lands.[13]

Tjokroaminoto's explanation suggests that if Muslims of the East Indies had a chance of self-government, the caliphate issue for them would be politically important. In light of this, the political future of Islamic nationalism proposed by the leaders of Sarekat Islam seemed to depend on whether or not Pan-Islamism would succeed. Finally, since there was no clear prospect for the future of the caliphate, the leaders of Sarekat Islam gave up on the campaign for Pan-Islamism in 1929 and shifted to favor Indonesian nationalism.[14] A year later, the organization's name was changed from Partai Sarekat Islam to Partai Sjarikat Islam Indonesia.[15] Adding the word "Indonesia" to the name of the party represented a clear shift of Sarekat Islam's orientation from Islamic internationalism to Indonesian Islamic nationalism.

Sarekat Islam concluded its debate on Islamic nationalism by the late 1920s, and another Islamic organization, the Persatuan Islam (Persis), established in 1923, took over the discourse in the early 1930s. This Muslim organization, which was primarily founded for discussions on religious issues, furthered the articulation of Islamic nationalism vis-à-vis Indonesian nationalism. In fact, the discourse developed by the activists of Persis is relevant to this study, since their opinions and criticisms addressed the issue of the legal system of the prospective self-governing Indonesia. Persis' criticisms were due to the fact the proponents of Indonesian nationalism ignored the use of Islamic elements in their movement for Indonesia's independence. In fact, for Indonesian nationalists, as Federspiel wrote, "Islam could not be the basis of the nationalist movement since Christians, Hindus, Buddhists and even animists were also involved and would not support a movement intended to favor Islam and place themselves in a subservient position." [16]

The Muslim leaders, according to Ricklefs, were basically not able to understand that in a country where the majority was Muslim there could be anything other than Islam seriously proposed as the basis of unity.[17] Therefore, the criticisms launched by Persis figures such as Ahmad Hassan and Mohammad Natsir were largely based on the fact that almost 90 percent of the Indonesian population was Muslim and that Islam was the bond that unified people from diverse places and ethnic and language backgrounds in the East Indies. For this reason, while Hassan queried as to why the 90 percent Muslim majority must be overlooked because of the 10 percent non-Muslim minority, Natsir contended that without Islam there was no Indonesian nationalism, since Islam had first planted the seeds of Indonesian unity and removed attitudes of isolation in remote islands.[18] Once again, it is clear here that the arguments presented by these Muslim leaders were more about the psychological nature of nationalism than about its political future.

The political future of Islamic nationalism described by Persis activists was unfortunately to return to the universal religious state of the medieval ages. This position was clear since Persis continued to support the idea of Pan-Islamism even though many other Muslim organizations had discarded this political obsession.[19] It was only after Indonesia's independence in 1945 that Persis abandoned this aspiration and acknowledged that the national state was the practical political organization for the current age.

Between Natsir and Soekarno

The polemic between Natsir and Soekarno in early 1940s clearly articulated the different views on the political future of Indonesian nationalism. On the one hand, Natsir placed heavy emphasis on Islamic, rather than Indonesian, nationalism. With this emphasis, Natsir sought for the state to assist Muslims in observing their religious duties. On the other hand, Soekarno preferred to see Indonesian nationalism as having a neutral position toward religion that would liberate the state from the intervention in religious affairs.

Natsir distinguished the political goals of Muslims in an independent state of

Indonesia from those of groups who supported the idea of neutrality toward religion, saying that:

> The objective of Muslims to fight for independence is to achieve the independence of Islam, in order that the Islamic rules and structures of Islam can be applied, for the salvation and the dignity of Muslims in particular and all God's creatures in general.[20]

It is no wonder that Natsir rejected the concept of a religiously neutral state proposed by the nationalist group. In Natsir's eyes, the state's guarantee for protecting Islam was not adequate if this meant only that:

> Muslims will be given freedom to pray at home and in the mosque, [that they] will not be prohibited from fasting and celebrating the 'Id [Islamic festivals], [they] will be permitted to go on pilgrimage and to pay zakat voluntarily (no attention paid to those who evade zakat payment), [that they] will be allowed to make arrangements for the dead, for marriages and divorces and similar other cases according to their preference.

It seemed that for Natsir this kind of guarantee would not balance the sacrifices that Muslims had already made because these rights were available under any government, including the colonial government. Moreover, he said, "it is not proper for Islam to receive protection; it is Islam which should give this protection." [21]

Natsir saw Soekarno's suggestion that Indonesian Muslims should dominate the parliament to be able to set and determine the state agenda, resulting ultimately in the formulation of policy decisions imbued with Islamic values, as irrelevant since Islam already embraced the majority of Indonesian inhabitants in any case.[22] For Natsir, Indonesia must be automatically a Muslim country. Soekarno's suggestion, he thought, might be appropriate for Muslims who live in a predominantly non-Muslim democratic country.[23] Moreover, Natsir further sought to convince people that the implementation of *shari'a* in Indonesia would not spoil or endanger other religions. For this, he contended that a refusal to implement Islamic law in Indonesia because it would hurt non-Muslims feelings would tyrannize Indonesian Muslims, whose population dominates the country, and would thus violate the rights and the interests of the majority.[24]

Responding to Natsir's argument, Soekarno contended that there was dissonance between the concept of democracy and the notion of unity of religion and state. For Soekarno, such a notion would only create a sense of discrimination, particularly among non-Muslims. In his essay titled "Saya Kurang Dinamis" [I am less dynamic], he wrote:

[The] reality shows us that the principle of the unity of state and religion for a country whose inhabitants are not 100 percent Muslim could not be in line with [the principle of] democracy. In such a country, there are only two alternatives; there are only two choices; the unity of state-religion, but without democracy, or democracy, but the state is separated from religion! The unity of religion and state, but authoritarian and betray democracy, or committed to democracy yet disregard the unity of religion and state![25]

[. . .]

How do you put your ideals (about the unity of religion and state) into practice in a country in which you will uphold democracy, where some of its population are not adherents to Islam, like Turkey, India and Indonesia, [and] where [in these countries] there are millions of Christians or other believers and their intellectual groups in general do not subscribe to Islamic thought? . . . If you rule the country in which many of the people are non-Muslims, will you decide by yourselves that Islam is the basis of the state, the constitution is an Islamic constitution, [and] all laws must be Islamic *shari'a?* If the Christians and other believers do not want to accept [your decision], what will you do? If the intellectual groups do not want to accept [your decision], what will you do? Do you want to force them . . . to agree with your decision? . . . Do you want to play dictator, to force [them] with arms and cannons? If they will still not obey, what will you do? You do not want to eliminate them all, [do you?] for the present is a modern period and not a period of annihilation of each other as was the practice of former days.[26]

Soekarno's remarks suggest that it is not acceptable in a modern nation-state to enact a national law by looking only at one source of religion to apply to various people with different backgrounds. Soekarno, however, acknowledged that every element of society would have a chance to contest, influence, and introduce their religious views in state regulation. Thus, the result that might come from this process was a single uniform law applicable to all citizens, regardless of their backgrounds.

In the polemic between Soekarno and Natsir, it is interesting to note that Deliar Noer, an Indonesian political scientist, has concluded that both lacked clear detail in their writing on the political future of Indonesian nationalism once independence arrived. While Noer criticized Soekarno for his inconsistency in applying democracy (his Presidential Decree of 5 July 1959 shifted parliamentary democracy to 'guided democracy'), he regretted that Natsir did not offer a comprehensive account of the rights and the status of non-Muslims in Indonesia. In other words, Noer considered that both interest groups, albeit united in the national movement to fight colonialism, did not set up a robust foundation for shaping the political future of Indonesian nationalism. In my view, Noer's assessment was unfair, since it is clear that Soekarno was more conscious of, and hence more prepared to anticipate, the political implications of the national state by proposing democracy. What Natsir understood about democracy at that moment was only majoritarianism, while Soekarno emphasized the important role of procedures in democracy, which, according to many political scientists, is much more significant than any other aspect of democracy.[27]

∿

The foregoing discussion shows that the awareness of many Muslim leaders of the shift from the traditionally universal religious states to the modern secular nation-states was a long process that had taken more than two decades. However, although Muslim leaders eventually acknowledged the necessity of a nation-state, they were still unaware of the implications of this shift—that is, equality. This lack of awareness can be clearly seen in the circular issued in 1941 by the Daily Board of the Majelis Islam A'la Indonesia (MIAI), a federation of Muslim organizations, regarding the amendment of the draft of the Indonesian constitution prepared by the Indonesian Political Alliance (GAPI), a federation of political parties that struggled for Indonesia's independence. The MIAI circular proposed that adherence to Islam be required for the head of state and for two-thirds of the ministers of the cabinet. In addition, the MIAI requested that there be a ministry to administer religious affairs. Finally, they demanded that the flag of Indonesia be red and white with a crescent.[28] Although this circular generated protests among the members of MIAI itself, it might indicate that a concept of equal rights between different religious believers was still absent among Muslim leaders, thus suggesting the fault lines in their understanding of the concept of the nation-state, even if they already accepted it as an inevitable fact.

It is difficult to confirm that there was a correlation between the political developments in Turkey (the decline of the millet system and the abolition of the Ottoman caliphate) and the discourse of nationalism developed by Indonesian Muslim leaders during the early period of Indonesia. However, this is in a sense not the point. The fact that Muslim leaders in Turkey and Indonesia faced a comparable situation, and expected a similar solution, suggests a common experience of the global Muslim community in the era of nation-states, and certainly of many Turkish and Indonesian Muslims. At that time, Islam became the defining characteristic of a global community that increasingly came to be seen as a nation for many Muslims in Indonesia. They therefore considered themselves as a political community whose goal was to achieve political power and to rule a country based on Islamic precepts, thus positioning Muslims as the principal citizens of the country.

The next chapter shows that in the wake of Indonesia's proclamation of independence, Muslim leaders were keen to realize this goal by introducing provisions into the Indonesian constitution that benefited Muslims. Although their efforts were not completely successful, they achieved an important concession never granted during the Dutch colonial period: the founding of the Ministry of Religious Affairs. Since its inception, as discussed in chapter 8, this ministry has been a device for the expansion and consolidation of Islamic institutions in Indonesia.

7

Formation of the Indonesian State

Because a successful interrelation between Islam and the state depends largely on the extent to which *shari'a* is implemented by the state, fierce discussions on whether Indonesia as a modern nation-state should implement *shari'a* for its Muslim citizens emerged during the months prior to Indonesia's independence on 17 August 1945. Many studies have focused on the perspective of Muslim nationalists as opposed to secular nationalists and have put aside the conceptions of state offered by both camps.[1] This chapter, therefore, will discuss the same subject but with a particular emphasis on the concepts of the unitary state and the so-called fragmentary state. The chapter posits that there has been an ongoing contest between efforts to implement the unitary state ideal and attempts to turn Indonesia into a fragmentary state since the first years of Indonesia's independence. It now seems, however, that the latter model may be more politically successful.

'Unitary State' vs. 'Fragmentary State'

Before going any further, let me explain what I mean by 'unitary state' and 'fragmentary state.' The former refers to a vision of Indonesia shared by most of the founding fathers[2] as a "state which neither fuses itself with the largest group in society nor allies with the strongest (political or economical) group, but [in fact] . . . transcends all groups, over individuals; it bonds all levels of society."[3] The 'fragmentary state' is understood as the exact opposite of the unitary state, that is, a state that links itself to the largest group of the country's population by offering degrees of autonomy either to particular religious communities or regions.

The discussion of the state format for a new Indonesia began seriously when the Japanese occupation promised Indonesia independence several months before August 1945. Although the Japanese had given a privileged position to Islam during their occupation,[4] there was no clear plan for the Japanese to initiate the establishment of a new state colored by a strong religious sentiment. As far as the position of Islam in the new Indonesia was concerned, the Japanese authorities, as described by Benda, "have not the slightest blueprint or plan concerning the place which the Islamic religion should occupy in the government, or what the relationship should be between Islam and other religions."[5] The Japanese claimed only to facilitate the efforts of Indonesian people to realize their own goal of founding the new state. However, it was suspected that the Japanese were likely to back the secular ideas propounded by the nationalists during the decolonization period.[6]

In early 1945, there was already hot debate over the character of the future Indonesian state between Islamic and nationalist leaders in the Sanyo Kaigi (Advisers Council), an official body of the Japanese government. According to Lev, the Gunseikanbu (military administration headquarters) was curious to know what was Sanyo Kaigi's vision regarding the relationship between religion and the state in an independent Indonesia, which promptly led to the polarization of competing ideologies between Muslims and nationalists. From February to April 1945, the focus of much of the discussion was on Muslim institutions, such as the status and jurisdiction of an Islamic court, the roles of the chief mosque administrator (*kepala masjid*), and whether *penghulu* (the Islamic religious official) would continue to counsel the first instance of the ordinary courts and remain adviser to the heads of regencies (*bupati*).[7]

Abikusno Tjokrosuyoso, the leader of the Indonesian Islamic Union Party (PSII), advocated that Islamic courts not only must remain—he took this for granted—but should also be strengthened through the provision of better-educated and government-paid judges. Moreover, their original jurisdiction over inheritance, which was transferred to the state court in the Dutch colonial period, should be restored. Above all, Abikusno not only defended the formal existence of the Islamic religious advisers, but also "argued forcefully for granting the Islamic *umma* its full due, which amounted to something very close to an Islamic state."[8] For Abikusno and other Muslim leaders, Islam could only survive and grow stronger and be fulfilled as a religion if it had the state behind it.

Meanwhile, although Mohammad Hatta, the secular nationalist[9] and the first vice president, welcomed the existence of *kepala masjid* and *penghulu,* he was not in favor of the Islamic courts. Apparently, Hatta felt it was sufficient to have all cases tried by an ordinary court, which could seek the advice of *penghulu.* In fact, Hatta also did not support the idea that national law should be derived solely from the Qur'an. As quoted by Lev, Hatta wrote:

> [a] healthy sense of logic tells us it is not possible [to base national law purely on the Qur'an]. . . . The Qur'an is especially the basis of religion, not a book of law (*kitab hukum*). The various legal needs of today find no regulations in the Qur'an. . . . If all these legal needs must be filled from the Qur'an through interpretation, how difficult government will be; and how many men are capable of doing it? Of course

the Qur'an establishes a basis for justice and welfare, which must be followed by Muslims. But this basis . . . is only a guiding goal. . . . The people of the state themselves must establish orderly law by their mutual deliberations. Of course, every person will express his conceptions based on his religious convictions. But the resulting law will be *state* law, not religious law. Possibly it will be state law much influenced by religious law or its spirit may be infused with religious spirit.[10]

On the relationship between religion and the state, Hatta's stance was certainly different from that of the Islamic groups who wanted no separation between the private and public spaces in Islam. Hatta stated:

[w]e will not establish a state with a separation of religion and state, but a separation of religious affairs and state affairs. If religious affairs are also handled by the state, then the religion will become state equipment and . . . its eternal character will disappear. State affairs belong to all of us. The affairs of Islam are exclusively the affairs of the Islamic *ummah* and the Islamic society.[11]

It must be kept in mind here that the nationalist group was predominant. Most of them were university graduates and thus more politically skilled and articulate, and they were in control of the direction of Indonesian politics prior to and during the independence period. However, the fact that Islam was rooted in the majority of the population of Indonesia was too overwhelming to be ignored. This was because, as Ricklefs explained, the political isolation of Islam would only generate the isolation of the nationalist elite from the masses, for at this time only Islam could offer the organizational link between the educated urban leaders and the rural society.[12] For this reason, it was no wonder that Muslim leaders were invited to participate in the Investigatory Committee for the Independence of Indonesia (BPUPKI), created by the Japanese occupation to draft a constitution for the proposed independent Indonesian state.

At the first round of meetings of the BPUPKI, which lasted from late May to mid-July 1945, both contending camps were openly confrontational in debating the basis for the new state of Indonesia. Three speeches of the nationalist group, presented by Muhammad Yamin, Soepomo, and Soekarno on 29 May, 31 May, and 1 June respectively, argued that the Five Principles (the Pancasila) [13] would be the foundation of Indonesia. Although these three speeches were slightly different in formulating what should constitute the Five Principles, they shared a similar opinion that the Indonesian state should not be solely based on Islam.

Among these three speeches, the most detailed one was Soepomo's. Unlike Yamin and Soekarno, Soepomo explained more specifically what a non-Islamic state of Indonesia would look like. Having analyzed various theories of states in the world history, Soepomo came up with the idea of the state that requires "the unity between the leader and his/her people and the unity of all in the state." [14] However, as Soepomo emphasized, this kind of state was not meant to deny the interests of various groups or individuals in the society. Instead, "it recognizes and respects those interests in the sense that groups and individuals should be conscious that they are an organic part of the state totally and feel obliged to strengthen the unity and harmony among those parts." [15]

Criticizing the idea of an Islamic state propounded by the speakers from the Islamic groups, Soepomo highlighted the importance of the unitary model for the new independent state of Indonesia. For Soepomo, there were differences between "an Islamic state" and "the state that is founded on the high ideals of Islam." In the former, "the state cannot be separated from religion. State and religion are one, a whole." [16] To create this Islamic state, according to Soepomo, would mean "not setting up a unitary state," but "the state that is going to link itself to the largest group, the Islamic group." He further argued that

> [i]f an Islamic state is created in Indonesia then certainly the problem of minor-
> ities will arise, the problem of small religious groups, of Christians and others.
> Although an Islamic state will safeguard the interests of other groups as well as
> possible, these smaller religious groups will certainly not be able to feel involved in
> the state. Therefore, the ideals of an Islamic state do not agree with the ideals of a
> unitary state which we all have so passionately looked forward to. [17]

Having said this, Soepomo expressed his agreement with a national unitary state that acknowledged the rights of every group, both large and small, and individuals to subscribe to any religion. Thus, everyone, regardless of religious background, would feel at one with the state and feel at home in his or her state. For Soepomo, a national unitary state did not mean a state without a religious character. Instead, this kind of state would have a lofty moral basis, such as that advocated by Islam. Declaring his concurrence with the notion of "the state founded on the high ideals of Islam," Soepomo said:

> [I]n the state of Indonesia[,] citizens must be stimulated to love their fatherland, to
> devote themselves to and sacrifice themselves for the sake of the country, to gladly
> serve the fatherland, to love and serve their leaders and the state, to bow down to
> God, to think of God every moment. All this must constantly be promoted and
> used as a moral basis for this national unitary state. And I am convinced that Islam
> will strengthen these principles. [18]

Soekarno, who delivered his speech the day after Soepomo, underscored further the possibility of Islam giving its high ideals to influence the direction of a national unitary state. In this national state, according to Soekarno, Islam finds fertile soil, for "this is the best place to promote religion." Islam can be defended by "mutual agreement, achieved by deliberation, namely in the Parliament." Soekarno elaborated:

> [i]f we really are an Islamic people, let us then work as hard as we can, to see that the greatest number of seats in the Parliament, which we shall form, will be held by Islamic representatives. . . . If we take it that Parliament has one hundred members, then let us work, work as hard as possible, so that sixty, seventy, eighty, ninety of the representatives sitting in Parliament will be Muslims, Islamic leaders. Then the laws, which Parliament promulgates, will naturally be Islamic laws. Yes, I am even convinced that only when something like this happens, only then can it be said that Islam really lives in the soul of the people.[19]

The counterarguments of the Islamic groups during this first round of the BPUPKI meeting came from Ki Bagus Hadikusumo, the leader of Muhammadiyah.[20] In his remarks, presented on 31 May 1945, Hadikusumo demanded the establishment of a state on the basis of Islamic principles for two reasons.[21] First, he claimed that Islam is strongly embedded at the heart of the Indonesian people. Addressing an audience that was mostly of the nationalist camp, Hadikusumo challenged them to look into the people's hearts to discover what actually resided there. What was to be found, according to Hadikusumo, was that the majority of Indonesian people would have Islam in their hearts. Second, Hadikusumo mentioned that the fight against the colonial Dutch, which Muslims mostly initiated, was an incentive for Islam to be a formal religion in the new state.[22]

Responding to the idea of national unity presented by the nationalist group, Hadikusumo quoted various Qur'anic verses[23] implying that Islam is an effective device to achieve strong unity.[24] It seemed, for Hadikusumo, that Islam has been the largest and the most important part of the unity of Indonesia for a long time. He apparently assumed that the unity of Indonesian people under Islam was naturally identical to the national unity of Indonesia. Accordingly, Hadikusumo saw no serious obstacle to the establishment of an Indonesian state based on Islamic principles.

The Jakarta Charter

There was no immediate consensus from this first round of the BPUPKI meeting. Instead, nine members were chosen to look for a solution to the increasing tension between the nationalist and Islamic camps regarding the basis of the new state of Indonesia. They were Soekarno, Mohammad Hatta, A. A. Maramis, Achmad

Subardjo, Muhammad Yamin, Abikusno Tjokrosuyoso, Abdul Kahar Muzakkir, Agus Salim, and Wahid Hasjim. The first five represented the nationalist camp, while the rest represented the Islamic groups (Abikusno and Agus Salim were from Sarekat Islam; Abdul Kahar Muzakkir from Muhammadiyah, and Wahid Hasjim from Nahdlatul Ulama).[25]

At the meeting on 22 June 1945, these nine leaders managed to arrive at a compromise. The nationalist group had an assurance from the Islamic group that the state of Indonesia would not be based on Islam, while the Islamic group received a concession from the nationalist group that the practice of Islamic *shari'a* would be obligatory for Muslim citizens. This compromise, later well-known as the Jakarta Charter, constitutes the 'seven words' *dengan kewajiban menjalankan syariat Islam bagi pemeluk-pemeluknya* [with the obligation for adherents of Islam to practice Islamic *shari'a*] inserted in the formulation of the Pancasila as part of the preamble of the 1945 constitution.[26]

However, in Boland's view, this compromise was vague since there was no clarity about what the seven words would actually mean in practice. Boland inquired, "Does this formula mean a more or less Islamic state? Does it have legal consequences . . . or does this formula only carry meaning as a pious stimulus for the Muslims? . . . in other words, what has the state to do with it?" [27] The compromise was therefore interpreted differently according to the interests of the respective parties. For the Islamic groups, the compromise meant that the government had to actively put *shari'a* into practice. For the nationalist groups, the practice of Islamic *shari'a* was a duty of Muslims, not of the state. Instead, the nationalists put the words "in accordance with the principle of a righteous and moral humanitarianism" immediately after the seven words in the draft preamble to prevent the possibility of an overly rigorous application of *shari'a*.[28] Whatever the implication of this formula and its precise interpretation, however, the Jakarta Charter was a successful device to invite all elements of Indonesian society (and especially Muslims as members of the majority population) to join the effort to achieve the independence of Indonesia and to participate in the new state.

The compromise reached in the form of the Jakarta Charter was not, however, the final consensus. This temporary consensus then had to be brought to the second round of the BPUPKI meeting (10–16 July 1945) for deliberation by all BPUPKI members. On the second day of the meeting (11 July 1945), three members raised objections to the Jakarta Charter. The first was Latuharhary, a Protestant representative from Maluku, who demanded its revision, since it could have a big impact on other religions and might create difficulties with customary law (*adat istiadat*). The other two members were Wongsonegoro (a liberal Javanese) and Hoesein Djayadiningrat (the first Indonesian head of the Office for Religious Affairs during the Japanese occupation), who alleged that the Jakarta Charter would lead to religious fanaticism because Muslims would be forced to practice Islamic law. To Latuharhary's objection, Agus Salim replied that the conflict between religious law and *adat* law was not new and in fact had been already resolved. He added that non-Muslim citizens did not need to worry about "[t]heir safety," because it was "not dependent on the power of the state, but on the tradition of the Islamic community, which includes 90 percent of the population.[29]

In response to Wongsonegoro and Djayadiningrat's objection that the seven words may create fanaticism because Muslims would be forced to apply *shari'a,* Wahid Hasjim reminded the audience of the importance of the principle of mutual deliberation (*permusyawaratan*) in Indonesia and that therefore there would be no compulsion. He further contended that if some members considered these seven words were going too far, there were other members as well who regarded the Jakarta Charter as not going far enough.[30]

During this second BPUPKI meeting, the Islamic groups tried to go further beyond what they had obtained in the Jakarta Charter. Realizing that their demand for Islam as the basis of the state had failed, Muslim leaders insisted on unambiguous concessions in connection with the Jakarta Charter. There were two maneuvers undertaken by Muslim leaders to achieve more political rights and comparative advantages for Muslim citizens in place of Islam for the state ideology.

The first was the idea suggested by Hadikusumo on 14 July 1945 that the words *bagi pemeluk-pemeluknya* [for the adherents of Islam] should be deleted from the seven words so they would only be *dengan kewajiban menjalankan syariat Islam* [with the obligation to practice Islamic law]. By suggesting the deletion of the words *bagi pemeluk-pemeluknya,* Hadikusumo wanted the government to be made responsible for implementing Islamic law, thus guaranteeing that there would be no legal dualism for the citizens and implying that Islamic law would be the law of the land for citizens of all religions. It seemed that Hadikusumo interpreted the original seven words (including *bagi-bagi pemeluknya*) as stipulating that Muslim themselves should practice Islamic law without the government's involvement. However, the floor did not accept Hadikusumo's proposal.[31]

On the evening of the next day, 15 July 1945, Hadikusumo once again pressed for this idea even though a day earlier the members had unanimously accepted the draft of the Jakarta Charter. Hadikusumo argued that what he sought today was not the seven words in the preamble, for it had been already finalized a day before, but the seven words in Article 28 (later Article 29) of the constitution (*Batang Tubuh*).[32] Hadikusumo returned to this issue perhaps because the interpretation of the seven words given by Soepomo at the morning meeting was not clear to him. Soepomo explained that as a compromise between the nationalist and the Islamic groups, the seven words "did not mean that the Indonesian state would exist only for one group (Muslims), but simply that the state would be heedful of the spe-

cial identity of the largest section of the population."[33] Soepomo further emphasized that none of the Muslims or the nationalists were allowed to go beyond this
compromise.[34] Since Hadikusumo was not involved in the special committee that
drafted the Jakarta Charter, it seemed he did not personally feel obliged to firmly
hold to such a compromise. In fact, not only he did ask Soepomo to explain the
clear meaning of the seven words in Article 28 of the constitution, but he also contended that the decision made at the special committee might need to be changed
at the plenary meeting. Given that his request was not sufficiently addressed, Hadikusumo finally said that he was in disagreement with the compromise reached in
the form of the Jakarta Charter.[35]

The second maneuver was the proposal put forward by Wahid Hasjim at the
meeting of the Working Committee of the Constitution (*Batang Tubuh*) on 13 July
1945. Hasjim proposed that in Article 4 paragraph 2, the words *"yang beragama
Islam"* [Muslims] be added, thus making adherence to Islam one of the qualifications for eligibility for the position of president or vice president of Indonesia.
Another of Hasjim's suggestions was that the article on religion in the constitution should read as follows: "The religion of the state is Islam, with the guarantee
of freedom for adherents of other religions to profess their own religion . . . etc."
The reason given by Hasjim for his proposals was based on the strong influence of
Islamic symbols (the president is Muslim and the religion of the state is Islam) on
the regulations issued by the state. With this strong influence of Islamic symbols,
any policy or regulation would make people obedient to it. This was particularly
important for the defense of the country from external attack, because Hasjim suggested that Muslims would only sacrifice themselves for their religion.[36]

The Islamic group in this subcommittee meeting was not unanimous in its
response to Hasjim's proposal. Although Sukiman supported Hasjim's proposal,
Agus Salim opposed it, saying it would undermine the compromise between the
nationalist and Islamic groups. Agus Salim added, "If the president has to be a Muslim, then what about the vice president, the ambassadors, etc., and what then was
the point of our promise to protect other religions?" The nationalist groups (those
of Djayadiningrat and Wongsonegoro) rejected all Hasjim's proposals. In fact, to
counter Hasjim's proposal for an article on religion, Oto Iskandardinata suggested
that a repetition of the seven words from the preamble be put into the article on
religion. Soepomo, as a chairman of this working committee, accepted Iskandardinata's suggestion and adopted it into the revised draft of the constitution.[37]

Because the draft was provisional and still needed to be confirmed by the plenary meeting the next day, the Islamic groups once again came up with a suggestion on the religious qualifications of the president. On the evening of 15 July 1945,
Kiyai Masjkur, a Nahdlatul Ulama activist, repeated the previous ideas proposed

by Wahid Hasjim at the working committee that the president must be a Muslim and that the religion of the state should be Islam. Masjkur argued:

> If in Indonesia there is an obligation to practice Islamic law for the adherents of Islam, whereas the president was not Muslim, would this be conducive [to the implementation of Islamic law], or would Muslims accept this situation in general, and would not the situation as such be terrible [because there was a conflict between articles]? [38]

In view of this, Masjkur offered two options to solve the problem. First, if Islamic faith was not a presidential qualification, then the article on religion must be changed from the seven words taken from the preamble to the stipulation that "Islam is the official religion of the Republic of Indonesia." Or, second, the Muslim qualification was to be added to the article on the president and the article on religion was to be left unchanged.

Responding to this suggestion, Soekarno sought to assure the Islamic groups that the president of Indonesia would obviously be a Muslim. He once again referred to the compromise, saying that this draft of the constitution was a reflection of such compromise. But Masjkur continued to demand clarity between two options, not only for himself but for the whole people. In this heated debate, Muzakkir worsened the situation by propounding a wholly new compromise, as he himself called it. Thumping the table with his fist, he importuned on behalf of the Islamic groups that "everything, from the beginning of the preamble to articles in the constitution that mention the name of God (Allah) or Islam or anything else that related to it, be deleted so that nothing [of Islam] would remain." [39] It is interesting to note here that immediately after Muzakkir spoke, Sukarjo Wirjopranoto, a former leader of Parindra (Partai Indonesia Raya), a nationalist party, responded to what Masjkur suggested. In his view, the suggestion actually contradicted Article 27 on equality. Wirjopranoto said that according to Article 27 there should be no discrimination between Indonesian citizens so that everyone in the country would have the same rights including the right to be the president. He finally added that Islam should protect this kind of justice. [40]

Worsening the already tense situation and pushing the Islamic groups' demands further, Hadikusumo interrupted the argument between Soekarno and Muzakkir, remarking irritably:

> I seek refuge in God from Satan who brings destruction. More than once it has been explained here that Islam includes a state ideology. The state, therefore, cannot be separated from Islam. . . . If the ideology of Islam is not accepted, all

right then! Then it is clear that this state is not based on Islam and therefore will be neutral. That at least is clear. Let us not accept a bit of compromise, as Mr. Soekarno calls it. As far as justice and religious duties are concerned, there is no compromise at all. Let us be clear about this. If there are objections to accepting the ideology of the Islamic community . . . then there must be neutrality as far as religion is concerned. That is clear and more explicit. [However,] if the state is religiously neutral, do not take any words from Islam that would be used only on the surface. . . . [Because] if this is so, without reflecting the meaning [of the words], it would [lead to] a bad impression for Muslims.[41]

Hadikusumo's remarks led to a deadlock that night. And perhaps because of the strong insistence of the Islamic groups, the next morning (16 July 1945), the suggestion that the president of Indonesia must be a Muslim was finally accepted for inclusion in the draft constitution. On this last day of the second round of the BPUPKI meeting, the version of the constitution that included the seven words in the preamble and in the article on religion, and the religious qualification of the president of Indonesia, was completed. For the Islamic group, this was still not enough, but it was the best they could get.

The Deletion of the Seven Words

The foregoing discussion shows that neither side was able to completely achieve its objectives. The Islamic groups failed to introduce Islam as a state ideology, while the nationalists were disappointed that there were provisions in the constitution that Muslim citizens would be obliged to practice Islamic law and that to be eligible for the position of president of Indonesia, one must be a Muslim. Under these conditions, the inequality between citizens became clear, as Muslims were given more political rights and a higher status than others. For that reason, many non-Muslim citizens did not feel bound by the draft constitution and viewed themselves being discriminated against by these provisions. Consequently, the nationalists and non-Muslim leaders decided on a countermaneuver to reverse the situation.

The rapid political developments that followed the declaration of the independence of Indonesia (17 August 1945), especially those that occurred on the day after that, 18 August 1945, cracked the compromise reached in the Jakarta Charter and wiped out all concessions given to the Islamic groups. The seven words in the preamble as well as in the article on religion were deleted and replaced with "Ketuhanan Yang Maha Esa" (One Almighty God). In addition, the religious qualification for the president was withdrawn entirely from the constitution. The most important factor mentioned by many historians to describe this change was Hatta's encounter with the Japanese navy (*Kaigun*) official on the evening of the day of independence, 17 August 1945,[42] in which Hatta was warned that Christians and the Protestants in the eastern islands of the archipelago would separate from the Republic of Indonesia if the seven words were included in the constitution. This threat to the unity of Indonesia directly changed Hatta's stance over the compromise. He promised that he would convey this message to the members of the Preparatory Committee for Indonesian Independence (PPKI) that would meet the next morning. After more than two hours of lobbying between Hatta and the Islamic groups (those of Hadikusumo, Wahid Hasjim,[43] and Kasman Singodimedjo[44]), the meeting of PPKI on 18 August 1945 revoked all decisions based on the Islamic groups' demands made in the previous BPUPKI meetings. As Boland says:

> [the meeting] finally came to the conclusion that in fact Indonesia only could become and remain a unity if the Constitution contained nothing that was directly connected with Islam. Therefore articles on Islam as the official religion of the state, the condition that the President must be a Muslim and "the obligation for adherents of Islam to practice Islamic law" had to be removed.[45]

The new consensus of 18 August 1945 regarding the deletion of the seven words of the Jakarta Charter would become one of the most controversial issues in the history of modern Indonesia. Debates on this issue have taken place at least three times since 1945, the latest as recently as the People's Consultative Assembly (MPR) Annual Session of 2002. As can be seen in chapters 10 and 11, the different stances between the Islamic factions and the nationalist factions in the MPR regarding the constitutional amendment to reinsert the seven words of the Jakarta Charter and in interpreting the events that occurred on 18 August 1945 have remained largely static. While the Islamic factions saw the consensus on that day as temporal or conditional, the nationalist factions conceived it as a substantial agreement made by the founding fathers for the sake of Indonesian unity. In light of this, the failure of the Islamic factions in the MPR Annual Session of 2002 was actually repeating history.

8

Reproducing the Millet System

The Foundation of the Ministry of Religious Affairs

The debate over the foundation of the Ministry of Religious Affairs (MORA) took place during the meeting of the Preparatory Committee for the Independence of Indonesia (PPKI) from 18 to 19 August 1945. The draft on the ministries for the new Indonesian government, provided by a subcommittee consisting of Subardjo, Sutardjo, and Kasman, included the MORA. However, at the plenary meeting, Latuharhary objected to its establishment, saying that if, for instance, a Christian became the minister of religion, Muslims would naturally be discontented, and vice versa. Other members, such as Iwa Kusumasumantri, a former activist of the Indonesian National Party (PNI), supported Latuharhary's objection. Kusuma-sumantri further asserted that since Indonesia would be a nation-state, the MORA was irrelevant. Meanwhile, Abdul Abbas, a representative from Sumatra, suggested that religious affairs should not form a single ministry, but should instead be under a so-called "Ministry of Training, Education and Religion." The proposal to estab-lish a ministry that exclusively managed religious affairs was eventually rejected after only six of twenty-seven members voted for it.[1]

These developments at the PPKI meetings demonstrated that Indonesia was not going to embark on the path to a fragmentary state but was firmly on track to become a unitary state. But this was not coming true and new compromise was needed, which inadvertently paved the way for the fragmentary state to start oper-ating.[2] By January 1946, the MORA was set up. For the nationalists, the foundation of the MORA was considered a tradeoff for the Islamic groups' support for the sec-ular state of Indonesia. Although for many Muslims the MORA was too limited a concession since it was initially proposed to replace the office for indigenous affairs (*Het Kantoor voor Inlandsche zaken*) that existed during the Dutch government, it at least gave Islam and Muslims in Indonesia more than they had had during colo-nial times. As discussed below, the MORA had more mandates than the colonial office for indigenous affairs had, since the latter's concern with Muslim needs was limited to the organization of pilgrimages to Mecca (*hajj*).[3]

In short, in order for Indonesia as a secular nation-state to gain full legitimacy, it would be forced to concede at least partial authority to Islam. Meanwhile, for Islam to be able to secure its interests, it would have to espouse the existence of a secular nation-state. As can be seen later, however, the establishment of the MORA actually blocked Indonesia's path on the track toward a true unitary state.

Following a proposal sent by religious officials from Banyumas (central Java) to the Central National Committee of Indonesia (KNIP), the MORA was founded on 3 January 1946, under the cabinet of Sjahrir. Approval of this proposal was partly a result of feelings of lingering discontent among many Muslim leaders regarding the exclusion of the seven words from the constitution. It was believed that this bad feeling would be a disincentive for Indonesian people in dealing with the threat posed by the returning Dutch.[4] Indonesian Muslims, as Hasjim had already argued in the BPUPKI meeting, would not sacrifice themselves to defend something that had no religious character. In this light, the objectives behind the concession given in the form of the foundation of the MORA by the national state in the wake of Indonesia's independence were parallel with the Ottoman Empire's objectives in setting up the millet system in the aftermath of the conquest of Constantinople, as explained in chapter 4.

According to Boland, there had previously been suggestions that the new ministry should be named the Ministry of Islamic Affairs. Yet it eventually became a Ministry of Religion with several sections: Islamic, Protestant, Catholic, and Hindu-Buddhist. The minister, however, has always been a Muslim, and naturally the Islamic section is the largest.[5] At present, a director general who is responsible to the minister runs each religious section, except for Islam. The Islamic section, by contrast, has two director generals: Islamic affairs and Islamic education. Given that the ministry has primarily paid attention to Muslims, it is not totally wrong to say, as Martin van Bruinessen once did, that the ministry is indeed a Muslim institution,[6] or as Geertz put it, "the Ministry of Religion is for all intents and purposes a *santri* affair from top to bottom."[7]

Centralizing Islamic Affairs

For some, the MORA had from the very beginning turned out to be "a bulwark of Islam and an outpost for an Islamic state,"[8] although its foundation in 1946 did not include a portfolio. This assessment was, however, probably true only in the first decade after independence. During this time, many Muslim leaders regarded the MORA as a starting point in the struggle for an Islamic state backed by Islamic parties. These parties expected that the first general election would allow them to change the state ideology. However, the result of the 1955 election made it clear that this struggle had reached an impasse.[9] Instead, after the 1950s, the MORA became the locus of the internal strengthening of the Islamic institutions, the Muslim community, and the spread of Islam (*da'wa*).

Seen through a sociopolitical framework, a number of observers consider the MORA important because it allows religions (Islam in particular) to function as effectively as possible in the state as well as within religious communities and because it is a symbolic intermediary between a secular state and an Islamic state.[10] Another author, Bruinessen, looking from a political economy perspective, saw the MORA as a source of "patronage in the form of jobs, funds and facilities, and often . . . a powerful machine for cooptation."[11] However, both these appraisals might be accurate only as far as the MORA in a particular period was concerned.

All these views—in a sense—ignore the reality that the real task of the MORA has been to accelerate the unification of Islamic affairs throughout Indonesia. Lev has aptly argued that the MORA has been a vehicle "to consolidate the entire administration of Islamic affairs into a single national authority controlled by Islamic groups, thus leading to specialization, centralization and autonomy for the Islamic institutions unimaginable without the new ministry."[12] More importantly, Lev not only pointed out that the MORA is "a critical foothold pending further Islamization of Indonesia," but also that the existence of the MORA was the highest achievement of Islam in terms of corporate autonomy[13]—something central to the millet system—in the nation-state of Indonesia. This was actually the opposite of what had happened in the Middle Eastern Muslim countries, where nationalism and nation-states generally weakened religious administrative institutions (via the millet system). In many Muslim countries, such as Turkey, the corporate autonomy of each religion was reduced in favor of expanding civil bureaucracies under several departments, such as the Ministry of Justice, the Ministry of Education, and the Ministry of Home Affairs. In contrast with this, in Indonesia, according to Lev, "the logic of growing institutional autonomy for Islam was inherent in the Ministry of Religion."[14] However, Lev was not bold enough to argue that the MORA in reality has created Islam as "the dominant millet" in Indonesia.

A Replica of the Millet System

It is my contention that the MORA appears to be a replica of the Ottoman millet system, albeit in a new form, in the nation-state of Indonesia. Moving beyond Lev, I would contend that the MORA has not only helped reinforce national legal development by eliminating the remnants of the Dutch colonial legal structure that was based mostly on racial or ethnic groups,[15] but has actually initiated attempts to develop a new legal system that differentiates citizens based on their religions. Extracting some functions related to Islam from other departments, such as the religious courts, education, and information services, the MORA rode the paradigm of nation-state to transform the Ottoman millet system into its new Indonesian version.

Having argued this, a brief explanation regarding the difference between the old millet system of the Ottoman Empire and the new millet system in the Indonesian nation-state is needed here. They are not identical, for two reasons. First, in the old system, it was the clerics, be they patriarch, rabbi, or *shaykh al-Islam,* who retained autonomy in administering religious affairs such as education, justice, and economics. However, in the new Indonesian version of the millet system, neither the clerics nor the *shaykh al-Islam* are central. In this era of nation-states, they have been replaced by a modern religious bureaucracy, which manages religious affairs based mostly on rational objectives and common (not divine) rules. Within this bureaucracy, each religion is given relative autonomy to manage the various religious institutions that serve the needs of that religious community. However, this kind of bureaucracy has limited interest in the religious duties that people have to observe.

Second, as far as the implementation of Islamic law was concerned, the *fatwa* (legal opinion) in the old millet system played a dominant role within the Muslim community. In this connection, the office of *shaykh al-Islam* was responsible for issuing *fatwa*s regarding administrative affairs and the general public issues. Conversely, in the new millet system, the *fatwa* is no longer the main focus because *fatwa* is applied restrictively to individuals or particular cases. For a bureaucracy in the nation-state, homogeneity in a particular territory is required in some aspects of citizens' lives. The *fatwa* was therefore replaced by Islamic legislation, which is, according to Schacht, "an important, if it is not the most important, manifestation" of Islam in the modern world.[16]

Apparently, the presence of the MORA is a reproduction of the Ottoman millet system in the Indonesian context. The MORA not only developed the types of bureaucratic expertise it needed at its early years in the 1950s, but it has now also successfully expanded into a modern religious bureaucracy.[17] The expansion was vertical as well as horizontal. The vertical expansion included setting up the local offices of religious affairs throughout the country from the level of provinces (*provinsi*), districts (*kabupaten*), and subdistricts (*kecamatan*) down to village religious officials (*naib, modin,* etc.), who were incorporated into the hierarchy.[18] The horizontal expansion placed in the hands of the MORA authority in areas like

Muslim marriage, religious education, religious courts, endowment (*wakaf*), the pilgrimage to Mecca (*hajj*), religious taxation (*zakat*), mosque empowerment, and *halal* food supervision.

One cannot overestimate the impact of the MORA in Islamic legislation within the national legal system. Lev noted that the first major statute initiated by the MORA was Law 22/1946 on the Administration of Marriage and Divorce,[19] but the breakthrough was Law 7/1989 on the Religious Courts. This law opened the gate for further enactments not based on citizenship in general but on religious adherence in particular. The promulgation of three statutes exclusively for Muslims (Law 17/1999 on the Hajj Service, Law 38/1999 on the Zakat Management, and Law 41/2004 on Wakaf) was possible partly because a precedent had already been established.

Engendering Dissonance

The Islamic national legislation initiated by the MORA creates an ambiguity in the paradigm of the nation-state, because those particular statutes are principally applied to Muslims, not to all individuals who live in the same territorial jurisdiction of Indonesia. This undoubtedly engenders inequality between citizens and generates dissonance in the application of religious law in a nation-state. While the nation-state has the ultimate objective of standardizing legal products, the MORA has built a religious block among the people, since most of the legislation it initiated is expressed in religious categories. The key to this predicament is that *shari'a* is not about *where* you are but *who* you are. *Shari'a* rules, therefore, apply only to Muslims no matter whether they live, in a secular state or in an Islamic one. Accordingly, Islam usually encounters difficulty in steering the modernization program of a nation-state. Equality still generates problems even for the new version of the millet system, in this case the MORA, when dealing with the case of minority groups, the non-Muslims. The discussion of the nationalization of *shari'a* in part IV will confirm this contention.

Neither non-religious-oriented nationalists nor non-Muslim leaders could fully accept the foundation of the Ministry of Religious Affairs. This religious bureaucracy was considered inappropriate in a modern state, and hence it became a hindrance to the establishment of a real unitary state in the sense meant by Soepomo: a state that neither fuses itself with the largest group in society nor is allied with the strongest political or economical group, but transcends all groups and individuals and bonds all levels of society.

It is interesting to note that the "imperfection" of the concept of the unitary state, especially with regard to the religious plurality of Indonesian citizens, has provided an opportunity for the fragmentary state to be influential, and the MORA played a major role in strengthening this influence. This was possible with the support of the New Order regime that shifted its legal policy in general in conjunction with its leaning toward Islamization in the 1990s. For more than two decades (1966–1989), the legal policy of the New Order government was to promote the unitary state, which was based on two principles: the unification of law and the archipelagic perspective (*wawasan nusantara*). This emphasizes that the Republic of Indonesia is a nation-state, not a state founded upon a racial, cultural, or religious base. Therefore, there should not be any regulation that discriminates between people based on ethnic group, class, race, religion, or the like. In addition, it requires that the whole archipelago be an integrated, compact unity of fatherland (*tanah air*). This requires that laws are valid for the whole country, all the regions should have the same rights and responsibilities, and no region should be discriminated against or privileged over another.[20]

However, this legal policy was gradually neglected. Munawir Sjadzali, the New Order minister of religion from 1983 to 1993, was among the state officials who sought to expressly override the policy by emphasizing the principle of 'legal distinction.' Responding to objections raised by the nationalists and non-Muslims regarding the Bill on the Religious Court in 1989 on the grounds that the bill discriminated against citizens based on their religion, Minister Sjadzali said to the legislative members that:

> [not] every legal distinction should be perceived as inequality before the law. It cannot be said either that the principle of equality before the law is valid only if all factual conditions are similar. Therefore, there should be certain specific laws for particular groups of citizens." [21]

Sjadzali justified this principle of 'legal distinction' by referring to the official state motto (which is, of course, not necessarily a legal principle) of *Bhinneka Tunggal Ika* (a Sanskrit phrase that means "Unity in Diversity"), which appears on the banner clutched by the legs of the Garuda Pancasila, the official icon of the state.

The People's Consultative Assembly (MPR) further reinforced the principle of legal distinction in the 1993 Broad Outlines of National Policy (GBHN). The presence of the principle of legal distinction in the 1993 GBHN overrode previous provisions in the GBHNs of 1973, 1978, 1983, and 1988 that stated the codification and unification of law was a basis for the development of national laws. The provisions for legal distinction in the GBHN of 1993 provided a new direction for Indonesian legal development, namely, that all processes of lawmaking should pay attention to the "plurality of the legal awareness of the citizens." [22] With this new policy, Indonesia embarked, whether knowingly or not, on the path toward a fragmentary state by allowing a variety of legal subsystems, especially Islamic legal codes, to be accommodated in the national legal system and to serve the national interest.

Finally, as far as the implementation of law in Indonesia is concerned, the upshot of the rivalry between the unitary state and the fragmentary state in steering the development of the national legal system is that the latter has gradually surpassed the former. The pathway toward the fuller fragmentary state has become smoother in Indonesia, especially in the post–New Order era. In addition to a number of statutes that had been enacted exclusively for Muslims citizens in the past seven years, such as Law 17/1999 on the Hajj Service, Law 38/1999 on the Zakat Management, and Law 41/2004 on Wakaf, there are other drafts of regulations—mostly related to Muslim concerns—being presented to the legislature: the Bill on Islamic Shari'a Banking, the Bill on Applied Islamic Rules (*Hukum Terapan Islam*), and the Regulation on Halal Food. If passed, these Islamic statutes may further the process of segregation based on religion and would intensify the process of Islamization in Indonesia in the years to come.

PART III

The Constitutionalization of *Shari'a*

9

Constitutional Dissonance

Islamic Constitutionalism

Ann Elizabeth Mayer has defined Islamic constitutionalism as based on "distinctively Islamic principles."[1] What "Islamic principles" entail here, however, remains in disagreement. In spite of this, to identify whether or not a country has an Islamic constitution depends much on how Islam is defined in the constitution. The constitutional position of Islam as a state religion, therefore, always becomes pertinent during the process of constitution making or political reform in Muslim countries.

There are at least four types of Muslim countries with regard to the constitutional recognition of state religion.[2] The first is states that proclaim themselves as 'Islamic states,' such as Afghanistan, Bahrain, Brunei, Iran, Maldives, Mauritania, Oman, Pakistan, Saudi Arabia, and Yemen. The second is those states that have declared Islam to be the 'state religion,' like Bangladesh, Egypt, and Malaysia. The third is states that have no constitutional declaration about the state religion, such as Indonesia, Syria, and Uzbekistan, among others. And the fourth is states that acknowledge themselves to be secular states. Examples of this kind of state are Azerbaijan, Senegal, and Turkey. According to the 2005 estimate made by the United States Commission on International Religious Freedom, of the 1.3 billion Muslims in the world, approximately 58 percent of them live in the first and the second types of state listed above.[3] This means that almost half the Muslims in the world are not living in countries controlled by Islamic constitutions.

In addition to constitutional recognition of Islam as the state religion, the acknowledgment of the status and the role of *shari'a* in the constitution of a Muslim country has been another decisive criterion for distinguishing Islamic constitutions from others. In fact, Hasan Turabi makes the highly questionable statement that the "*Shari'a* is the higher law, just like the constitution."[4] The way an Islamic constitution refers to the *shari'a* and attributes its significance differs markedly from one Muslim country to another. A number of Islamic countries explicitly define the *shari'a* as the source of national legislation. They are Bahrain, Egypt, Iran, Kuwait, Oman, Qatar, Saudi Arabia, Syria, United Arab Emirates, Yemen, and Sudan. Other countries maintain that any law enacted cannot be contrary to Islamic tenets, such as Iraq,[5] Afghanistan, the Maldives, and Pakistan. There are also a few countries that constitutionally acknowledge the partial impact of the *shariʿa* in certain legal matters (mostly personal or family laws), for example Gambia, Malaysia, and Jordan.[6]

It must be noted here, however, that there is no consensus in those Muslim countries over what should be the authoritative body that determines whether or not enacted laws, either passed by the legislature or decreed by the executive government, are *shariʿa*-compliant or have sufficiently referred to the *shariʿa*. According to Ghai and Cottrell, some states leave this decision to the legislature itself; others give it to a constitutional council; some give it to regular or special constitutional courts.[7] In Egypt, for instance, the role of assessing the conformity of legislation with the *shariʿa* falls to the Supreme Constitutional Court, while in Pakistan, the Federal Shariat Court plays this role. In Iran, uniquely, the Council of Guardians (*wilaya al-faqih*), consisting of several prominent *ulama*, has been responsible for this role.

It is clear from the above discussion that the status and the role of *shariʿa* in the constitution is central to what is called 'Islamic constitutionalism.' The position of *shariʿa* in a constitution largely determines whether it is Islamic or not. For this reason, it is not surprising to find that what Islamic groups are most concerned with during the process of constitution making, as in Afghanistan and Iraq,[8] is the status and the role of *shariʿa* law, and that, accordingly, constitution making in Muslim states does not usually follow the path of constitution making in non-Muslim states.

In many non-Muslim states, there are two basic issues constantly emerging: (1) the limitation of the state in the form of a set of rights and freedoms of the citizens, and (2) separation of powers within the state.[9] By contrast, the two quite different issues that largely attract political attention throughout the debate on constitutional law in most Muslim countries are (1) the religious rights of Muslim citizens to freely apply *shariʿa*, and (2) the obligation of the government to arrange properly for the implementation of *shariʿa* rules in the country.

The high priority placed on the issue of Muslim rights and on *shariʿa* in particular is mostly based on the classical juristic traditions that emphasize that the ultimate goal of the state is to apply *shariʿa* to guarantee the happiness of its subjects in this world and to avoid punishment in the hereafter.[10] The classical juristic tradition, however, did not address which institutions and procedures are necessary to prevent the rulers from oppressing and exploiting their subjects. In fact, it was disposed to look at the relationship between ruler and ruled solely in terms of an ideal scheme, where rulers are conceived as pious Muslims eager to follow the *shariʿa* entirely.

Accordingly, the constitutional law in Muslim countries becomes unrealistic and does not provide appropriate institutional mechanisms to deal with reality. Indeed, as pointed out by Mayer, when legal means are needed to overthrow despotic and oppressive rulers, Western models often become the key references.[11] In light of this, it is little wonder that constitutional provisions that defend individual rights vis-à-vis the state are minimal in the constitutions of many Muslim countries.

Religious Rights or Religious Duties?

To clarify the term 'religious right' employed in this chapter, let me first discuss briefly the concept of 'right' in Islam. As explained by Ebrahim Moosa, the term 'right' is closest to the word *haqq* in Arabic, though the latter has a wider meaning. The word *haqq* can mean 'right,' 'claim,' 'truth,' 'reality,' or 'duty' depending on its use in a specific context.[12] There are two types of rights in Islam: 'rights of God' (*haqq Allah*) and 'rights of persons' (*haqq al-insan*). The 'rights of God' can be fulfilled either by observing religious rituals or performing actions that benefit the entire community. The 'rights of persons' are those rights to a decent living and to hold property. Included in this type of rights are freedom of opinion, profession, movement, and many others.[13]

It is often found, however, that human rights in Islam are only related to religious obligations (*al-takalif al-shar'iyya*). The Islamic human rights are then mostly understood as "the corollaries of duties owed to God and to other individuals."[14] As a result, the duties of Muslims toward God are given more emphasis than the rights of individual vis-à-vis the ruler. It is for this reason that when the freedom of the individual (*haqq al-insan*) and religious rule (*haqq Allah*) are in conflict, it is the former that should give way. This conception, however, has been challenged by Khaled Abou El-Fadl, a professor of Islamic law at the University of California at Los Angeles, USA. He argues that the right of individual is above the right of God (*haqq al-insan muqaddam 'ala haqq Allah*), largely because God is more than capable of defending his rights in the hereafter, while human beings must secure their own rights in this world. For this reason, the violation of human rights is not pardonable, even by God himself, unless those victims of human rights abuse would forgive the perpetrator. Meanwhile, the infringement of God's rights might be pardoned through a serious repentance and a strong willingness to not repeat a similar infringement.[15]

Tension within the constitutional law of some Muslim countries partly originates from the fact that it tends to emphasize not human rights and freedoms, but rather the duties of (Muslim) citizens to obey the divine law or *shari'a*. That duties and obligations usually have priority over the rights in most interpretation of Islam is also observable in the Universal Islamic Declaration of Human Rights (UIDHR). Given this, it is perhaps more appropriate to say that the UIDHR is better described as the Universal Islamic Declaration of Human *Duties,* instead of Rights.[16] In sum, religious rights in the constitutions of many Muslim countries are, in most cases, essentially religious duties, and they rarely guarantee individual rights to freedom in general.

Individual Rights vs. Collective Rights

Having clarified the concept of religious rights, I will now discuss the difference between the individual right and the collective right of religious freedom. Looking more closely, individual religious rights and collective religious rights seem essentially related to religious duties, except that one is observed individually and another is performed collectively.

As pointed out by Izhak Englard, Justice of the Supreme Court of Israel, the principle of freedom of religion has both individual and collective dimensions. The individual dimension of religious freedom requires the state neither to ban religious beliefs and practices of the citizens nor to impose duties that contravene their religious injunctions, while the collective dimension of religious freedom implies that the state should allow the practice of religious duties through a community of believers. In fact, the state in some cases grants degrees of religious autonomy for a particular community, largely religious minorities. In these senses, the collective religious right appears to be no more than a natural extension of each individual's religious freedom. In other words, provided that one is allowed to observe a religious duty individually, to do it collectively must be freely welcomed.[17] This obviously underlines the fact that, again, what are often entailed in collective religious rights are, in reality, collective religious duties.

It follows then that the dissonance often observable within the constitutional law of many Muslim countries is that individual rights are frequently suppressed at the expense of collective rights. As argued by Coulson, the principles of original freedom and the inviolability of life, honor, and property in Islam were often treated as principles which merely secure the general order and well-being of the whole community (*umma*), but were not regarded as fundamental liberties of Muslim individuals.[18] For this reason, the formulation of lists of the specific rights of Muslim individuals in the constitutions of Muslim countries seems more symbolic than actual. This can be clearly seen through conditional phrases that curb individual freedoms which are frequently mentioned. Words or clauses like "if it is not contrary to *shari'a,*" "provided that they are not detrimental to the fundamental principles of Islam," and "in accordance with Islamic criteria" are examples of the sort of qualifications added to individual rights provisions in constitutional texts. According to Mayer, "imposing Islamic qualifications on rights sets the stage not just for the diminution of these rights, but potentially for denying them altogether." [19]

A case related to fasting in Ramadan month presented by Englard effectively demonstrates the dissonance between the aspiration to collective autonomy and the religious freedom of individuals. This case took place during the British Mandate in Palestine (1917–1948). During this period, the millet system of the Ottoman Empire was basically maintained.[20] Article 83 of the Palestine Order-in-Council, 1922 (as amended in 1939) acknowledged both the principle of individual rights and collective right of religious freedom, as follows.

> All persons in Palestine shall enjoy full liberty of conscience, and the free exercise of their forms of worship subject only to the maintenance of public order and morals. Each religious community shall enjoy autonomy for the internal affairs of the community subject to the provisions of any Ordinance or Order issued by the High Commissioner.[21]

Englard tells how a Muslim, Sharif Shanti, was brought to the court for publicly breaking his fast without a legitimate religious excuse contrary to the then-valid Ottoman Penal Code. The defendant contended that this provision was null and void, being in conflict with Article 83 of the Order-in-Council mentioned above. The District Court rejected his argument, saying: "[The law] aims at the maintenance of public morals among the Moslems and in this sense carries out the spirit of Article 83." [22] This court's decision seemed to put an individual under siege by the community, which itself has superior rights. This communal imposition of a religious duty as a matter of public morals among Muslim individuals was hardly consistent with modern notions of individual rights of religious freedom.[23] Shanti's case, however, was not a dispute between collective religious rights versus individual freedom of religion, but religious duties versus individual freedom of choice. That collective rights, namely religious duties, are above individual rights not only reflects a situation where a Muslim lacks individuality and autonomous existence, but also shows the rejection of individualism in favor of communalism.

The Ambiguity of Collective Religious Rights

Based on the foregoing discussion, it is fair to state that constitutional dissonance would exist in Indonesia if the attempts of Islamic parties to amend the constitutional provision on religion (Article 29 of the 1945 constitution) were successful, at least as between the amended Article 29 on Religion and Article 28 on Human Rights. It is easy to imagine that individual rights would be suppressed in the name of religious collective obligations if the seven words "with the obligation of carrying out Islamic *shari'a* for its adherents," as proposed by some Islamic parties, were successfully inserted into the constitution. Although the call to amend Article 29 might be seen as a proposal for collective religious rights, that is, the collective right to practice *shari'a*, such demands are ambiguous since the collective rights are essentially religious duties to be imposed on Muslim citizens.

The same could be said of the proposed amendment formula, which affects Article 29 on Religion by requiring every religious adherent to practice their religious duties according to their respective faiths. It seems here that if the original text of Article 29 were amended in this way, that is, even without any reference to the seven words of the Jakarta Charter, the state would be leaning toward a religiously legal polycentrism, where citizens would be treated not as autonomous individuals but more on the basis of membership of a religious community. What is more, the state would have to arrange a standardized religious practice for each religious community (or this task would be delegated by the state to relevant religious authorities). As a consequence, a citizen would no longer be free to exercise his or her religious liberty based on his or her own religious consciousness or interpretation, as guaranteed by Article 28E (2) of the 1945 constitution: everyone has the right "to possess conviction and beliefs, and to express his or her thoughts and attitudes in accordance with his or her conscience."

Above all, the collective religious rights proposed by Muslims as a majority population in Indonesia is inappropriate, since these constitutional protections are usually granted to the minorities instead of to the majority group.[24] There are two ways a constitution recognizes religious rights, or, more precisely, the right to perform religious duties. First, a constitution can confer religious rights on individuals because they belong to a religious community. Second, a constitution can grant religious rights to a religious community as a group of people. The former is undertaken individually, while the latter is exercised collectively and is usually granted to minorities for their protection, and hence is often called 'minority rights.'[25] It must be immediately noted, however, that the way the Indonesian constitution mentions religious freedom without mentioning Islam is meant to afford equal rights for all citizens *regardless* of their religious backgrounds.[26] That the Indonesian constitution fails to recognize the majority religion indicates that there is no minority religion, in principle, which implies that Indonesia deals with its nationals individually and not collectively as religious groups.

10
Bringing Back
the 'Seven Words'

After the fierce debate in the BPUPKI and PPKI meetings in 1945, described in chapter 7, attempts to reintroduce the Islamic *shari'a* into the Indonesian constitution have been made at least three times. The first attempt was in the meetings of the Constituent Assembly (*Dewan Konstituante*) from 1957 to 1959. The second effort took place in the first years of the New Order era (1966–1998), during the meetings of the Provisional People's Consultative Assembly (MPRS) Annual Session of 1966 to 1968. Finally, the third attempt occurred during the process of constitutional amendment in the People's Consultative Assembly (MPR) Annual Sessions of 2000, 2001, and 2002. All these attempts were, however, unsuccessful.

The Constituent Assembly, 1957–1959

In the aftermath of the 1955 election, a Constituent Assembly was established to draft a new permanent constitution for Indonesia. By late 1957, a number of Islamic parties, including Masyumi, Nahdlatul Ulama (NU), Partai Sarekat Islam Indonesia (PSII), and Perti (which together won slightly less than half of the votes) joined to propose Islam as the foundation of Indonesia. Meanwhile, non-Islamic parties such as Partai Nasional Indonesia (PNI), Partai Komunis Indonesia (PKI), Partai Kristen Indonesia (Parkindo), Partai Sosialis Indonesia (PSI), and others (which together won slightly more than half of the votes) were united in rejecting the proposal of Islamic parties and, instead, promoted Pancasila as the basis of the state.[1] Given that a decision on the state ideology required a two-thirds majority, it was assumed that the contending views of Islamic parties and non-Islamic parties would result in an impasse. This assumption was then employed to support a proposal of the government, backed by the military, to reintroduce the 1945 constitution without amendment. Non-Islamic parties supported the proposal without any reservation, but Islamic parties were adamant in their persistence. In fact, they even put forward a proposal that to return to the 1945 constitution, the seven words of the Jakarta Charter must be reinserted into the preamble and Article 29 of the constitution.[2]

By mid-1959, neither the Islamic parties nor the non-Islamic parties could attain a two-thirds majority in the Assembly. This situation led President Soekarno to issue a Presidential Decree on 5 July 1959 to dissolve the Constituent Assembly and to return to the 1945 constitution. In order to attract support from Islamic parties, the Presidential Decree accommodated the Jakarta Charter by stating it not in the body of the decree, but in the 'Considerations' section intended as 'inspiration' but not as substantive law.

It is worth noting here the explanation, given by Roeslan Abdul Gani, a former aide to Indonesia's first president Soekarno and a key player in the formulation of the Presidential Decree, of the intended meaning of the words contained in President Soekarno's decree (*Piagam Jakarta menjiwai UUD 1945 dan merupakan suatu rangkaian kesatuan dengan konstitusi tersebut,* "The Jakarta Charter inspires the 1945 constitution and it forms an integrated framework with that constitution"). At a meeting with some members of the MPR, Gani explained that it was he who was requested by Soekarno to prepare the draft of the decree. According to Gani, Soekarno believed that the Jakarta Charter inspired the 1945 constitution, but was not part of the constitution. Soekarno therefore advised Gani that this belief should not be expressed in the dictum of the decree, but rather in the 'Considerations' of the decree, thus making it not a formal part of either the decree or the constitution. When Gani lobbied Muslim leaders regarding this inclusion of the Jakarta Charter, he did not notify them that the Jakarta Charter was located only in the 'Considerations' of the decree. Additionally, to emphasize that the Jakarta Charter was not part of the 1945 constitution, Muhammad Yamin advised Gani that the word *rangkaian* [framework] should be inserted in the decree. This word, according to Gani, signified that the Jakarta Charter is not automatically integrated with the text of the constitution.[3]

Thus, for the government, the Jakarta Charter was not part of the 1945 constitution, regardless of how the Islamic parties viewed it. Despite a number of contending interpretations that relied on the important position of 'Considerations' (*Pertimbangan*) rather than the 'Body' (*Batang Tubuh*) in the civil law system to imply that the Jakarta Charter had, in fact, been officially ratified,[4] the standpoint of the government that the Jakarta Charter was not part of the reinvigorated 1945 constitution was widely accepted.

The MPRS Sessions, 1966–1968

In the first years of the New Order regime (1966–1998), Islamic parties once again demanded the implementation of the Jakarta Charter as an integral part of the preamble of the 1945 constitution, as stated in the 1959 Presidential Decree. Unlike the Constituent Assembly debates in 1957–1959, where Islamic parties were unanimous in promoting Islam as the state ideology and in giving the seven words of the Jakarta Charter a constitutional status, Islamic parties (NU and Parmusi) during the MPRS Sessions of 1966–1968 had a different opinion regarding the constitutional position of the Jakarta Charter.

During this period, the NU party was less concerned with the constitutional position of the Jakarta Charter. Although this party had previously struggled for recognition of the Jakarta Charter, their aim now was no longer to amend the 1945 constitution. Rather, it focused on the new position and role of the Jakarta Charter they saw as arising from the issuance of the Presidential Decree. This decree implied, some NU leaders argued, that the Jakarta Charter should be considered a *source* for Indonesian laws, regardless of its position in the constitution. In this role, as NU leaders believed, the Jakarta Charter could be used to promote the unification of laws among Muslims, and this was more important than obliging Muslims to practice *shari'a*.[5] With this, as Samson observed, the issue of the Jakarta Charter was deliberately downplayed by the NU, possibly to avoid a renewal of acrimonious debate regarding the relationship between Islam and Pancasila.[6]

Contrary to NU's stance, however, the Partai Muslimin Indonesia (Parmusi)[7] remained keen to reinsert the seven words of the Jakarta Charter, either into the preamble to the 1945 constitution or into Article 29 of the constitution, thereby giving *shari'a* legal force and designating the state as being responsible for its implementation.[8] These efforts by Islamic parties to force discussion of the constitutional position of the Jakarta Charter in the early years of the New Order era were, however, rejected when the army prohibited it from being discussed in the MPRS session of 1966. In the MPRS sessions of 1967 and 1968, an attempt was repeatedly made to implement the Jakarta Charter into the preamble to the 1945 constitution. But, again, these efforts proved fruitless due to lack of support.[9]

The MPR Annual Sessions of 2000, 2001, and 2002

The fall of the Soeharto regime in 1998 ushered in new opportunities for widespread change in Indonesia. Many Indonesians expressed a strong desire for a revision of the 1945 constitution, which many observers perceived as the root cause of authoritarianism.[10] Calls for a revival of the seven words (with the obligation to carry out *shari'a* for adherents of Islam) were greatly increasing as well, as some Muslim groups struggled for a fuller incorporation of *shari'a* into the constitution in the MPR Annual Sessions of 2000, 2001, and 2002. In particular, the post–New Order Islamic parties,[11] for example, the United Development Party (PPP) and the Crescent Moon Star Party (PBB), wanted to see implementation of *shari'a* formally acknowledged in Article 29 of the constitution.

Unlike the Islamic parties in the 1950s that fought for Islam to be the state ideology and then to reinsert the seven words of the Jakarta Charter into the preamble of the 1945 constitution, the post–New Order Islamic parties have largely abandoned these objectives. Many of their leaders have accepted that the Presidential Decree issued by Soekarno on 5 July 1959 acknowledged the position of the Jakarta Charter as being 'inspirational' and 'linked' to the 1945 constitution. Perhaps because of this, Islamic parties believed that the constitution's preamble did not require the amendment. This was one of five preliminary conclusions reached by Islamic parties and other parties in 2000 regarding the constitutional amendment procedure. The four other conclusions were (1) to maintain the form of the state as a unitary republic, (2) to retain the presidential system, (3) to amend the constitution by addendum (inserting more paragraphs), and (4) to incorporate norms and principles as found in the elucidation of the 1945 constitution into the Articles of the constitution.[12]

Issues around the Amendment

Article 29 on Religion consists of two paragraphs (shown in Table 10.1). In fact, this is still the form of Article 29 since it was not, in the end, amended.

The amendment debates over Article 29 centered on four issues. The first was the proposal for the reinsertion of the seven words of the Jakarta Charter into the

TABLE 10.1 Article 29 on Religion

Paragraph One	*Negara berdasar atas Ketuhanan Yang Mahaesa* [The state is based on belief in one almighty God]
Paragraph Two	*Negara menjamin kemerdekaan setiap penduduk untuk memeluk agamanya masing-masing dan untuk beribadat menurut agama dan kepercayaannya itu.* [The state guarantees the freedom of each citizen to adhere to religion and to worship according to his or her religion and belief]

first paragraph, so that it would be "the state is based on belief in One God *with the obligation to carry out Islamic shari'a for its adherents.*" The second was the title of Article 29. Some factions wanted to replace the title Agama [Religion] with "Ketuhanan Yang Maha Esa" [Belief in One God]. The third was the deletion of the words *dan kepercayaannya* [and his or her belief] in the end of Article 29 (2), so it would become "[t]he state guarantees the freedom of each citizen to adhere to religion and to worship according to his or her religion." The last issue was the addition of a new paragraph to Article 29. Each of three factions, the F-PG (the faction of Golkar party), the F-PPP (the faction of United Development Party), and the F-PKB (the faction of National Awakening Party), sought to add various different paragraphs, each with its respective wordings. However, all dropped the idea before the 2002 Annual Session.[13] For the purpose of this study, the first issue will be the main focus. Nevertheless, where necessary and relevant to the main focus, the other issues will be discussed as well.

The debate over the constitutional amendment to Article 29 fluctuated during the last three MPR Annual Sessions of 2000, 2001, and 2002. In the 2000 Annual Session, there was an increasing demand to insert the seven words. Debate took place not only during the meeting of the Panitia Ad Hoc I (Ad Hoc Committee One) of the Working Group of the MPR in June 2000, but throughout the meetings of the MPR Annual Session in August 2000.

However, in the 2001 session, the debate between MPR members over the wording "with the obligation to carry out Islamic *shari'a* for its adherents" into Article 29 of the constitution was restrained compared to the previous session. This was because the 2001 Annual Session (1–10 November) was held just three months after Abdurrahman Wahid had been impeached and dismissed from the presidency and Megawati Soekarnoputri, the leader of the Indonesia's Struggle Democratic Party (PDI-P) and Hamzah Haz, the leader of the United Development Party (PPP), were appointed as new president and vice president respectively. The appointment of Haz might perhaps have lessened PPP's passion for the inclusion of seven words into Article 29 of the constitution.[14] It appears that his position as subordinate to President Megawati, the leader of a party (PDI-P) that strongly opposed the inclusion of the Jakarta Charter into the constitution, had much to do with this change.

Unlike the previous MPR annual meetings, a heated debate between various MPR factions over the issue of amending Article 29 took place mostly in the 2002 Annual Session. Since the first meeting of the Ad Hoc Committee One (28 January 2002), the amendment of Article 29 had been discussed for more than six months. The upshot of this discussion was that the plenary meeting of MPR Annual Session on 10 August 2002 finally decided to leave the original text of Article 29 as it stood. Chapter 11 will present this debate in detail.

The Nationalist Faction vs. the Islamic Faction

The nationalist faction consisted of a faction of the Indonesia's Struggle Democratic Party (F-PDI-P), a faction of the Golkar Party (F-PG), a faction of a number
of tiny nationalist parties (F-KKI), a faction of Christian parties (F-PDKB), and
a faction that represented Indonesian military and police forces (F-TNI/POLRI).
The nationalist faction rejected the idea of amending Article 29 on Religion.

The Islamic faction were those Islamic parties that joined together to propose
and support the amendment of Article 29. This Islamic faction consisted of two
groups: (1) parties that advocated the insertion of seven words of the Jakarta Charter into Article 29, such as the PPP, the PBB, and those tiny Islamic parties (PKU,
PNU, and PSII) that formed an MPR faction of Perserikatan Daulat Ummat (F-
PDU), and (2) those parties that sought to make religious teaching obligatory for
respective believers, such as the National Mandate Party (PAN), the Justice Party
(PK), and the National Awakening Party (PKB).

While the Islamic faction took the view that the preamble to the constitution
was inspired by the Jakarta Charter, as the Presidential Decree of 1959 put it, the
nationalist faction did not share this opinion. The nationalist faction hardly made
reference to the substance of the Presidential Decree of 1959. During their discussion of the amendment of Article 29 in the MPR Annual Sessions (2000, 2001, and
2002), the nationalist faction seemed, in fact, to disregard the implications of that
decree entirely. Instead, they considered it a historical document that might function as a formula for political compromise rather than as a formal accommodation of the interests of Islamic parties. This was perhaps reasonable enough given
that constitutional amendment inherently creates a chance for drafters to add to or
subtract from the constitution whatever they wish without necessarily being bound
by history.

With regard to the amendment to Article 29 (1) 'Negara Berdasarkan Ketuhanan Yang Maha Esa,' there are three alternative drafts. The nationalist faction,
which included parties such as F-PDI-P, F-PG, F-KKI, F-PDKB, and F-TNI/POLRI,
formed the contra-amendment camp, which suggested that the original text of the
constitution be maintained (Alternative One). The Islamic faction, which can be
identified as the pro-amendment camp, proposed two alternative drafts to amend
Article 29 (1). One of them (Alternative Two) stated, "The state is based on belief
in One God *with the obligation to carry out Islamic shari'a for its adherents*," while
the other (Alternative Three) proposed, "The state is based on belief in One God
with the obligation to carry out religious teachings for respective believers."

There were at least three basic differences between the nationalist faction and
the Islamic faction regarding amending Article 29 to reinsert the seven words of
the Jakarta Charter into the constitution. First, both camps were in disagreement

in interpreting the historical fact of the deletion of the seven words of the Jakarta Charter that took place on 18 August 1945. One conceived it as a substantial agreement made by the founding fathers of the country for the sake of Indonesian unity. The other side viewed the deletion that day as a temporal or conditional consensus, and hence a tentative agreement. The second difference occurred over the question of whether the body of the constitution should restate the critical clause from the preamble: "the state is based on belief in One Almighty God." One view preferred to leave Article 29 on Religion in the constitution alone as it needed no elaboration. The other view saw the clause as needing further clarification to specify more accurately to what extent it applies constitutionally. The third difference related to the state's function in the modern era. For the nationalist faction, the state is not established to intervene in the religious life of its people. Instead, the state is required to uphold rules effectively so that people will respect law and order. But for the Islamic faction, it is the task of the state to promote religiosity in public life and to enhance the piety of its citizens, thus, the faction claimed, providing a solution to the various crises that had hit Indonesia.

The Islamic faction presented four arguments for the amendment of Article 29 with the inclusion of the seven words. First, the proposal was closely related to the Presidential Decree of 5 July 1959, which acknowledged the position of the Jakarta Charter to have inspired and influenced the current constitution. Second, every religion teaches about faith and piety, and hence to include the seven words into the constitution would be a solution to the perceived moral decadence of the country. Third, Islamic *shari'a* would be applicable only for Muslim adherents, so followers of other religions had no need to be concerned. And fourth, the reinsertion of the seven words of the Jakarta Charter into Article 29 would clarify the constitutional position of *shari'a*. Thus, any proposal for incorporating an aspect of Islamic *shari'a* in the Indonesian legal system would be justified. These four arguments can be clearly seen later when discussing the stance of each member of the Islamic faction in the next chapter.

Meanwhile, the anti-amendment camp of the non-Islamic faction also offered four reasons to oppose the amendment to Article 29 and to maintain the original text. First, they considered national integrity much more important than the political interests of any particular group of citizens.[15] Second, since Indonesia is a Pancasila state and not a theocracy, the state has no right to control the observance of religious duties by its citizens.[16] Third, provisions in the body of the constitution should not contradict what has been already stated in the preamble. For this reason, both the preamble and the text of Article 29 must be consistent and coherent. Because a preliminary consensus had been reached for not amending the preamble of the constitution and because the text of Article 29 (1) already precisely copied the preamble's words, "the state is based on belief in One Almighty God," Article

29 (1) should also not be amended.[17] The final reason for resisting the effort to amend Article 29 was because to mention the rights and obligations of one particular religion in the constitution at the expense of other religions would violate the principle of equality.[18] This problem would, it might seem, be avoided if Alternative Three as proposed by the F-Reformasi was adopted, but, as will be discussed later, this proposal remained problematic.

What Kind of *Shari'a*?

A peculiar problem that appeared from the running debate at the MPR Annual Sessions was that the meaning of *shari'a* remained unclear.[19] Even the Islamic parties seemed to have different understandings about its meaning. If one reads carefully through the proceedings of the Ad Hoc Committee One meetings in the 2002 MPR Annual Sessions, it becomes evident that there was no clarity about what kind of Islamic *shari'a* the Islamic parties actually proposed. It seems that all elements of Islamic *shari'a* would be included in their proposal. In that case, they wanted the constitution to formally declare that Muslim citizens are obliged to perform religious duties, without any precision as to what those duties might be.

One explanation about what kind of *shari'a* would be officially implemented in Indonesia came from Lukman Hakim Saifuddin, a legislator for the PPP. He argued that his party viewed Islamic *shari'a* in three categories. The first is 'universal *shari'a*,' which comprises the principal values embraced by all religions, such as justice, equality, and *musyawarah* (consultation). The second is '*shari'a* norms,' which includes all ideals of Islamic beliefs and practices that are applicable only to Muslims and not to other believers. And the last is '*shari'a* rules,' most of which are *fiqh* or legal interpretations of *shari'a*. Some Muslims might accept this last category, but most would reject it and argue over its content. According to Saifuddin, the PPP put high priority on the first two categories and struggled for their inclusion into the Indonesian legal system through legislative procedures. However, as for the third category, such as the obligation to wear *jilbab* and severe punishments for criminals, the PPP was not, he said, in a position to struggle for it any further.[20]

It was always unlikely that a consensus over the meaning of *shari'a* could be reached among Islamic parties. While the Justice Party (PK) emphasized universal *shari'a* as a stepping-stone for further introduction of the Islamic *shari'a* into the public sphere,[21] Hamdan Zoelva (F-PBB) contended that the *whole* of *shari'a* must be legalized. In his words, "a Muslim should carry out Islamic *shari'a* not only in terms of rituals but also in all legal aspects including penal, civil, foods and trade.

All these aspects of *shari'a* law require the support of the state if successful implementation is to be achieved." [22]

It is interesting to note here that the F-PBB, as represented by Zoelva, was ironically leaning toward 'secularizing' Islamic law by acknowledging that the official implementation of *shari'a* in Indonesia "depends much on the outcome of debates in the legislature." [23] He added that "the final result of this debate would not be a Shafi'i Law, Hanafi Law or Hanbali Law, but a National Law produced by the Indonesian legislature." For Zoelva, the final wording regarding the application of *shari'a* does not belong to a council of *ulama* like that in Iran. In fact, it is legislative members that hold decisive authority, while the *ulama* are just invited to present their opinions before a decision is made. Zoelva finally concluded that it does not matter that the legislated *shari'a* is actually a human product, so long as it is still based on God's revelation.[24] Zoelva's pragmatic stance raises the question of how *shari'a* can be referred to as God's law and its implementation strongly demanded when the laws in question are basically products of human deliberation—that is, they are mostly products of legislatures. As Khaled Abou El-Fadl has pointed out, "[a]ll laws articulated and applied in a state are thoroughly human and should be treated as such. These laws are a part of *shari'a* law only to the extent that any set of human legal opinions can be said to be a part of *shari'a*." [25] Given this, it is no wonder that a huge number of Indonesian Muslims, at least as represented by the two biggest Islamic organizations: Nahdlatul Ulama and Muhammadiyah, have very different visions of *shari'a* [26] and opposed the proposal of the Islamic parties to amend Article 29 in the 2002 MPR Annual Session.[27]

I I

The Failure of Amendment

This chapter describes in more detail the arguments put forward by each member of the Islamic faction regarding the amendment of Article 29 on Religion, particularly in the meetings of Ad Hoc Committee One of the 2002 MPR Annual Session. Of the forty-five members of Ad Hoc Committee One, thirteen representatives came from the Islamic faction. The United Development Party faction (F-PPP) and the National Awakening Party faction (F-PKB) each put four representatives on this committee, while the Crescent Moon Star Party faction (F-PBB) and a faction of small Islamic parties (F-PDU) could each send only one representative. Although F-Reformasi was a merger of two parties, the National Mandate Party (PAN) and the Justice Party (PK) and could place three representatives in the committee, all of them were from the PAN and none were from the PK.

It is interesting to note here that although members of the Islamic faction shared a similar objective of amending Article 29, their individual stances varied over time. As is shown below, some members of the Islamic faction were eager to speak more about collective than individual rights. Debate on the amendment to Article 29 on Religion attracted their attention much more than did Article 28 on Human Rights. In fact, discussions on human rights by Islamic parties during the period of constitutional amendment were generally unsatisfactory and largely figurative.

The United Development Party Faction (F-PPP)

The F-PPP obtained sixty-seven seats in the People's Consultative Assembly. Four members were sent to represent the faction in Ad Hoc Committee One; Lukman Hakim Saifuddin, Zein Badjeber, Ali Hardi Kiaidemak, and Ali Marwan Hanan. The last representative later resigned because of his appointment as state minister for cooperatives and small-medium enterprises in President Megawati's cabinet. In the MPR Annual Session of 2001 and 2002, his place was taken by Abdul Aziz Imran Pattisahusiwa.

Since the 2000 Annual Session, the F-PPP had committed itself to reintroduce the seven words of the Jakarta Charter into Article 29 (1) of the constitution. For the F-PPP, amendment of Article 29 was not meant to change the state ideology, but was merely to redefine the wording of the preamble, making it more clearly elaborated in the body of the constitution. In addition, the F-PPP suggested the deletion of the word *kepercayaan* in Article 29 (2) to prevent this article from accommodating non-religious beliefs. And finally, the F-PPP proposed a new third paragraph: "The state should not allow the spread of the views that contradict One Almighty God." [1]

The F-PPP reasserted this position in the MPR Annual Session of 2002. In the Ad Hoc Committee One meeting on 21 March 2002, Lukman Hakim Saifuddin argued that although state and religion can be distinguished, they cannot be separated. Emphasizing the state's role in the spiritual aspects of human life, Lukman contended that the state is authorized and capable of supervising the implementation of religious doctrine because the term 'religious doctrine' (*ajaran agama*), in his view, not only meant rituals but also implied social relations.[2] Summarizing the final stance of the F-PPP in the Ad Hoc Committee One meeting on 13 June 2002, another spokesman for the F-PPP, Ali Hardi Kiai Demak, also stressed what had been put forward by previous F-PPP speakers (Zein Badjeber and Lukman Hakim Saifuddin). In fact, he went further by illustrating that since there are laws that include Islamic *shari'a,* such as the Marriage Law (UU 1/1974), the Pilgrimage Service Law (UU 17/1999), the Zakat Management Law (UU 38/1999), the Religious Court Law (UU 87/1989), and the Nanggroe Aceh Darussalam Law (UU 44/1999), all these legal developments should be ratified officially by the reintroduction of the Jakarta Charter into Article 29 of the constitution.

By referring to such laws, the F-PPP asserted that Muslim citizens have already acquired particular collective religious rights, so constitutional status for the *shari'a* would be merely a symbolic acknowledgment.[3] However, things may not be that simple. The enactment of those laws has led to the creation of an ambiguous legal system that is not solely based on citizenship, but on religious beliefs. This is certainly in contradiction to the basic conception of the modern nation-state, which purports to treat its citizens equally, regardless of their religious background.

The Crescent Moon Star Party Faction (F-PBB)

Due to the small number of votes (1.9 percent) they obtained in the 1999 election, the F-PBB was only able to place fourteen members in the MPR. Of this, there was only one member sent to speak on behalf of the F-PBB, namely Hamdan Zoelva, in the meetings of Ad Hoc Committee One of the MPR Annual Session from 2000 to 2002.

The F-PBB's insistence on insertion of the seven words into Article 29 of the constitution was clear from the 2000 MPR Annual Session.[4] In the MPR Annual Session in November 2001, the F-PBB firmly and solely advocated the reinsertion of the seven words. It did so alone because the F-PPP was silent at this time, partly because Hamzah Haz, the chairman of PPP, had now become vice president to Megawati Soekarnoputri. The 2002 MPR Annual Session provided more time for the F-PBB to discuss in depth the amendment to Article 29.

In the meeting on 21 March 2002, Zoelva reasserted the necessity of state intervention and emphasized the distinction of Islam, in the sense of Islam-state relations, from other religions.[5] Zoelva further argued, in the next Ad Hoc Committee meeting on 4 April 2002, that there is always a need for state support for the implementation of *shari'a*. He cited two Qur'anic verses on two different Islamic injunctions: the obligation of fasting (*siyam*) and the obligation of retaliation (*qisas*). Both obligations are clearly described in Qur'an with the same Arabic words *kutiba 'alaykum* [prescribed for you], meaning Muslims are obliged to follow both these directives.[6] According to Zoelva, the obligation of fasting will cause no harm if observed, and hence it may not need state intervention. However, the obligation of retaliation will lead to anarchy if Muslim individuals are free to carry it out. For this reason, the F-PBB argued that to maintain law and order, the state should involve itself in implementing this Islamic obligation.[7] In other words, Muslim religious duties are impossible without state intervention.

The F-PBB's proposal thus implied that Islamic *shari'a* was compulsory for both Muslims and for the state. It is obvious here that the proposal of Islamic parties concerning the amendment to Article 29 has much more to do with religious duties rather than with rights.

The problem with the argument of the necessity of state intervention is that in order to support its claim, it brings together two Islamic injunctions (fasting and retaliation) that are totally different from each other, in the sense of the respective levels of obligation attached to them in Islamic legal theory. While the nature of the obligation of Muslims to fast during the month of Ramadan is unquestionable, with regard to the obligatory nature of retaliation, there is a set of intricate qualifications and requirements, and there are a great number of disagreements among Islamic jurists on what is lawful retaliation.[8]

In addition, there is a third verse in the Qur'an (2:180) that includes *kutiba 'alaykum* and relates to *wasiyya* [last will and testament]. But, although this verse uses the words *kutiba 'alaykum*, a Muslim is not obliged to make a last will and testament; the status of *wasiyya* in Islam is not an obligatory religious duty, but a recommended one.[9] Given this, the grammatical argument provided by Zoelva is not entirely convincing.

Aware that an exclusive reference to Islamic *shari'a* in the constitution would offend non-Muslim feelings, Zoelva stated that his faction would welcome a compromise and was ready to discuss a new formula for Article 29. At the meeting on 13 June 2002, he was ready to accept that all other religions could be mentioned in the constitution as well, thus making Article 29 (1) not exclusively applicable to Muslim citizens. Zoelva also proposed another draft either to be inserted as a new third paragraph or as additional clause of Article 29 (2): *Negara menjamin dapat dilaksanakannya syariat Islam yang diwajibkan bagi para pemeluknya* [The state guarantees that Islamic *shari'a* that is obligatory for its adherents can be implemented].[11] However, in the meeting on 28 June 2002, Hamdan Zoelva cancelled his compromise draft after realizing that it was not welcomed by other factions in the MPR. The F-PBB then returned to its previous position, which was similar to that of the F-PPP.[12]

The Union of the Umma Sovereignty (F-PDU)

This faction was an alliance that consisted of eleven individuals from various small Islamic parties, like the Muslim Community Revival Party (PNU), the Muslim Community Awakening Party (PKU), the Indonesian Islamic Union Party (PSII), the Partai Masyumi, the PDR, and two deserters from the PBB (Hartono Mardjono and Abdul Qadir Djaelani). Both joined this faction after disappointments with internal policies of their own party in 2001. In the meetings of the Ad Hoc Committee One of the MPR Annual Session from 2000 to 2002, this faction was solely represented by Asnawi Latief of the PKU.

As far as the amendment to Article 29 (1) was concerned, the stance of the F-PDU changed from time to time. Initially, in the 2000 MPR Annual Session, the F-PDU's position was that there should be no amendment to Article 29 (1). But in the Ad Hoc Committee One meeting on 21 March 2002, Asnawi Latief explained that his faction supported what Yusuf Muhammad (the F-PKB speaker) proposed regarding Alternative Three. However, Latief immediately added that if the assembly could not accept the F-PKB's proposal, his faction was ready to return to the original text of Article 29 (1), for there would be nothing new.[13] At this juncture, it seemed that the F-PDU hesitated to take a clear position.

In the following Ad Hoc Committee One meetings (13 June 2002 and 28 June 2002), the F-PDU clarified its stance toward the amendment to Article 29. Basically, the F-PDU wanted to see Islamic *shari'a* become mandatory in the constitution, but preferred to place this obligation in Article 29 (2), not in Article 29 (1). In the F-PDU's opinion, Article 29 (1) was about the state ideology and was already final, thus any attempt to amend the first paragraph would also be a change to fundamental state ideology and this was undesirable.[14] In the finalization meeting of

25 July 2002, Latief declared that his faction was ready to return to the original text of Article 29 (1) so long as the Islamic *shari'a* would be acceptable in Article 29 (2).[15] The F-PDU's stance here was similar to that of the F-PPP and the F-PBB, except that they differed as to the question of which paragraph of Article 29 the seven words of the Jakarta Charter should be inserted into.

However, the F-PDU's stance changed again in the plenary meeting of the 2002 MPR Annual Session. Ahmad Sjatari, a representative of the F-PDU from the PNU, when conveying F-PDU's General Remarks (Pemandangan Umum) on 3 August 2002, demanded that Article 29 (1) accommodate the obligation of *shari'a* for Muslim citizens.[16] Later on, in the Meeting of the Commission (Rapat Komisi) on 6 August 2002 and in the Final Remarks (Pendapat Akhir) on 9 August 2002, both Asnawi Latief and Hartono Mardjono reasserted the position taken by Sjatari.[17] Seen from the perspective of political game analysis, it may be assumed that this final stance of the F-PDU was an extravagant negotiating stance taken to get the MPR Annual Session to accommodate Islamic *shari'a* in Article 29 (2) instead of in Article 29 (1), as the F-PDU had sought earlier in the finalization meeting.

One may wonder why there was a shift in F-PDU's stance over the amendment to Article 29 during the years of constitutional amendment. According to Latief, the shift was due to the continuous call for the implementation of *shari'a* raised by radical Muslim groups, such as the Defender Front of Islam (FPI), Hizbut Tahrir, and Indonesian Council of Muslim Fighters (MMI), who met his faction and pushed for the insertion of seven words into Article 29.[18] Nevertheless, it could also be speculated that the change took place in the F-PDU's stance because of two deserters from the F-PBB, Hartono Mardjono and Abdul Qadir Djaelani, who joined the F-PDU in mid-2001.[19] Both were die-hard campaigners for the implementation of *shari'a* in Indonesia. From then on, the voice of the F-PDU gradually changed to strongly advocate the formal implementation of *shari'a*.

To support the inclusion of the seven words into Article 29, the F-PDU presented the argument of religious rights, which was the collective rights of Hindus in the island of Bali to exercise the religious day of silence (*Nyepi*) for twenty-four hours.[20] During this time, which occurs once a year, there are no public activities allowed, including flights to or from Bali. What is more, according to Asnawi Latief, the electricity in all regions of Bali is switched off for the day. He further underscored that no non-Hindus raise an objection or feel religiously discriminated against by this ritual.[21] Given this, the F-PDU sought to assert that as the state and non-Hindus tolerate this condition for Hindus in Bali, the same thing should be applied to Muslims if they wish for the constitutional implementation of *shari'a* in Indonesia.

At a superficial level, one might consider the F-PDU's argument to be credible. However, if we look closely at the nature of the *Nyepi* Hindu ritual in Bali with a comparative reference to the implementation of *shariʻa,* the argument becomes much weaker. First, what differentiates the *Nyepi* tradition from the formal implementation of *shariʻa* is that the former is mostly ritual and has little to do with legal matters, and thus does not require any formal legal apparatus, such as judges or police, to carry it out. It is voluntary. On the contrary, the formal implementation of *shariʻa,* as demanded by Islamic parties, is almost entirely about legal matters, and it needs the involvement of legal apparatus. Second, the *Nyepi* ritual is a Hindu obligation, but there is no sanction provided by the state for those who are recalcitrant. By comparison, the formal implementation of *shariʻa* contemplated by the F-PDU requires the state to uphold it by force. Thus, any Muslim who fails to perform the obliged *shariʻa* would be punished.

In essence, the fact that the state facilitates the *Nyepi* ritual in Bali by shutting down all public activities for a particular period is similar to what the state does for other religions for their rituals and holidays. The Islamic festive day of *Idul Fitri,* which falls a day after the fasting month of Ramadan ends, for example, is recognized by the state, which closes public activities for two days nationally, one day longer than other religious holidays such as Christmas Day or the Buddhist *Waisak.* Indeed, that the *Nyepi* ritual involves the disconnection of electricity, for instance, is a requisite of that particular ritual, not an example of the state's preferring a Hindu ritual over other religious rituals.

The Reform Faction (F-Reformasi)

The F-Reformasi consisted of forty-one members from the PAN and PK parties, with thirty-four legislators coming from the PAN and seven from the PK. In the meetings of the Ad Hoc Committee One, no member appeared from the PK. Instead, all three representatives of the F-Reformasi in those meetings were PAN activists, A. M. Luthfi, Patrialis Akbar, and Fuad Bawazier.

The early stance of the F-Reformasi, which supported Alternative Three, regarding the amendment of Article 29 was observable in the 2000 MPR Annual Session. At the meeting of 14 June 2000, the F-Reformasi speaker, Luthfi, originally proposed adding a new paragraph to Article 29: *Tiap pemeluk agama diwajibkan melaksanakan ajaran agamanya masing-masing* [every religious believer is obliged to carry out their respective religious teachings].[22]

In the MPR Annual Session of 2001, the F-Reformasi further developed this proposal. When delivering the General Remarks in the plenary meeting on 4 November 2001, the F-Reformasi speaker, TB Soemandjaja, came out with a newly developed draft for Article 29 (1): *Negara Berdasar Ketuhanan Yang Maha Esa dengan Kewajiban Melaksanakan Ajaran Agama bagi masing-masing Pemeluknya* [the state is based on belief in One Almighty God with an obligation upon the followers of each religion to implement their respective teachings].[23] The proposal of the F-Reformasi was referred to as the 'Piagam Madinah' or the Medina Charter since it was believed to mirror the plural policy established during the time of the Prophet Muhammad in Medina.[24]

The main argument put forward by the F-Reformasi to support its proposal was the 'moral decadence' of Indonesians. In the meeting of the Ad Hoc Committee One on 21 March 2002, Luthfi maintained that Indonesia was now one of the most corrupt countries in the world, and that there must be an effort to end this condition. For the F-Reformasi, the answer was simple: restoring the morality of the leaders and of the people. To this end, Luthfi emphasized that the state should recommend—not oblige—that all people carry out what their religions required them to do.[25] Or as another speaker of the F-Reformasi, Patrialis Akbar, said, "a constitutional statement such as [Alternative Three] is (simply) to remind people that the performance of religious duties is compulsory."[26] Once again, it appears that the proposal has nothing to do with rights, but with religious *duties.*

It is obvious that what the F-Reformasi proposed above involves the same goal as the three other Islamic parties (the F-PPP, the F-PBB, and the F-PDU), though their proposals differed in wording. Mutammimul Ula, a prominent figure among the seven representatives of the Justice Party in the MPR (1999–2004), explicitly acknowledged that drafts of Alternative Two and Alternative Three shared a similar goal in practice.[27] If the ultimate goal of both drafts was not altogether different, why then did the F-Reformasi not support the reinsertion of the seven words into Article 29 (1), rather than proposing Alternative Three?

There are two explanations. First, the PAN chose to suggest an alternative over the seven words, according to A. M. Fatwa, a leader of the PAN and former vice chairman of the DPR, because PAN sought to resolve a dilemma between fulfilling what was required of an inclusive party seeking non-Muslim support that should act neutrally toward religions and showing Islamic solidarity toward its majority Muslim supporters, especially those who were also Muhammadiyah members.[28]

Second, the PK decided against reinserting the seven words of the Jakarta Charter into Article 29 and instead preferred to promote the Medina Charter, for three reasons: (1) The Jakarta Charter is not final, since it is not the sole legitimate expression of the implementation of *shari'a* in Indonesia; (2) the text of the Jakarta Charter appears exclusive to Muslims, which was not in line with the spirit of Islam as merciful to all the world (*rahmatan lil-'alamin*); (3) the Medina Charter is much closer to the core of Islam than is the Jakarta Charter, as the former would acknowledge the legal autonomy of each religion while the latter would only give legal privilege to particular believers.[29]

It appears that the PK paid more attention to this proposal than did the PAN.

In fact, it was PK leaders who often referred to the Medina Charter when making a political statement regarding the formal implementation of *shari'a*. Outside the assembly meetings, the leader of PK, Hidayat Nur Wahid, introduced and supported Alternative Three on many occasions in writings and speeches as well as in media interviews. Nur Wahid argued that the role of the Jakarta Charter in the early history of Indonesia, as a compromise between those who struggled for a state based on Islamic ideology and those who wanted the secular state of Indonesia, was over. Now, for Nur Wahid, it was time for the Medina Charter to be the solution or middle way between those who wanted to amend Article 29 and those who opposed any effort to amend it.[30] He also added that the Medina Charter was capable of being a framework for establishing religion in daily life. In Nur Wahid's words: "We highlight [this issue] and we wish the Medina Charter to be the reference, [where] religion [not only] becomes a solution to correct the [condition of] society, [but also] it can be a warranty for national integration, as well as for no discrimination before the law."[31]

Obviously, the PK had been leaning toward religiously legal polycentrism in Indonesia, which, as I have argued in chapter 4, would closely resemble the millet system of the Ottoman Empire. Under this system, the state dealt with its citizens based on their membership in a religious community, not as autonomous individuals. It would be hard to imagine that under this system citizens could freely exercise their religious liberties since the state would either directly arrange a standardized religious practice for each religious community or indirectly delegate this task to respective religious authorities.

The National Awakening Party Faction (F-PKB)

The 1999 election made the PKB one of the five biggest parties along with the Indonesia's Struggle Democratic Party (PDI-P), the Golkar Party, the United Development Party (PPP), and the PAN. With fifty-one elected legislators at the MPR, this party was able to send four of its members to the meetings of the Ad Hoc Committee One of the MPR from 2000 to 2002. They were K. H. Yusuf Muhammad, Ali Masykur Musa, Erman Suparno, and Ida Fauziah.

The early stance of the F-PKB regarding the amendment to Article 29 in the 2000 MPR Annual Session was to support Alternative Three. However, at the last stage of the Annual Session of 2002, the F-PKB returned to the original text of Article 29 (Alternative One). What prompted this change? One needs to look at F-PKB's basic argument in order to understand it. According to Yusuf Muhammad, the F-PKB speaker, the primary objective of the F-PKB was to build a bridge between the different drafts proposed by various factions.[32] Muhammad took the view that Article 29 essentially meant that as the state is religious, so the people must be religious too. This condition of being religious must be reflected not only in theory, but, more importantly, in practice as well. Thus, for the F-PKB, it was the state's task to persuade, and not to compel, people to be loyal or observant toward their respective religious duties.[33] With this underlying notion, the F-PKB distinguished itself from other Islamic parties. While others emphasized political interests and long-term strategies, the F-PKB wished to accommodate all different outlooks with a single formula. The following discussion will describe F-PKB's effort to bring different opinions of the MPR factions into a compromise.

Realizing there were three alternative drafts (the original text and the other two amended drafts) for the constitutional reformulation of Article 29 (1), the synchronization meeting on 13 June 2002 attempted to encourage various factions to come to a preliminary agreement. It was Yusuf Muhammad from the F-PKB who first suggested a compromise. He suggested that the word *kesungguhan* [a sincere intention] might replace the word *kewajiban* [obligation] in the seven words of the Jakarta Charter, thus making it *dengan kesungguhan menjalankan syariat Islam bagi pemeluk-pemeluknya* [with a sincere intention to implement Islamic *shariʿa* on the part of its adherents]. According to Muhammad, the word *kesungguhan* is merely ethical and not imperative. This suggestion, Muhammad assumed, would deactivate the legal implications of Article 29 on Religion,[34] thus achieving a middle ground between the three alternative drafts discussed above.

Another member of the F-PKB, Ida Fauziah, later elaborated on Yusuf Muhammad's suggestion to avoid misunderstanding from other factions, especially the Golkar Party faction. She said that if the word *kesungguhan* could not be accepted to replace *kewajiban* in Article 29 (1), then it would be better to leave Article 29 (1) untouched. However, the F-PKB wanted Article 29 (2) to include the clause: *Negara menjamin kemerdekaan tiap-tiap penduduk untuk memeluk dan melaksanakan ajaran agamanya masing-masing dan untuk beribadah menurut agamanya* [The state guarantees the freedom of each individual to adhere and to carry out their respective religious teachings and to worship according to their religions].[35]

The proposed words of the F-PKB above were close to what the F-PDU had earlier put forward in the synchronization meeting on 13 June 2002.[36] Responding to the situation on that day, the F-PDU, through its representative Asnawi Latief, sought to find a way out by offering an amendment draft for Article 29 (2) as follows: *Negara menjamin kemerdekaan setiap penduduk untuk melaksanakan kewajiban agamanya masing-masing dan beribadat menurut agamanya itu* [The state guarantees the freedom of all citizens to carry out their respective religious obligations and to worship according to their religion]. This proposal would leave Article 29 (1) unchanged and it would only modify Article 29 (2) in line with the suggestions submitted by a number of factions that all religious believers are to be equally treated.

On 28 June 2002, at the last meeting of the Ad Hoc Committee One for discussion of Article 29, Yusuf Muhammad sought to reassert his previous proposal. The F-PKB now preferred that Article 29 (1) be left unchanged and there be modifications to Article 29 (2): *Negara menjamin kemerdekaan tiap-tiap penduduk untuk memeluk dan melaksanakan ajaran/kewajiban agamanya masing-masing dan untuk beribadah menurut agamanya itu* [The state guarantees the freedom of each individual to adhere and to carry out their respective religious teachings or obligations and to worship according to their religions]. According to Muhammad, these modifications of Article 29 (2) would lay down an ideal pattern of relationship between the state and religion. This kind of relationship would be cultural rather than institutional. Thus, it would provide an equal opportunity for each religion to develop and build a new harmony, while the state would only encourage the religiosity of people.[37] This proposal sought to bring all the three different drafts of alternatives into a single formula. Compared to the earliest proposal put forward by the F-PKB in the 2000 MPR Annual Session, there was not much change. The only change made was to relocate its position from the first paragraph to the second paragraph of Article 29.

The F-PKB's proposal seemed to attract much attention and support. For one thing, the proposal would leave the original text of Article 29 (1) as it originally stood (Alternative One). For another, it would accommodate and relocate both Alternative Two and Alternative Three into Article 29 (2). Although the chairman of the meeting, Harun Kamil, and two speakers from the F-PG, Amidhan and Theo L. Sambuaga, supported the proposal, other members of Islamic faction appeared hesitant. The F-Reformasi, whose proposed draft was similar to F-PKB's first proposal, carefully considered the latest suggestion of the F-PKB.[38] In the view of the F-Reformasi, F-PKB's suggestion that left the original text in Article 29 (1) unchanged and accommodated other alternative drafts in Article 29 (2) would be acceptable if it formed a final compromise.[39] However, this was not the case. A later debate showed that there was, in fact, no unanimous consensus supporting the F-PKB's proposal.

Other members of the Islamic faction, such the F-PPP and the F-PBB, may have had thoughts similar to the F-Reformasi's position. Ali Hardi Kiai Demak and Lukman Hakim Saifuddin from the F-PPP and Hamdan Zoelva from the F-PBB expressed the same concerns.[40] Perhaps if a consensus to accept the F-PKB's proposal could be achieved, it would be likely that the F-PPP and the F-PBB would withdraw their proposal to insert the seven words of the Jakarta Charter into Article 29 (1). However, these expectations were not met. The F-PDI-P, through Pataniari

TABLE 11.1. The Last Meeting of Ad Hoc Committee One

F-PDIP F-PG F-KKI F-PDKB F-TNI/POLRI	Alternative One (No change)	*Negara Berdasarkan Ketuhanan Yang Maha Esa* [The state is based on belief in one almighty God]
F-PPP F-PBB F-PDU	Alternative Two	*Negara berdasar atas Ketuhanan Yang Mahaesa* *dengan kewajiban menjalankan syariat Islam bagi* *pemeluk-pemeluknya* [The state is based on belief in one almighty God with the obligation to carry out the Islamic *shari'a* for its adherents]
F-Reformasi F-PKB	Alternative Three	*Negara berdasar atas Ketuhanan Yang Mahaesa* *dengan kewajiban melaksanakan ajaran agama bagi* *masing-masing pemeluknya* [The state is based on belief in one almighty God with an obligation upon the followers of each religion to implement their respective teachings]

Siahaan, wanted to see various alternative drafts made for Article 29, thus making the F-PKB's proposal not the sole alternative draft.[41] In addition, Khohirin Suganda of the F-TNI/POLRI, which represented armed and police forces, opposed the F-PKB's proposal since it would eliminate the word *kepercayaan* from Article 29,[42] thus removing a constitutional basis for non-religious beliefs.

As the time for amending Article 29 was running out, there was a tentative agreement resulting from these Ad Hoc Committee One meetings to present three draft alternatives to Article 29 (1) as shown in Table 11.1.

Political Trade-Off

Aware that amending Article 29 in the 2002 MPR Annual Session would be difficult since there was only limited support for change, the Islamic faction, the F-PPP in particular, sought to alter their strategy by reversing their short-term political goals. The F-PPP now considered relinquishing its proposal to amend Article 29 in exchange for the insertion of the words *meningkatkan keimanan dan ketakwaan* [to increase faith and people's consciousness of God] into Article 31 on Education. Article 31 (3) would then become: "The government shall develop and maintain a national system of education that increases faith (*keimanan*) and the people's consciousness of God (*ketakwaan*) and noble conduct (*akhlak mulia*), in the course of improving the people's intelligence, which is to be regulated by law."

The effort to insert the words *meningkatkan keimanan dan ketakwaan* [to increase faith and people's consciousness of God] into Article 31 on Education had begun in the 2000 MPR Annual Session. However, it was only in the 2002 Annual Session that the F-PPP overtly attempted to make a trade-off. The F-PPP was ready to return to the original text of Article 29 so long as those words *meningkatkan keimanan dan ketakwaan* were mentioned in Article 31 (3) of the constitution.[43] The amendment to this article by inserting the words "to increase faith and people's consciousness of God" was more desirable than adding the seven words of the Jakarta Charter since it would make religious education in every school in the country the medium by which the Islamic *shari'a* could be expanded.

This trade-off was welcomed by non-Islamic faction because the national goal of education, to improve the people's intelligence (*untuk meningkatkan kecerdasan bangsa*), remained unaltered.[44] In fact, the manual for disseminating the outcome of the constitutional amendments clarified this by stating that the ultimate goal of national education was to improve the people's intelligence, while increasing faith and people's consciousness of God (*untuk meningkatkan keimanan dan ketakwaan*) was only a part of that ultimate goal.[45]

However, the Islamic faction believed they had achieved an important political gain by the assembly's insertion of the clause into Article 31 (3) on Education. In the view of the Islamic faction, these words were a constitutional reference point for lawmaking on Islamic education and, indeed, in October 2003, this Article 31 (3) enabled the Islamic faction in the legislature to successfully pass the National Education System bill. Law 20/2003 has been seen as leaning to Muslim interests at the expense of others, Christians in particular, as it underscored the importance of providing Islamic education for Muslim students even if they attend Christian schools.[46] As education is an effective means of enhancing the understanding of Muslims about the *shari'a*, this success was considered a crucial gain in the struggle for Islamization of the country. Islamic parties, therefore, retained optimism that in the long run the formal implementation of *shari'a* might eventually be acknowledged constitutionally.

The Final Drama of the Amendment

By the time of the plenary meeting of the MPR Annual Session on 10 August 2002, in which the agenda was to ratify a number of draft MPR decrees, the decision of each member of the Islamic faction regarding the amendment to Article 29 differed. Even though the proposal to insert the seven words of the Jakarta Charter was not formally withdrawn, the F-PPP, in the national interest, granted the MPR full authority to opt for any of the three alternative drafts regarding the amendment to Article 29.[47]

The F-Reformasi seemed to take a similar stance as the F-PPP. After an extensive argument in favor of amending Article 29 (1) by inserting Alternative Three, the F-Reformasi finally came to realize that the political atmosphere in the assembly would not welcome any amendment of the original text of Article 29. The spokesman for the F-Reformasi and the leader of the PAN, Andi Mappetahang Fatwa, explained his faction's final stance that it would not impede the process of decision making by the assembly and that, accordingly, the F-Reformasi was ready to accept the decision to return to the original text of Article 29.[48] Soon after this, however, Mutammimul Ula, the other member of the F-Reformasi but from another party (PK), interrupted the meeting and expressed a different view held by seven members of PK within the F-Reformasi. Ula said that seven members of PK in the F-Reformasi wished to abstain from making a decision over the return to the original text of Article 29.[49]

They were not alone. Though there was strong resistance from the majority of the assembly members, the F-PBB insisted on proposing the seven words and stated that should the assembly unanimously agree to leave Article 29 unchanged, the assembly had to make an official note that all members of the F-PBB had dissented. The F-PDU and the other three members of the F-UG took the same position. They interrupted the meeting and wanted their names to be formally recorded as abstaining.

The end of the MPR plenary meeting showed that there were three camps of Islamic parties concerning the constitutionalization of *shari'a*. The first camp—the PKB—preferred to maintain Article 29 as it was. This party initially sought amendment, but only because of its strong commitment to seek a compromise between the different drafts of the alternatives. The second camp—the PPP and the PAN—finally decided to allow the assembly to return to the original text of Article 29. Both parties had been struggling to amend Article 29, partly due to a renewed need to protect their image as defenders of Muslim political interests in the eyes of their constituency. The third camp was a number of parties (the PBB, the PK, and other smaller parties like the PKU, the PNU, the PSII, organized under the F-PDU) that insisted on amending Article 29, either with Alternative Two or Alternative Three. As the majority of the assembly members were not in line with their wishes, they eventually declared themselves officially hands-off from the final decision-making process. Table 11.2 shows the concluding position of each faction with regard to amending Article 29 in the final meeting of the MPR Plenary Session in August 2002.

TABLE 11.2. Concluding Position in the MPR Plenary Meeting

F-PDIP	Alternative One	*Negara Berdasarkan Ketuhanan Yang Maha*
F-PG	(No change)	*Esa* [The state is based on belief in one
F-KKI		almighty God]
F-PDKB		
F-TNI/POLRI		
F-PKB		
F-PPP		
F-Reformasi (PAN)		
F-PBB	Alternative Two	*Negara berdasar atas Ketuhanan Yang*
F-PDU		*Mahaesa dengan kewajiban menjalankan*
		syariat Islam bagi pemeluk-pemeluknya [The
		state is based on belief in one almighty God
		with the obligation to carry out the Islamic
		shari'a for its adherents]
F-Reformasi (PK)	Alternative Three	*Negara berdasar atas Ketuhanan Yang Mahaesa*
		dengan kewajiban melaksanakan ajaran agama
		bagi masing-masing pemeluknya [The state is
		based on belief in one almighty God with an
		obligation upon the followers of each religion
		to implement their respective teachings]

In conclusion, the Islamization of Indonesia was clearly a living agenda for Islamic parties during the MPR constitutional debates. This is the main reason why the issue of the constitutional implementation of *shari'a* has never fully left the political agenda. In the eyes of Islamic parties, a constitutional status for Islamic *shari'a* is necessary, since only then could Islamic *shari'a* be officially implemented in Indonesia. From the previous discussion, it is clear, however, that Islamic parties have not been able to agree on *how* to give *shari'a* constitutional legitimacy. It remains true, nonetheless, that the tenaciousness of the Islamic parties in trying to place Islamic *shari'a* into the constitution shows that they are still important agents for Islamization of Indonesia. Indeed, Islamic parties such as PPP and PBB still insist they will keep on struggling for the implementation of *shari'a* despite gaining only marginal support from voters in the 2004 election.[50]

12

Limiting Human Rights

Having considered the failed attempt to amend Article 29 on Religion in the last chapter, I will demonstrate here how Islamic parties sought, in a debate that took place two years earlier at the 2000 MPR Annual Session, to undermine religious liberty by imposing limitations on Article 28 on Human Rights. This chapter compares the efforts of the Islamic faction in the MPR to amend Article 29 on Religion with their stance on the amendment of Article 28 on Human Rights. That Islamic parties accepted individual rights as mentioned in Article 28 while demanding the amendment to Article 29 to grant collective 'rights' to Muslim citizens creates an inherent contradiction. The struggle of Islamic parties for what they saw as religious rights, through insertion of the seven words of the Jakarta Charter into Article 29 of the constitution, was inconsistent with Article 28.

It must be borne in mind that discussions on human rights had begun earlier, at least since the MPR Special Session held in November 1998. On that occasion, the MPR promulgated Decree 17/1998 on Human Rights. The new constitutional provisions on human rights (Chapter XA) that formed part of the Second Amendment were mostly based on this MPR decree. A year later, the Habibie government (May 1998–October 1999) issued Law 39/1999 on Human Rights as well. Only one Islamic party, the PPP, was involved in the enactment of both MPR Decree 17/1998 and Law 39/1999. Other Islamic parties that entered the legislature only after the 1999 election were not able to participate in discussing constitutional provisions regarding human rights until the 2000 MPR Annual Session. This means that formal public debate *within* Islamic politics on this issue only really began in 2000.

There were two important meetings that specifically discussed an amendment to Article 28 on Human Rights at the 2000 MPR Annual Session. The first was the 43rd Plenary Meeting of the Ad Hoc Committee One that took place on 13 June 2000. The second was the 5th Commission Meeting of the MPR Annual Session on 13 August 2000. The meeting on 13 June 2000 was more important, as the discussion in that meeting proposed and drafted provisions on human rights, while the meeting on 13 August 2000 seemed to deal mostly with the systematic formulation of human rights provisions in the constitution. The following paragraphs will present the discussion on human rights provisions in both those meetings.

Religious Values as Limiter

Before the Second Amendment, the original Article 28 was very short. It stated that "freedom of association and assembly, of verbal and written expression and the like, shall be regulated by law." According to Lindsey, this phrase was "not a guarantee of rights at all, but the conferral on the state of the right to deal with such rights as it saw fit."[1] For this reason, it is little wonder that many factions in the MPR, except the F-PDI-P, strongly emphasized the need for amending it to include more general rights.

The Islamic faction, for example, sought to amend it in two ways. First, the F-PBB and the F-PPP required that the MPR Decree 17/1998 and the enacted laws on human rights should be the basic reference for the drafting of human rights provisions in the constitution.[2] While some speakers from non-Islamic factions often referred to a number of international conventions on human rights, such as Universal Declaration of Human Rights (UDHR) and International Covenant of Civil and Political Rights (ICCPR), the speakers from various Islamic parties seemed to be hesitant to do so. In general, they felt content with the existing regulations on human rights in Indonesia, or perhaps the Islamic faction thought that those international charters might contravene Islamic injunctions.

Second, the Islamic faction emphasized that constitutional provisions on human rights should be qualified. Two members of the Islamic faction, the F-Reformasi and the F-PPP, demanded that any constitutional provision on human rights should not contradict religious values. Neither Islamic faction, however, overtly proposed Islamic *shari'a* as a filter. Instead, they proposed the words "religious values."

According to Hosen, the words "religious values" do not refer to the *shari'a* in the sense of its formal meaning, but rather to its substantive meaning.[4] For Hosen, the words "religious values" were only one element among others that the constitution should take into account, such as justice, morality, security, public order, and the concept of a democratic country.[5] Hosen therefore argued that Islamic parties did not seek to establish *shari'a* over and above the constitutional provisions on human rights, as the only limitation to human rights is the law itself. Hosen's interpretation was based on the final draft of Article 28J (2) that stated:

> In the enjoyment of their rights and freedoms, each person is obliged to submit to the limits determined by *law,* with the sole purpose of guaranteeing recognition

and respect for the rights of others and to fulfilling the requirements of justice by taking into consideration morality, *religious values,* security and public order in a democratic society. (Emphasis added.)

In my view, Hosen did not pay enough attention to the details of the proceedings of the amendment to Article 28 and hence failed to see that Islamic factions were in fact seeking to qualify human rights with religious values. As a matter of fact, some speakers from Islamic parties in the Commission Meetings (Sidang Komisi) of the 2000 MPR Annual Session had even proposed that the words "and religious values" be moved to immediately after the word "law," which would imply that limitations on constitutional provisions on human rights emanate from both legal and religious values.[6] That the Islamic faction sought to undermine the constitutional provisions on human rights by religious values suggests that they attempted to put *shari'a* on a higher level than the constitution. If successful, this would imply a significant restriction of the individual rights to religious freedom mentioned in Article 28, which was introduced earlier. It is clear, therefore, that Islamic parties aimed to subordinate Article 28 to Article 29 of the Indonesian constitution. This effort, however, was unsuccessful.

Given this description, it is clear that the Islamic faction was less concerned with individual rights (Article 28) and more interested in religious collective rights (Article 29). The fact that the Islamic faction was mindful of the rights and freedoms as stipulated in Article 28 had much to do with assuring that the human rights abuses of the New Order period (which often targeted Muslim activists) would not recur in the post-Soeharto era.[7]

Threat to Internal Diversity

As discussed above, the attempts of the Islamic faction to achieve collective religious rights (namely the formal implementation of *shari'a* for Muslim citizens) and to limit individual human rights by religious values were unsuccessful. In spite of this, the Islamic faction was able, at least, to formulate Article 28J (2) of the constitution so that religious values must be taken into account in the implementation of human rights. In doing so, the Islamic faction sought to indirectly subordinate individual rights to communal rights. This could lead to a situation where embracing or practicing a particular religious interpretation that is different from the established practice of a mainstream religious group would be considered unlawful. This is certainly inconsistent with Article 28E (2) of the constitution, which states that everyone has freedom "to posses convictions and beliefs, and to express his or her thoughts and attitudes in accordance with his or her conscience."

Ironically, although the Second Amendment to the 1945 constitution adopted

a progressive formula of civil liberties, Indonesian citizens still fail to enjoy extensive individual rights relating to religious freedoms. This has partly to do with the
lack of effective instruments provided by the constitution to ensure the protection
of individual rights. As observed by Hyung-Jun Kim, it has long been the case in
Indonesia over many decades that individual rights relating to religious freedom
have been undermined, and this has greatly concerned religious groups collectively.[8] The prosecution in 2005 of Yusman Roy, for example, for reciting an Indonesian translation of the required first chapter of the Qur'an (*al-fatiha*) following
its Arabic version in his daily prayer, indicates that constitutional guarantees of
religious liberty, especially relating to the rights to embrace a different religious
interpretation than that of the mainstream religious group, remains vague in
implementation, to say the least.[9]

With regard to the Roy case, Roy had simply embraced a particular practice allowable according to the diversity of legal opinion in Islam.[10] For example,
observing daily prayers in a language other than Arabic is considered religiously
lawful in the opinion of Imam Abu Hanifa.[11] Therefore, from an Islamic legal
perspective, to regard Roy's practice as a deviation from Islamic tenets was incor-
rect. Likewise, from the constitutional point of view, to accuse Roy of disgracing
Islam by having a differing view of a clear religious injunction, as the prosecutor
believed, was groundless because it contravenes Article 28E (2) of the constitution,
which guarantees the right "to possess conviction and beliefs, and to express his or
her thoughts and attitudes in accordance with his or her conscience."

What the government's legal apparatus could have done in this situation is
basically be impartial to all the different interpretations of the same religion. The
state apparatus is required to consider that diversity is not only to be found *between*
different religions, but also *within* the same religion (intrapluralism). Unfortunately, the reality often reveals otherwise: The legal apparatus, such as the police
and public prosecutors, repeatedly side with one party in disputes between believers regarding the interpretation of a religious doctrine.

These challenges to the constitutional provisions on religious freedoms are
increasingly on the rise, as the Council of Indonesian Ulama (MUI) in mid-2005
issued a number of *fatwas* (legal opinions) concerning, among other things, the
reconfirmation that Ahmadiyya was a heretical sect and the banning of the idea of
religious pluralism.[12] Although what is meant by pluralism in the *fatwa* remains
unclear, it questions the variety of Islamic interpretations. This upsetting case
shows how, even under a non-Islamic constitution, proponents of the formal
implementation of *shari'a* could effectively constrain religious liberty. The current
ambiguous condition of religious freedom in Indonesia would be of much more
concern if Islamic parties were able to constitutionally place *shari'a* or religious
values on a higher level of importance than those of human rights.

PART IV

The Nationalization of *Shari'a*

13

The Institutionalization of *Zakat*

Zakat in Theory

The lexicological meaning of *zakat* is 'to purify.' It also comes with the connotation of 'growth' or 'increase.'[1] Technically, *zakat* means to give up a fixed proportion of one's wealth to certain determined recipients.[2] What is meant to be purified is the accumulated wealth, thus *zakat* is both a kind of tax on wealth, as well as a pious act (*'ibadah*). It is prescribed for every Muslim who possesses or keeps certain assets such as gold, silver, jewelry, cash, livestock, and agricultural produce to pay *zakat* for each one-year period in their ownership. The required duty for these assets amounts to 2.5 percent annually. The exception to this is for agricultural produce, which is levied as a tithe.[3]

In addition, there are two types of assets liable to *zakat:* apparent wealth (*al-amwal al-zahira*) and hidden wealth (*al-amwal al-batina*). While the state may forcibly levy *zakat* from Muslims who own apparent wealth, it is left up to the owner's conscience to pay the *zakat* on hidden wealth. This category of wealth was supposedly introduced by the caliph 'Umar b. Khattab (d. 644).[4] However, there was no consensus on what is considered apparent wealth and what is hidden wealth. Even in the time of the caliph Uthman b. Affan (d. 656), the definition given for hidden wealth contradicted its literal meaning, as it included highly visible assets such as housing and slaves. Meanwhile, certain easily concealed goods such gold and jewelry were deemed apparent wealth. It seems that this categorization was driven by expediency of the time rather than being based on strictly religious grounds.[5]

In spite of its high position as one of the five pillars of Islam, *zakat* is perhaps the religious duty least complied with by Muslims. For instance, a study conducted in rural Egypt shows that while 96 percent of farmers were aware of the obligatory nature of *zakat* payment, only 20 percent of them paid *zakat* on their crops.[6] There are two reasons that may account for this. First, regardless of their awareness of the obligatory nature of *zakat* payment, many Muslims lack adequate knowledge about the procedures for paying *zakat*: when, where, and how it should be conducted. This is due to the common reality that religious teachers rarely supply instruction on *zakat* to Muslims. Moreover, although the literature on *zakat* is huge, there is no substantial agreement over the practical meaning of the *zakat* requirement. As pointed out by Timur Kuran, King Faisal Professor of Islamic Thought and Culture at the University of Southern California, "there has never existed a single source that offers an authoritative account of how *zakat* should be paid or disbursed. . . . [T]he system has never been applied consistently over either time or space. . . . [Indeed], during Islam's first few centuries the application was never uniform."[7]

Zakat in Practice

The disagreement over the practice of *zakat* among Muslims anywhere and anytime is due to the nature of *zakat* itself. This is perhaps because the Qur'an does not elaborate on the issues of administration and the enforcement of *zakat*. There is no precise directive as whether to centralize or decentralize, or institutionalize or personalize, the application of *zakat*. Although the Qur'an mentions eight recipients of *zakat* of which a *zakat* agency (*al-'amilin 'alayha*) is one,[8] there is no further instruction on how *zakat* should be collected, whether Muslims are obliged to pay their *zakat* to this agency, or whether they can voluntarily give their *zakat* directly to the poor and the needy.

Another problem for *zakat* practice stems from the multifaceted function of *zakat* as it has developed since early Islam. Given that the purpose of *zakat* is mentioned in the Qur'an[9] and that it was clearly a historical response to the necessities of the Medina city-state and circumstances of the poorer *muhajirun* (Muslims who were migrants from Mecca to Medina),[10] the practice of *zakat* includes spiritual, political, and economic objectives. It is spiritual in the sense that by giving *zakat* one purifies the remainder of his or her wealth as well as his or her soul through a restraint on one's greed and imperviousness to others' sufferings. The recipient of *zakat*, likewise, is purified from jealousy and hatred of the well-off.[11] It also has political goals in that *zakat* in the first centuries of Islam was designed to raise revenue for the Islamic state, which allowed it to spend *zakat* revenue on public works and territorial expansion.[12] And, finally, *zakat* has economic purposes as it intends to reduce poverty and inequality.[13]

Taken together, the *zakat* payment is a purification of soul and wealth, as well as support for certain sociopolitical and socioeconomic structures that were necessary in early Islam. These three goals are, however, not easily achieved at the present time. In fact, the application of *zakat* in the modern period has never been the same

from one Muslim country to another. There is a range from complete incorporation of *zakat* as a regular tax of the Islamic state (Pakistan, Sudan, Saudi Arabia)
to the establishment of intermediary financial institutions that receive voluntary
payment of *zakat* (Jordan, Egypt, Bahrain, Kuwait, Indonesia) to the marginalization of *zakat* as a matter for each individual's private conscience (Morocco,
Oman).[14]

Pakistan's Experience of Centralizing *Zakat*

In what ways could the implementation of *zakat* in this regard parallel the agenda
of an Islamizing nation-state? It is noticeable that there has been an attempt in some
Muslim countries, including Indonesia, to simplify the variety of *zakat* practices by
subordinating its spiritual function into its political and economic purposes and by
centralizing its administration. In this way, a shift from conceiving *zakat* primarily
as an act of piety to an emphasis on *zakat* as the foundation of the Islamic political
and economic system is now being made. Likewise, there is a strong demand that
Muslim governments alone must assume the responsibility "of collecting *zakat*
and not leave its payment and distribution to the conscience of individuals . . .
for *zakat* is now seen as [an] entirely viable alternative to secular tax." [15] In short,
efforts to centralize the administration of *zakat* in the hands of the government
apparatus and its integration into the modern taxation system are clear stages on
the path to Islamizing the nation-state.

At the present time, there are already six Muslim countries (Saudi Arabia,
Libya, Yemen, Malaysia, Pakistan, and Sudan) that enforce the implementation
of *zakat*. Three of these have made a clear reference in their constitutions to the
responsibility of the state to implement *zakat* (Art. 10 of the Sudanese constitution,
Art. 21 of the Yemeni constitution, and Art. 31 of the Pakistani constitution).[16] Of
these Islamic countries, Pakistan has perhaps attracted most the scholarly attention since the implementation of *zakat* in Pakistan has become an exemplary part
of the greater agenda of Islamizing the nation-state.[17] The implementation of *zakat*
in Pakistan suggests how *zakat* collection and disbursement is characterized by a
centralized structure that serves as a pillar for the economic and political interests of the Islamic state. The intervention of the Pakistani government in *zakat*
administration has not, however, necessarily guaranteed the success of this mode
of Islamization.

Since it was introduced through the *Zakat* and Ushr Ordinance No. 17 of
1980, the centralization of *zakat* management in Pakistan has not come close to
achieving any complete socioeconomic or political transformation.[18] The real lives
and economic conditions of millions of Pakistani citizens have been completely

unchanged,[19] but a great number of socioreligious and political problems have arisen from state involvement in *zakat* administration. There are at least five effects of this centralized management that have proven deleterious. First, the incorporation of *zakat* into the Pakistani legal system has fixed the nature of *zakat* from a previously voluntary act to a compulsory religious duty.[20] In fact, the state has instituted "an official version of Islamic law in the face of differences of opinion among members of different schools and sects as to what Islam requires." [21] In the first days of the formal application of the *Zakat* Ordinance to all Pakistani Muslim citizens, strong opposition was raised by members of the Shi'i community. They argued that the provision of centralized *zakat* violated the right to distribute *zakat* as dictated by their religious awareness and their particular understanding of *shari'a* jurisprudence.[22] In April 1981, the government finally made a decision to allow Shi'i Muslims to file for their exemptions from paying the compulsory *zakat*.[23] However, as Kepel noted, the exemption created indignation among more conservative Sunni *ulama*, who were afraid that many Pakistani Sunni Muslims would convert to Shi'i for the purpose of *zakat* evasion.[24] This demonstrates that it is unrealistic for the state to officially acknowledge any single version of Islam.

Second, the institutionalization of *zakat* formally levied only on Muslims has enhanced the growing sense among a minority of non-Muslim Pakistani citizens that the state discriminates against them, even though they are exempt from payment. The Pakistani government program of Islamization was seen by non-Muslims as a sign that adherence to Islam was becoming the real basis of political community in the country, and they were considered only second-class citizens.[25] This suggests that any program of Islamization of a nation-state is likely to result in the prioritizing of particular religious groups at the expense of others.

Third, the integration of *zakat* rules into the Pakistani taxation system had transformed *zakat* payment from being simply and easily fulfilled into something with all the accessories of modern systems of taxation, which are, of course, difficult to understand for many Pakistanis, particularly the illiterate.[26] The Law of Zakat has created complex rules by adopting the vocabulary of formal tax regulations, which is not familiar to the majority of ordinary Muslims. This implied also the depersonalization of the payment of *zakat*. As the government automatically levied the *zakat* from the bank accounts of Muslim citizens each year during Ramadan, Pakistani Muslims who had previously paid their *zakat* directly to those they considered eligible recipients now felt that money payable under the ordinance was just like any other tax demanded by the government. Therefore, some Pakistanis thought their *zakat* obligation was not yet fulfilled and felt compelled to make another, traditional payment of *zakat*.[27] This illustrates how the spiritual purpose of *zakat* has been absorbed by the overwhelmingly political and economic objectives of the Islamic state that merely treats *zakat* as a source of official revenue.

Fourth, as the consequence of the depersonalization of *zakat* and its being religiously delegitimized, many Pakistani Muslims sought to evade all or part of the *zakat* payment. They did so "by not keeping [their] assets in forms taxable under the *zakat* law, or by removing assets from the taxing institutions just before the assessment [was] made on the first day of Ramadan."[28] As explained by Malik, a few days prior to the *zakat* deduction date, many Muslim *zakat* payers transferred their funds to the accounts of those who were not obliged to pay *zakat,* such as non-Pakistanis, non-Muslims, and Shiʻi citizens. In doing so, they decreased the amounts in their accounts to below *nisab* (a certain minimum amount required for the *zakat* payment), thus rendering their funds exempt from the levy. After the deduction date, these funds were then transferred back to their original accounts.[29] Here, the formalization of *zakat* payment by the state has detracted from the sincere character needed to perform religious duties, which in turn may have led to the spread of recusancy among Muslims.

Finally, the official implementation of *zakat* by the Pakistani government has created a competition between political parties for control over the *zakat* funds. This has much to do with the fact that the Pakistani *zakat* system, which is institutionalized from the high level of state to the lower levels of village or town, is a significant source of economic and political power for either the ruling regime or the opposition party. The local *zakat* committees have fallen under the control of political parties because the committees have become a source of financial support and, under certain conditions, can function as a mobilizing center or cash cow for political party activity.[30]

Viewed through the lens of the core argument of this book, namely that there are legal and political dissonances in the formal application of *shariʻa* in a modern nation-state, the problematical centralized administration of *zakat* in Pakistan is an example of how this arises. This Pakistani case shows that the belief that Islamization would enhance Muslim religiosity was unfounded. With regard to Indonesia, it is fair to say that the *zakat* administration in Indonesia would likely suffer the same fate as in Pakistan if current efforts toward centralizing *zakat* and making it compulsory were realized.

14
Managing the Collection of *Zakat*

Zakat before Indonesia's Independence

The nature of *zakat* practices in the early centuries after the coming of Islam to Indonesia remains largely unknown. There is no evidence that *zakat* had been formally transformed into an official tax regularly collected by Muslim kingdoms. Instead, *zakat* was voluntarily practiced and no Muslim was compelled to pay it. Snouck Hurgronje explained this situation by referring to the unusual process of Islamization in Indonesia, namely, that it was not militarily conquered by Arabs. The nature of *zakat* practice might have been different, he argued, if the process of Islamization in Indonesia had taken place through Arab conquest, in which case *zakat* would probably have become a political payment as a form of recognition for Arab rulers taking control of territory.[1]

Later, some local rulers, after they became Muslim, assisted religious officials in collecting *zakat* payments from Muslim subjects, although the payment was never considered a form of Islamic taxation or levied for political purposes.[2] In fact, it appears that Muslim kingdoms in Java never intended to establish official institutions to collect and to distribute *zakat,* let alone to force people to pay *zakat.* Additionally, there remains little if any evidence regarding how often the local Muslim rulers themselves paid *zakat.* The records available to us are too obscure to make any judgment. So, for example, Rouffaer suspected that "at the time of the first organizing of Mataramese land under Senopati (c. 1590) or more probably under Sultan Agung (c. 1625), of each 25 *cacahs* (units) of land, one was reserved for the religious people, as *waqf* [endowment], *perdikan*-land, (thus) as a sort of *zakat* on behalf of the king."[3] This vague information is still problematic and inconsistent with Islamic law, because land itself is not liable to *zakat* nor is a landowner required to pay *zakat* for possessing land. Why then did the Mataram kings reserve land for *zakat*? What kind of wealth did the Mataram kings seek to purify by giving such land as *zakat*? Based on this, it might be said that the practice of *zakat* under the Muslim kingdoms in Java in particular was not officially organized, at least not in accordance with official Islamic legal rules.

There is a dearth of information available to us regarding Dutch colonial policy on *zakat* and most of the little information available is restricted to Java and relies on Snouck Hurgronje's correspondence [4] containing his advice on the problems of *zakat*.[5] What we do know from his correspondence is that initial colonial policy on *zakat* probably stemmed from the fact that some native officials such as the regent (*bupati*), district chief (*wedana*), and head of village (*kepala desa*) misused the *zakat* funds for their personal benefit. The Netherlands East Indies government, realizing that such abuse by its own appointed officials might damage political stability in the colony, issued a regulation (*Bijblad* no. 1892) in 1866 prohibiting all officials of these classes from involvement in the collection and distribution of *zakat*.[6]

By and large, the Dutch policy on *zakat* practice ran parallel to Snouck Hurgronje's advice of neutrality and religious liberty,[7] which can be summarized as follows.

> To acknowledge and to protect religious practices wherever possible provided that [such] practices are considered indigenous, not because they are Islamic, that is to regulate such practices after having been sterilized from any abuse and custom that put heavy burdens on people.[8] . . . [The regulation that he meant was] to protect individual autonomy from any pressure in collecting *zakat* and *fitrah*, [in determining] their amount, or in choosing the agency that will allocate those religious funds.[9]

This relative lack of colonial intervention (either by obligation or management) in *zakat* practice meant greater freedoms were available to Muslims regarding their religious obligations. As Muslims were—in effect—largely free to choose to partake in religious duties or not, Snouck Hurgronje assumed they would overlook most religious practices because, in his eyes, various religious obligations were burdens for Muslims living in the modern world. In Snouck Hurgronje's view, *zakat* was mostly driven by a religious motive; that is, a failure to comply with this obligation would result in punishment in the hereafter. However, this motive had not become strongly embedded in the minds of Indonesian Muslims since they had had no adequate religious knowledge of the virtues of *zakat* payment.[10] This was consistent with the reality that there was a lack of attention paid by religious preachers or local Muslim teachers to the obligation of *zakat*. After all, various economic burdens including heavy taxation were already placed on the Muslim people of the East Indies by the colonial authorities and this obviously reduced the potential for *zakat* generosity.[11]

Zakat Administration in Post-Independence Indonesia

The *zakat* policy of the newly independent Indonesia adopted the previous Dutch colonial strategy. As mentioned previously, the Ministry of Religious Affairs (MORA), which effectively took the place of the Dutch colonial Office for Indigenous Affairs, was established in January 1946. The task of this ministry, among others, was to guarantee the freedom of people to observe their respective religious duties,[12] and at first it simply continued colonial policy on *zakat*. In 1951, for example, it issued a circular letter (*Surat Edaran* no. A/VVII/17367 dated 8 December 1951), stating that the ministry would not interfere in the *zakat* administration. It saw its task as simply to encourage people to observe their obligation to pay *zakat* and ensure that it was distributed properly in accordance with religious teachings.[13] This shows that from the very beginning, the Indonesian government never intended to initiate the establishment of an official institution to centrally manage *zakat* in Indonesia, but rather left it in the hands of the Muslim community.

A growing desire to make the Indonesian government responsible for the administration of *zakat* was observable, however, by the early years of the New Order regime. Following the issuance of President Soekarno's decree in 1959 that recognized the influence of the Jakarta Charter as inspiring and being linked in unity with the 1945 constitution, there was an increasing call for government engagement in *zakat* collection in the 1960s. Although the Jakarta Charter was excluded from debate in the MPRS sessions during 1966, 1967, and 1968 (as chapter 10 has shown), some Muslim figures believe it still had influence over the preamble of the 1945 constitution, as well as Article 29 of the same document. The belief that the Jakarta Charter remained valid as the underpinning of Indonesian religious life led a number of Muslim leaders to call for the administration of *zakat* by the government, which they saw as the first step in realizing the wording of the Jakarta Charter.[14]

Some prominent Muslim figures with key positions in the MORA formally proposed the legislation of *zakat*. In July 1967, Saefuddin Zuhri, then Minister of Religious Affairs, presented a draft *Zakat* Law to the legislature (DPRGR). The draft was also sent to both the Ministry of Finance and the Ministry of Social Affairs for feedback. Although the latter never responded, the minister of finance did reply with a suggestion that the *zakat* management would be better regulated by ministerial regulations instead of by a statute.[15] It was perhaps because of this suggestion that the legislature chose not to pursue discussion of the draft *Zakat* Law presented by the MORA. This suggestion may have also inspired the MORA a year later, now under the leadership of Mohammad Dachlan, to issue a ministerial decree concerning the foundation of the Badan Amil *Zakat* (the *zakat* agency) and the foundation of Baitul Mal (Islamic Treasury) that would be responsible for managing the *zakat* paid by Muslim citizens.[16] These regulations, which were issued in July 1968, provided that a governmental *zakat* committee would be established at all administrative levels (both district and subdistrict) across the country.

Soeharto's Approach

This ministerial regulation on *zakat* did not, however, last long. In fact, it ended even before any steps were taken to implement it. It was indirectly but effectively annulled three months later by President Soeharto's speech at the celebration of the Isra' Mi'raj (the Prophet's Ascension) on 26 October 1968. Instead of endorsing the establishment of official *zakat* agencies throughout cities and towns in Indonesia, as stated in the ministerial regulation, President Soeharto co-opted the administration of *zakat* by offering himself to take over the whole responsibility for collecting and distributing *zakat,* on a personal basis, as a private citizen.[17] In his official speech, President Soeharto stated:

> [a]s the first step, I would like here to announce to all Indonesian Muslims that I as a private citizen am prepared to take charge of the massive national effort of *zakat* collection. . . . From now on, I am *personally* willing to receive *zakat* payments made in the form of money orders from every single Muslim in the country. God willing, I will regularly publicize to all citizens how much money I receive and I will be responsible for its expenditure. I do really expect that this appeal will be fully paid attention and will have a positive feedback from the leaders and all Muslims.

Five days later, President Soeharto issued an instruction (*surat perintah*) assigning three high military officers to make all necessary preparations for a nationwide *zakat* collection drive.[18] Furthermore, he sent a circular letter (*surat edaran*) to all public offices and local governments, suggesting that they establish organizational apparatuses for *zakat* collection in their respective workplaces.[19] A week after this letter was issued, on 5 December 1968, the governor of the Capital Special Region of Jakarta, Ali Sadikin, decreed the foundation of a *zakat* agency (*Badan Amil Zakat*). Instead of referring to the regulations issued by the MORA, this governor's decree referred to President Soeharto's scheme, in which it stated that *zakat* should be deposited to the president's account and not to the Baitul Mal (Islamic Treasury) of the MORA.

The minister of religion seemed not to immediately understand the implications of President Soeharto's speech. Instead, the minister assumed that the speech was somehow confirming the ministerial decree on *zakat,* and so, in the same week as Soeharto's speech, further, more detailed rules on *zakat* implementation were released.[20] The MORA only came to the realization that Soeharto objected to the ministerial decree on *zakat* after receiving a letter, dated 16 December 1968, from the cabinet secretary. In January 1969, compliant with the cabinet secretary's letter, the minister of religion issued a ministerial instruction (No. 1 of 1969) for the deferment, or more precisely the revocation, of the ministerial decree on the *zakat* agency. Following that ministerial instruction, the MORA then circulated a letter (No. 3 of 1969) supporting President Soeharto's scheme on the collection of *zakat*. This letter announced that all results of *zakat* collection, instead of being sent to Baitul Mal (Islamic Treasury) of the MORA, would be deposited in President Soeharto's account at post offices throughout Indonesia. President Soeharto's offer to create a personally centralized system thus changed the nature of *zakat* administration from being official and institutional under ministerial regulation to something informal and personal, concentrated on an individual and not the state.

The operation of the *zakat* agency under the personal auspices of President Soeharto ran only for a few years. In 1974, President Soeharto concluded his role as a national personal *amil* (a person or institution that manages the collection and distribution of *zakat*). His last report on *zakat* was delivered in his *Idul Fitri* (the breaking of the fast of Ramadan) speech on 30 November 1970. It was reported that the collected *zakat* for the duration of two years amounted to Rp. 39.5 million in domestic currency and US$2,473 in foreign currency.[21] This meant that on average no more than Rp. 25 million per year had been collected from *muzakki* (*zakat* payers) since its inception in 1968. In President Soeharto's eyes, this figure was certainly a small amount given the number of Muslims in Indonesia. Based on this low response to his appeal for the *zakat* collection, President Soeharto justified his resignation from the *amil* position. It is not the main purpose of this study to scrutinize why there was such little attention paid to President Soeharto's appeal. What is important here is that the reason put forward by President Soeharto, though it may sound acceptable, was perhaps camouflage for his real objective in becoming a provisional *amil:* to thwart the MORA's attempt to implement the Jakarta Charter by creating a national *shari'a*-based mechanism to enforce *zakat* collection. As his real objective was achieved, in that he was able to sabotage the MORA plan, there was no need for President Soeharto to keep on collecting *zakat*.

This interpretation is supported by the fact that in 1982, after his resignation from the position of national personal *amil,* President Soeharto created the Pancasila Muslim Charity Services Foundation (YABMP), a foundation with the specific purpose of developing socioreligious resources for Muslims. This foundation levied almsgiving (*sedekah*[22]), not *zakat,* from all Muslim civil servants in Indonesia by automatically withholding small amounts of their monthly salaries. The collected funds were spent by the foundation to build hundreds of mosques all over the country.[23] Given that the concept of *sedekah* is very close to *zakat* in Islam, one may safely argue that President Soeharto had established a new *zakat* agency, though in a different fashion. One important question to be raised is why President Soeharto, when acting as national *amil* in the late 1960s and early 1970s, did not collect *zakat* in the same way he levied almsgiving through his foundation. If voluntary *sedekah* could be imposed by the president's foundation on civil servants, would not it be much easier for him to forcibly levy a compulsory religious duty (*zakat*) from the government employees? This suggests that it was likely that President Soeharto's political motive of opposing the introduction by stealth of the Jakarta Charter was the major reason for his brief assumption of the role of national *amil*.

The Rise of Various *Zakat* Agencies

Once President Soeharto ceased to be national *amil* in the mid-1970s, there was no clear legal basis for several government-sponsored or semiautonomous *zakat* agencies to exist. The only legal basis they had during that time was the president's circular letter issued in 1968, which suggested the foundation of an organizational apparatus to collect *zakat* in the respective host institutions of *zakat* agencies. Now that the president had withdrawn from this duty, would his circular letter remain valid? His maneuver left the legal basis of *zakat* collection in Indonesia non-existent, leaving the *zakat* agencies without a foothold. Lacking a regulatory foundation and without any clear national guidance, the *zakat* agencies had to struggle to exist locally at all.

Surprisingly, although there was no national policy as to the direction the *zakat* collection would go, the number of *zakat* agencies continued to increase gradually. Abdullah noted that even after the resignation of President Soeharto from the *amil* position, a great number of provincial administrations established government-sponsored *zakat* agencies (known as BAZIS or Badan Amil Zakat, Infak dan Sedekah) including DKI Jakarta (1968), East Kalimantan (1972), West Sumatra (1973), West Java (1974), South Kalimantan (1974), South Sumatra (1975), Lampung (1975), Irian Jaya (1978), North Sulawesi (1985), and South Sulawesi (1985), among others.[24] In addition, since 1986, new types of *zakat* organizations have emerged: private-company-sponsored *zakat* agencies (The Bontang LNG Company, Pertamina)[25] as well as *zakat* agencies created by Muslim community organizations in the 1990s (Dompet Dhuafa Republika, Pos Keadilan Peduli Umat, Yayasan Dana Sosial Al Falah, Muhammadiyah, Persatuan Islam). Besides these three types of *zakat* agencies, traditional *zakat* collection and distribution mechanisms, such as the establishment of temporary *zakat* committees by mosque administrators, or by giving *zakat* directly to the poor, are still widely found in Indonesia.[26]

Since 1989 the MORA has sought to facilitate the operation of this wide variety of *zakat* agencies. From this time, in conjunction with a gradual shift of the national political configuration that began to favor the Muslim community, general policy on *zakat* was gradually developed, even though its ultimate goal long remained unclear. The MORA, however, realized that even by the early 1990s the time was not yet ripe to propose any formal legislation on *zakat,* let alone set up any government apparatus to be a national or local official *amil.*[27] This was because many bureaucrats at the Ministry of Home Affairs and the state secretary regarded the involvement of government apparatus as a step toward implementing the Jakarta Charter, and this was considered politically unacceptable. In addition, although President Soeharto was happy enough to levy *sedekah* from state employees through the Yayasan Amal Bakti Muslim Pancasila, he was unenthusiastic about the formal involvement of the government officers in the *zakat* administration.[28] In this situation, all the MORA could do was to provide broad guidance and offer limited assistance to the existing *zakat* agencies, in the form of ministerial instructions (no. 16/1989 and no. 5/1991) and joint ministerial decrees (no. 29/1991 and 47/1991).[29]

It is interesting to note here that although this guidance gave the legal basis for the existence of a *zakat* agency in Indonesia, it actually weakened the formal attachment of the *zakat* agency to the provincial government structure. From then on, the governor functioned only as a patron of the *zakat* agency and could no longer directly engage himself in *zakat* collection. The regulation thereby changed the nature of *zakat* agencies from established government-sponsored to non-governmental and semiautonomous local *zakat* agencies. The provincial government only had the right to validate the *zakat* agencies established by Muslims, but not to initiate their foundation. Although the existence of non-governmental provincial *zakat* agencies was acknowledged and some partial regulations for *zakat* collection were arranged, there was no national agency that centrally organized the collection of *zakat* in Indonesia [30] because, after all, *zakat* payment still remains voluntary for Muslims in Indonesia.

In spite of the above, the issuance of a number of *zakat* regulations during Indonesia's New Order had great impact in the form of a rising consciousness among many Muslims regarding their *zakat* obligations. The willingness of President Soeharto to personally manage the collection of *zakat* during the early years of his regime provided a symbolic example of his piety as a Muslim, thus popularizing the institution of *zakat* among Muslim citizens. Though his stance on *zakat* collection was ambiguous at best, Soeharto did indirectly promote the practice of *zakat.* This can perhaps be seen as contradicting state policy on the importance of neutrality toward religious life and this is perhaps indicative of some support for a limited Islamization agenda.

15

Legislating *Zakat* Payment

The promulgation of Law 38/1999 on the Management of Zakat was clear evidence that the institutionalization of *zakat* had reached the point where the permeation of Islamic doctrines in the structure of the secular state had begun to deepen considerably and perhaps even irreversibly.

The process of drafting that law, however, was not easy. The existing law is actually the sixth draft prepared by the Ministry of Religious Affairs (MORA). The first draft was presented to the legislature in 1967, but it was withdrawn before it had a chance to be discussed. The other draft appeared in 1985, composed by a joint committee from the Ministry of Justice and the Ministry of Religion. There was, however, no follow-up to transform the draft into a Zakat Bill to be presented to the national legislature (DPR). What the MORA could produce in 1991 was only a joint ministerial decree, which had limited influence on the institutionalization of *zakat* at the national level.

At the national meeting of all provincial *zakat* agencies (BAZIS) facilitated by the MORA in Jakarta on 3–4 March 1992, many delegates from throughout Indonesia expressed their concern that a higher *zakat* institution was necessary to organize or facilitate *zakat* nationally.[1] They also requested that Rudini, the former minister of home affairs, be the chairman of a National Zakat Board. He agreed, subject to its being consistent with existing regulations.[2] The proposal, however, ended in failure because it was not welcomed by President Soeharto.

In the absence of a National Zakat Board, although there had been various local *zakat* agencies since the 1970s, some local *zakat* agencies attempted to establish an Association of Organizations for Zakat Management (Lembaga Pengelola Zakat), which was later named the Forum Zakat or FOZ, in September 1997. It was founded by eleven government-sponsored and private-company-sponsored *zakat* agencies.[3] Two years later, its membership had increased to 150 *zakat* agencies.[4] As an association of *zakat* agencies at the national level, the FOZ played an important role in member networking, mediating *zakat* issues with the government, disseminating information, coordinating activities, and being a consultant on various *zakat* problems. In fact, at its first congress in January 1999, the FOZ was assigned by its members to prepare a draft law on *zakat* management.

The Legislative Process

The enactment of Zakat Administration Law 38/1999 was as a result of contributions from both the MORA and the FOZ, although the former actually sought to dominate the enactment process. It was only after the downfall of President Soeharto in 1998 that the MORA revived its effort to introduce a *zakat* law in Indonesia. Even though the 1998 MPR's Decree on Religion and Socio-Cultural aspects implied that only a law on *hajj* services would be enacted, the MORA saw an opportunity to force through *zakat* legislation as well. Soon after President Habibie signed the bill on *hajj* services on 3 May 1999, the MORA finalized its draft law on *zakat* management and obtained a letter of *izin prakarsa* (permission to initiate legislation) from the state secretary on 15 May 2003.[5] Based on this, the bill was presented to the DPR on 24 June 1999 and discussion began on 26 July 1999.[6]

There were at least four reasons why the Zakat Administration Law was considered necessary in Indonesia. First, it was expected that the law would increase the amount of *zakat* payment in Indonesia. Second, it was intended to assign *zakat* funds for economic objectives, such as poverty eradication and social welfare. Third, it was needed for legal and political purposes, that is, to provide a stronger judicial foundation for a *zakat* agency in Indonesia and to establish a *zakat* agency at the national level. And finally, it stemmed from religious expectations that the legislation would boost participation levels and the religiosity of Muslims.[7]

Three important issues arose during the legislative process of the *zakat* bill. The first related to the nature of *zakat* collection in Indonesia. It is worth noting that the final draft of the bill prepared by the MORA contained a provision regarding *zakat* collection that may be interpreted as imperative. It was initially drafted in Article 12 (1) of the bill that:

> *Pengumpulan zakat dilakukan oleh badan amil zakat dengan cara menerima atau mengambil dari muzakki* [The collection of *zakat* is organized by the government-sponsored *zakat* agency by receiving or taking [the *zakat* payment] from the *zakat* payer].

However, this provision was criticized by the State Secretariat's officials, who claimed that it implied coercion in the *zakat* collection and would inadvertently lead to the realization of the Jakarta Charter.[8] Given this criticism, a phrase was added to the end of Article and it became:

*Pengumpulan zakat dilakukan oleh badan amil zakat dengan cara menerima atau mengambil dari muzakki **atas dasar pemberitahuan muzakki*** [The collection of *zakat* is organized by the government-sponsored *zakat* agency by receiving or taking [the *zakat* payment] from the *zakat* payer **upon notification by the payer**].[9] (Emphasis added.)

Although the MORA welcomed this change, there was heated debate over Article 12 (1) when it was discussed at the Panitia Kerja (Working Committee) stage of deliberation. Professor Dr. Umar Shihab, a member of the Golkar faction (F-KP), said that the article seemed to suggest the *zakat* agency would be passive in collecting *zakat*. For the Golkar faction, the *zakat* agency should be proactive in collecting *zakat* even without notification from the *zakat* payer. Therefore, the F-KP proposed a clause that explains this condition in the elucidation of the proposed bill. This proposal might be seen as evidence of Golkar's increasing tendency toward Islamization, or at least pro-Islamic rhetoric, during the 1990s. The F-KP's proposal was criticized by the military faction (F-ABRI) and the Persatuan Pembangunan faction (F-PP). Abdullah Hadi of the F-ABRI contended that the proactive proposal would create resistance from the people, and he believed it would have a fate similar to the tax levied on the possession of televisions, which proved fruitless due to widespread non-compliance. Referring to the *iman and takwa* (faith and piety) principles of *zakat* management, mentioned in Article 4 of the bill, Abduh Paddare of the F-PP argued that a proactive *zakat* agency was not in line with this principle. According to him, the "*zakat* payers should have their own awareness to purify themselves, as well as their wealth, without coercion. Only then would the *zakat* payers be rewarded by the paradise in the hereafter." [10]

Responding to these criticisms, Shihab replied by clarifying that what his faction meant by proactive was not violence, but merely reminding (*mengingatkan*) Muslims to pay *zakat*. Citing a Qur'anic verse and a fragment from the history of early Islam, he differentiated between to compel and to remind. Shihab further stated that his faction did not want to modify Article 12, but wanted to give the article an explanation in the elucidation of the bill.[11] The proposal was eventually accepted not only because the F-KP had a great majority in the legislature, but also because other factions found that the proposal would not change the voluntary nature of the *zakat* payment. As a result, a new clause was created in the elucidation of Zakat Administration Law Article 12 (1) stating: "In undertaking its tasks, the *zakat* agency should be proactive through communication, information and educational activities." Although the *zakat* payment was not made imperative, this new clause became the basis for a campaign that followed to popularize *zakat* institutions.[12]

The second issue that emerged in the legislative process was the rivalry between Badan Amil Zakat or BAZ (government-sponsored *zakat* agency) and the Lembaga Amil Zakat or LAZ (non-state-sponsored *zakat* agency). The draft prepared by the MORA was designed to provide the BAZ with full legal arrangements and did not include the LAZ. However, there were strong demands from the LAZ for acknowledgment in the bill. When the bill was passed by the DPR, it did in fact finally mention the existence of the LAZ, though in a limited way. Of the thirty-three articles mentioned in the minister of religion's Decree no. 581/1999, only four dealt with the LAZ. It seemed that the MORA did not want the bill to empower the LAZ, but rather to subordinate it into the lower structure of the BAZ as a task force of *zakat* collection (UPZ or Unit Pengumpulan Zakat).

The last issue was the idea of tax deductibility of *zakat* payment in the *zakat* bill. Article 13 (2) of the bill prepared by the MORA stated that *zakat yang telah dibayarkan kepada Badan Amil Zakat dikurangkan dari laba/pendapatan sisa kena pajak dari wajib pajak yang bersangkutan sesuai dengan peraturan yang berlaku.* [The *zakat* paid to the government-sponsored *zakat* agency is a deduction from the profit or taxable income of the taxpayer in accordance with the applicable regulation.] It seems the MORA ignored the Ministry of Finance when drafting this provision, and in May 1999, the Ministry of Finance sent a letter to the MORA objecting to the provision for two reasons: (1) it would lessen the annual tax received by the Directorate of Taxation, and (2) there was no existing regulation on taxation that supported the idea of tax deductibility for *zakat* payment as drafted in the bill. Since there was conflict between ministries, the problem was forwarded to the president to decide the dispute.[13] President Habibie appeared not to welcome the stance of the Ministry of Finance and therefore the essence of the provision remained untouched and was passed intact by the DPR.[14]

It is worth noting here that in an attempt to counter criticism from legislative members during deliberation on the bill regarding the particular provision discussed above, the MORA disseminated copies of the decree of the minister of finance, Ali Wardhana, and the circular letter of the general director of taxation, Sutadi Sukarya. The ministerial decree revived the colonial ordinances (the 1925 Company Tax Ordinance and the 1944 Income Tax Ordinance) stating that every donation given to certain social institutions appointed by the minister of finance would be eligible for a tax deduction, while the circular letter concerned whether the *zakat* payment was tax deductible.[15]

Attempts to Amend the *Zakat* Law

Although many Muslims welcomed the existing *zakat* law, some have complained about its legal enforcement and would like to amend the current *zakat* law. The idea of amending the *zakat* law has arisen publicly on a number of occasions. At a public hearing with the legislative members on 28 January 2002, the FOZ, presenting the bill to amend the *zakat* law, argued that *zakat* should be a mandatory duty for Muslims and if there are Muslims who evade *zakat,* then they should be prosecuted.[16] In addition, the FOZ emphasized the role of the state in managing *zakat* and argued that the government must carry out this function optimally. Indeed, the FOZ sought the foundation of a Ministry of Zakat and Wakaf (Endowment).[17]

The idea of amendment, as put forward by the FOZ, has much to do with seven problematic issues as follows: First, the nature of *zakat* in the existing law is still voluntary and hence the *zakat* payment has much depended on the religious awareness of rich Muslims. Second, since there is no punishment stated in the current law for those who refuse to pay *zakat,* it can be said that the role of the government is almost absent in the *zakat* administration. Third, the fact that anyone can establish a *zakat* agency has created unnecessary rivalries and inevitable conflicts between various *zakat* agencies, especially between the BAZ and the LAZ themselves. Fourth, because of the third problem, both the collection and distribution of *zakat* have been fragmented and less productive. Fifth, it is not clear which institution has a right to control and accredit a non-state *zakat* agency (the LAZ), which might have implied that the limits of the jurisdiction between one LAZ and another became blurred. Sixth, the position and the role of BAZNAS (National Zakat Agency) have remained unclear, and hence the establishment of a *zakat* collector unit (as a subordinate of BAZNAS) at a number of state-owned companies has been stagnant. And the last, the existing *zakat* law lacked a strong technical regulation at the lower level. Indeed, instead of a ministerial decree, the Government Regulation (Peraturan Pemerintah) issued by the president must support this law. Because of these problems, according to the FOZ, the advantages of *zakat* payment in empowering Indonesia's economy cannot be maximized.[18] Therefore, the FOZ has attempted to amend the existing Zakat Administration Law to transform *zakat* payment from a voluntary to a compulsory practice.[19]

As far as the idea of amending the current *zakat* law is concerned, many *zakat* agencies that became members of the FOZ paid attention to two issues: first, they demanded that *zakat* evasion by rich Muslims should be punished; and second, they asked that the collection of *zakat* be centralized in the hands of the government-sponsored *zakat* agency. Among their reasons were that since there is provision in the law for punishment for the *zakat* agencies that abuse *zakat* funds, the principle of legal equity requires that there should also be a formal punishment for *zakat* evasion by rich Muslims. As this idea would require the state apparatus to use its law enforcement powers on behalf of religion, such an amendment would naturally lead to the deepening of Islamization at the state level.

It is no wonder then that the Third National Congress of the FOZ in Balikpapan on 25–28 April 2003 chose the theme "Menggagas Amandemen UU no. 38 tahun 1999 tentang pengelolaan Zakat: Menuju Optimalisasi Dana Zakat" [Proposing the Idea of Amendment to the Zakat Law no. 38/1999: Toward Optimizing Zakat Funds]. Several non-government speakers in this congress strongly argued that amendment to the *zakat* law is urgent. They believe that the centralization of *zakat* under state management and the imposition of penalties for those rich Muslims who are unwilling to pay *zakat* are essential to optimize the collection of *zakat*.[20] However, the speakers from the government disagreed with this and instead argued for a priority on the effort to strengthen the position of BAZNAS, as regulated by the existing law, as a better means to achieve the same objectives.[21]

The idea of amendment also seems to be unpopular among legislators. A public hearing to discuss the possibility of the amendment to the existing *zakat* law resulted in fierce criticisms from the legislative members who argued that Indonesia is not an Islamic state. Although many members of the DPR rejected the FOZ' proposal, the idea of amendment has become widespread and is supported by nearly all the *zakat* agencies (which, of course, stand to benefit from the enhanced powers they would receive).[22]

Realizing that efforts to amend the Zakat Administration Law will not be simple, the FOZ has sought to empower BAZNAS. In the FOZ National Workshop held in September 2003 in Jakarta, it was proposed that BAZNAS should function as a policy maker, like Bank Indonesia (BI), to regulate and supervise either government-sponsored *zakat* agencies or private *zakat* agencies. BAZNAS would form a central pool of *zakat* funds, while the fund allocation itself to the eligible recipients would be the task of local *zakat* agencies. Although it might be too early to speculate whether this idea of central administration of *zakat* could ever succeed in Indonesia, such an effort is not necessarily consistent with the goal of enhancing the piety of Muslims.

16

Overlapping *Zakat* and Taxation

The religious awareness of Muslim adherents that they should pay *zakat* has increased gradually since the New Order period. However, their obligatory *zakat* payments have also overlapped with their commitment as citizens to pay taxes to the government of a modern nation-state.

Responding to this problem, the Council of Indonesian Ulama (MUI) held a seminar on *zakat* in 1988 and affirmed that *zakat* and tax are different obligations and that Indonesian Muslims are obliged to pay *zakat* as well as to pay tax. One of the reasons underlying this view was that *zakat* is a religious obligation mandated by God through the Qur'an and Sunna to all Muslims, while tax is another compulsory duty required by the nation-state but religiously justifiable on the basis of the principle of public interest (*al-maslaha al-'amma*).[1] In short, one must hand out *zakat* to realize the religious injunction, and at the same time one must also pay tax to show obedience as a citizen of the secular country. This opinion has burdened Muslims with a dual taxation system, and as a result, many Muslims have overlooked the *zakat* payment but chosen to pay tax, or vice versa.

'Like Soul and Body'

MUI's views concerning *zakat* and tax was challenged by Masdar F. Mas'udi, a Muslim intellectual and a leader of the Nahdlatul Ulama. In his controversial book *Agama Keadilan: Risalah Zakat (Pajak) dalam Islam,* first published in 1991, he proposed that paying tax be a replacement for *zakat.* According to Mas'udi, a Muslim who has paid tax is no longer obliged to pay *zakat,* since the paid tax is intended (*diniatkan*) to be the *zakat* payment.[2] For Mas'udi, "*zakat* internally is a human spiritual commitment to God, while externally it is in fact a tax, that is, a human social commitment. Zakat and tax, therefore, are one and the same." To use the metaphor of the human body, "*zakat* is the soul and tax is the body itself that together come to life. Soul (*zakat*) and body (tax) are distinguishable but are not to be separated; they have to be integrated."[3]

With the spirit of *zakat* imbued in taxes, Mas'udi wanted three things to materialize. First, Muslim taxpayers should understand that their taxes were no longer a secular obligation to the state, but more a requirement of belief in God, because the state upholds (or should uphold) universal justice, especially for the poor and the needy. Second, Mas'udi suggested there should be a shift in the perception of Muslim taxpayers from conceiving of the state as an almighty deity, absolutely capable of repressing them, to the view that the state is only the *amil* and must serve the interests of its citizens. Third, there should be a growing awareness among Muslim taxpayers that they have legitimate rights to supervise the government in administering the tax funds, so they can be confident that the tax/*zakat* funds are appropriately spent for the welfare of all the people, especially the most helpless among them.[4] Mas'udi's view seems to be revolutionary in terms of the existing practice of *zakat* and tax in Indonesia. It is no wonder then that his vision has attracted critiques from other Muslim scholars as well as from the *zakat* agencies themselves.

Three main criticisms have been made about Mas'udi's thoughts on *zakat* and tax. First, it is argued that his approach requires that a religious obligation (*zakat* as a tax) must be authorized by the state, and this would implicitly require the foundation of an Islamic state, given that only a religiously qualified government could levy the *zakat* (as a tax) from Muslim citizens. For many Muslims, the Indonesian nation-state certainly does not meet the criteria of an Islamic state,[5] although it may be called a Muslim country because the majority of its population is Muslim. These Muslims cannot accept the notion that a non-Islamic state could enforce religious teachings, such as *zakat*.[6]

This is mistaken. By integrating *zakat* and tax, what Mas'udi wanted was not the unification of two equal institutions or bodies that would result in the foundation of a formal Islamic state, but merely the integration "between soul and body, morality and action or vision and institution." Illustrating his point of view, Mas'udi says:

> The essence of the moral commandment of *zakat* is as follows: if with taxes the state builds, then build for the sake of Allah in the interest of the welfare of all the people, especially the weakest; if with taxes the state funds a bureaucracy and pays its civil servants, then let there be the bureaucracy and civil servants who for the sake of Allah loyally fulfill the needs of the people, especially the weakest; if with its taxes the state feeds the servants of the law (police, prosecutors, judges and so on), then let there be servants of the law who honestly for the sake of Allah protect the rights of all the people, especially the weak; and if with its taxes the state feeds its

soldiers and arms them, then let there be soldiers who for the sake of Allah loyally guarantee the security of all the people, especially the weak.[7]

This is actually intended to overcome the problematic relationship between the state and religion. In Mas'udi's view, although religion and the state are indeed different, they cannot be separated; "religion gives direction, the state gives form." While religion speaks of justice and the common good of all as a trust from God, the state speaks of matters of institutions for that trust and of making it a reality.[8]

Second, it is argued that Mas'udi's thinking on *zakat* and tax is not applicable to the Indonesian context because of the difficulty in distribution. As the allocation of *zakat* and taxes are different, the use of tax (*zakat*) funds for the benefit of particular religious adherents may generate objection from other religious people. On the one hand, the funds of *zakat* (tax) cannot be handed out to non-Muslims, except for *muallaf* (newly converted Muslims), while, on the other hand, it is commonly assumed that most tax funds stem from non-Muslim taxpayers (especially ethnic Chinese and foreign taxpayers), whose tax liabilities tend to be larger than Muslim taxpayers. This will, of course, raise concerns about disproportionality if most of the tax is taken from non-Muslims but eventually goes to benefit the Muslim majority. As the majority of Indonesians who live in poor economic conditions are Muslims, they are the most eligible to receive the benefit of such funds. Mas'udi sees this problem as a matter for *ijtihad* (the use of individual reasoning in matters of *fiqh*). In fact, it can be overcome by reaching a consensus among citizens themselves based on their particular situation. What is important is that the decision made must reflect the principal objectives of *zakat*, namely justice and the universal good, where those who are able to can fulfill their obligations to assist the weak and fund matters of public interest.[9]

Third, Mas'udi's proposal would likely result in the elimination of the existing *zakat* agencies, because the Taxation Service Office (Kantor Pelayanan Pajak) under the auspices of the Directorate General of Taxation, which operate in every district throughout Indonesia, would presumably take over the functions of the *zakat* agencies. Mas'udi argues this would not be the case since all the *zakat* agencies are still needed to collect almsgiving (*sedekah*) and donation (*infak*), which may be much more than *zakat*, especially because *zakat* is paid annually while almsgiving and donation can be given at any time. The fact is, however, that *zakat* is not *sedekah* and *infak*, so these agencies would need to withdraw the term "*zakat*" from their institutional names (Badan Amil Zakat Infak dan Sedekah or BAZIS), leaving only the phrase "*sedekah*" and "*infak*" in their office titles.[10]

The Idea of 'Deductible Tax'

Given these objections to Mas'udi's view, and the feeling that MUI's views regarding *zakat* and tax could create a heavy financial burden for Muslims, a solution to the prospect of dual payment has been constantly sought. It was Dawam Rahardjo, a prominent Indonesian Muslim intellectual and a former chairman of Muhammadiyah, who, at the national meeting of the Government Sponsored Zakat Agencies (BAZIS) of Indonesia in 1992, first put forward the idea that *zakat* payment should be deducted from tax.[11] The idea was then supported by the regional *zakat* agency of the Jakarta government and of Central Kalimantan and became a central issue at a national seminar held in Jakarta by the Faculty of Syariah of the State Islamic University on 25–26 March 1997. The seminar suggested that *zakat* paid should be tax-deductible to the value of at least 2.5 percent. This notion is a compromise between MUI's view and Mas'udi's thinking on *zakat* and tax. While Malaysia has been mostly referred to as an example of *zakat* management involving tax credits or deductibles, the practice in several Western countries (like the United States or Australia), where an individual or public company that makes donations to registered charity foundations can receive a tax deduction, surely helped inspire this notion in Indonesia.[12] However, there are two meanings of the term 'tax deduction' in Indonesia. The first is a tax reduction in which the amount of tax liability is reduced by the amount of the payments of *zakat* by rich Muslims. Generally referred to as a tax credit, this is what many *zakat* agencies in Indonesia have demanded. The second is what is more generally understood as a deduction, a tax reduction where the amount of *zakat* payment would be subtracted from taxable income to lower the amount of tax owed. This is what the current *zakat* law has implied.

The idea of tax deduction is not unfamiliar in the Indonesian context. As early as the twentieth-century colonial period, the 1925 Company Tax Ordinance and 1944 Income Tax Ordinance stated that every donation given to certain social institutions appointed by the minister of finance would be eligible for a tax deduction. It is not surprising then that in 1976 the minister of finance issued a decree to reinvigorate the ordinance. In 1979, the General Directorate of Taxation issued a circular letter welcoming the *zakat* payment as tax-deductible.[13] In fact, this idea is clearly stated in Article 14 of Law 38/1999 on Zakat[14] and Article 9 of Law 17/2000 on Taxation,[15] although its translation into practice has not proven to be easy.

Implementing the tax deductibility of the *zakat* payment is not as easy as simply inserting it into statute. Its complexity lies in the fact that this provision, in order to be properly implemented, requires full cooperation from both the sanctioned *zakat* agency and the taxation office at the local level. But this is not easy given that even the coordination at the national level between ministries (MORA and the Ministry of Finance) does not run smoothly. The enactment process of Law 17/2000 on Income Tax showed how coordination and cooperation between ministries was lacking. When the tax bill was presented to the DPR in May 2000, there was no provision supporting the tax deductibility of *zakat* payments that was now contained in the Zakat Administration Law, passed a year earlier. It seemed that the MORA was not involved at all in the development of the income tax bill. It was only after some legislative members of the F-Reformasi criticized the bill that the minister of finance finally revised the bill to conform to the Zakat Administration Law, but adding the words "provided that it does not contradict the principles of the Income Tax Law," whatever they mean.[16]

Another problem with the provision for tax deductibility of the *zakat* payment was observable on initial implementation. Zakat Law 38/1999 began to apply only after two years from its enactment, that is, from 2001. It was therefore expected that those Muslims who paid *zakat* would have a tax deduction by 31 March 2002 (the end of the Indonesian fiscal year 2001–2002). However, this was not the case, given that the tax form pack (*Surat Pemberitahuan Tahunan Pajak Penghasilan Wajib Pajak*) failed to list the *zakat* payment as tax-deductible.[17]

According to Didin Hafiduddin, chairman of the National Zakat Agency (BAZNAS), the problem lies in the implementing regulation under the Zakat Administration Law, which is in the form of a ministerial decree (KMA) issued by minister of religion. In his view, a Peraturan Pemerintah or Government Regulation is required to properly provide for the administration as between *zakat* and tax, as both issues involved two different ministries.[18]

In fiscal year 2002–2003, *zakat* finally was listed in the tax form, and the Directorate of Taxation issued a decree regulating the details of implementing the tax deductibility of the *zakat* payment. Nevertheless, there was still an obstacle for those paying *zakat* to obtain a tax deduction if they failed to receive a valid letter demonstrating *zakat* payment (*Bukti Setoran Zakat*) from the BAZNAS, as required by the Directorate of Taxation.[19]

Criticisms of Tax Deductibility of *Zakat*

It was believed that the tax deductibility for *zakat* payments would boost the amount of *zakat* funds paid by *muzakki* (*zakat* payers). However, this was an unrealistic expectation since the tax restitution system in Indonesia does not apply the self-assessment principle. For this reason, few people would be encouraged to pay *zakat,* report the amount in the tax form, and then apply for a tax deduction. The specter of tax corruption through *zakat* payment manipulation remains a reality.[20] In light of this, it is hard to imagine that Indonesian Muslim businesses would respond to the tax deductibility policy. Indeed, given the real problems with tax restitution in Indonesia, this policy is not likely to be successful in the short term. Perhaps attention should be given to improving the efficiency of the tax restitution system as a first step.

Tax deductibility of *zakat* payments does not eliminate the double burden for Muslims living in the nation-state. Indonesian Muslims are still required to pay both tax and *zakat*, though they may deduct 2.5 percent from their net taxable income. This is, however, only a small number and has little impact. Some officials of the *zakat* agency who were enthusiastic about including this provision in both the *zakat* law and taxation law have been disappointed by its implementation. They complained that what they wanted was a tax credit (a reduction from the amount of tax due), not a tax deduction, as is presently offered.[21]

It is worth emphasizing that with the introduction of the deductibility system, and despite all its shortcomings, criticism has arisen concerning discrimination between religious adherents in Indonesia. A *Jakarta Post* editorial fiercely questioned "why has the government singled out the Muslim community when it is well aware that followers of other creeds also pay religious donations."[22] Abdul Munir Mulkhan, a sociologist of religions at the State Institute for Islamic Studies (IAIN), Yogyakarta, and Astrid Soesanto, a legislative member from the Christian party (PDKB), strongly argued that the government should extend the same policy to followers of other religions, since other religions also have sacred duties to collect charitable donations from their communities.[23] However, the minister of religion in Megawati's government, Said Agil Husein Al Munawar, responded by stating that before the government could consider applying the tax-deductible *zakat* policy to similar kinds of almsgiving in other religions, the government would focus on administering the *zakat*. Reassuring other religious groups, Al Munawar said, "God willing, we will arrange it later. . . . We will do this one by one."[24] In light of this, it is again clear that Islam has enjoyed priority over other religions in Indonesia's sociopolitical life over the past few years, and this perhaps indicates a deepening of the Islamization process.

Dissonant Legislation

With regard to the main argument of this book—that there is dissonance in legislating for *shari'a* through the legal system of a modern nation-state—two aspects of dissonance, legal and political, are relevant to the institutionalization of *zakat*.

The implementation of *shari'a* in Indonesia, as expressed in the Zakat Administration Law, is legally dissonant, as some of its provisions are not independent of, but subordinate to, provisions of the Law on Taxation, which either obstruct or negate them. For a long time, Indonesian Muslims have importuned that by paying *zakat* they should have a tax reduction to avoid a dual financial liability as citizens as well as religious adherents. However, all they have obtained is the ability to reduce declarable income by a percentage of *zakat* paid, so that they do not recoup the full amount of *zakat* paid, but rather the small amount of tax that would have been payable had the *zakat* amount been counted as taxable income.

In addition, what now has been implemented regarding *zakat* payment could only be viewed as an implementation of *fiqh*, not *shari'a*, for it is the human interpretation (*ijtihad*) that dominates the formation of the rule. The example of *zakat profesi*, a religious tax paid by professionals such as civil servants, lawyers, doctors, lecturers, and others, shows this clearly. The largest source of *zakat* funds received by the *zakat* agencies in Indonesia is from this *zakat profesi*,[25] which was made a religious obligation by an interpretation that regards professionals as equivalent to farmers. Like farmers, who should make *zakat* payments after every harvest, professionals pay the *zakat profesi* after receiving their monthly salary. However, the *zakat* value these professionals should pay is not 5 percent or 10 percent as farmers pay, but 2.5 percent, equal to the *zakat* value paid by the traders or the owners of gold and silver.[26] Since this *zakat profesi* is considered not *shari'a* but *fiqh*, it is no wonder there has never been a consensus among Muslim scholars regarding it. In fact, the Nahdlatul Ulama, the largest Muslim organization in Indonesia, has opposed effort by the MUI to issue a *fatwa* making the *zakat profesi* compulsory for Muslim professionals.

The enactment of the Zakat Administration Law in Indonesia is politically dissonant for non-Muslims who feel discriminated against by some of its provisions. It has been suggested that the legislation has singled out the Muslim community when followers of other creeds also pay religious donations. This suggests that while Indonesia is not officially an Islamic state, it has the substance of a typical historical Islamic state, that is, a differentiation between citizens that ultimately favors Muslims as a sort of millet.

PART V

The Localization of *Shari'a* in Aceh

17

Formalizing *Shari'a* Locally Through *Ulama*

The Acehnese *ulama,* since the early years of the Indonesian republic, have played a major role in mobilizing the expression of Islamic identity to pursue special concessions from the central government of Indonesia, that is, to formalize the implementation of *shari'a* in Aceh. In so doing, the Acehnese *ulama* have sought to re-emphasize their significant role in influencing society and in asserting the discrete identity of the Muslim Acehnese. To this end, the *ulama* needed political power to implement *shari'a* and define and shape the life of Muslim Acehnese in compliance with Islamic *shari'a.*

In the first years after the independence of Indonesia in 1945, it became clear that the *ulama* controlled the local government in Aceh. As Benda pointed out, "[u]nder the banner of a distinctly Islamic local and ethnic patriotism, Aceh thus entered independent Indonesia as a virtually autonomous *imperium in imperio.*"[1] Having taken over the local administrative offices from the *uleëbalang* (aristocrats or self-governing rulers), the next challenge for the *ulama* was to continue the social revolution they had commenced.[2] The *ulama* regarded this as the struggle for the reassertion of an Islamic identity, that is, the implementation of *shari'a.* For the *ulama,* the social revolution in Aceh was not yet finished and hence it was now time to realize "their primary aim [which] was to apply as much Islamic law as possible in Acehnese society. The national revolution was, therefore, seen by [the] *ulama* as an opportunity to restore the validity of Islamic law in the region."[3] The willingness of the All-Aceh Association of *Ulama* (PUSA) to support the independence of Indonesia and their enthusiasm in fighting the Dutch attempts to reoccupy Indonesia was very much determined by their assumption that the Indonesian state would allow them to officially uphold Islamic law in their region.[4]

The *ulama* subsequently sought to realize their goals by proposing the establishment of Aceh province in 1949, which assumed a particular authority in religious matters. For the *ulama,* the establishment of Aceh province would be not only a basis of authority, but also a basis of protection for the entrenched identity of the Islamic Acehnese. The *ulama* were aware that provincial status for Aceh was necessary in order to apply Islamic law in Aceh. But provincial status for Aceh lasted only for one year due to a lack of the recognition from the central government, which regarded the province as founded not on statute, as would usually be the case, but merely on a subordinate regulation issued by Deputy Prime Minister Sjafruddin Prawiranegara. Aceh was then incorporated into the province of North Sumatra, with Medan as the capital, in 1950.[5]

The dissatisfaction among the Acehnese *ulama*, given the dissolution of the province of Aceh by the central government in 1950, was the fruit of their belated awareness of divergent identities. Initially, the Acehnese wanted to join the Indonesian unitary state because the majority of the population of the rest of Indonesia was Muslim. Hence, the new Republic of Indonesia was considered a unified *umma*, and merging with other Muslims was seen as an expression of Islamic solidarity.[6] However, there was a dilemma. While the Islamic leadership in Aceh attempted to build an Islamic society, the national leadership in Jakarta was seeking to have a religiously neutral state with Pancasila as the principal ideology. Now that the *ulama* in Aceh were forced to make a choice between national integration under a concept of Indonesian Pancasila and religious expression within a regional identity, they eventually chose the latter. Accordingly, it was no wonder that on 21 September 1953, only eight years after the independence of Indonesia, the Acehnese, under the leadership of PUSA leader Daud Beureu-eh, proclaimed that Aceh was separate from the Republic of Indonesia and was a part of Negara Islam Indonesia (Indonesian Islamic state) of Sekarmadji Maridjan Kartosuwiryo, and that two years afterwards Aceh was renamed "Negara Bagian Aceh Negara Islam Indonesia" (NBA/NII, The State of Aceh/Indonesian Islamic State).[7]

Founding the Council of *Ulama*

After the revolt of *ulama* led by Daud Beureu-eh was settled in the early 1960s, the *ulama* lost power and their political position declined across the whole province. The banning of the Indonesian Communist Party (PKI) that came with the downfall of President Soekarno in the mid-1960s, however, provided, another opportunity for the Acehnese *ulama* to return to local political space. This came as a consequence of the extermination of the PKI members in many areas of Indonesia. While the PKI had not been a strong threat locally in Aceh, with only minor support (mostly from non-Acehnese plantation and railway workers), that the PKI was present in Aceh at all not only allowed the *ulama* to destroy the communists, but also to mobilize support networks for *ulama*.[8] In this way, *ulama* and other elements of Muslim groups were able to establish an alliance with the local armed forces. Nevertheless, the resulting coalition was superficial and in fact proved to be the first step in a process by which many Acehnese *ulama* were coopted by the incoming military-backed government known as the New Order regime.

In an attempt to eliminate the few PKI in Aceh, the military forces in Aceh consulted three *ulama* to ask for a *fatwa* regarding this issue.[9] These three suggested that all *ulama* in Aceh must be invited to discuss such an issue. Through a decree by the military commander of Aceh, a conference of the Acehnese *ulama* was set up in late 1965 in Banda Aceh and lasted for two days (17–18 December 1965). Although this conference was attended by the *ulama* from different regions within Aceh, several military officers were among sixty-three listed participants in the conference.[10]

The deep involvement of the local military forces in this conference of *ulama* meant that its main outcomes seemed largely to support the military goal of eliminating the PKI. Regarding the issue of the PKI, the conference issued statements declaring that communism was unlawful (*haram*) and that those people who adhered to this ideology were infidels (*kafir*) and must be fought. Additionally, the *ulama* condemned the PKI's coup d'état and demanded its abolition. In fact, while the PKI was declared illegal in March 1966, it was in Aceh that it was formally banned for the first time (in December 1965). Finally, the *ulama* released a *fatwa* on the martyrdom status for anyone who died in fighting the PKI.[11] Although the *ulama* did not intend to support the political interests of the military, they were quickly manipulated for the purpose of making the armed forces unrivaled in local politics.

Another outcome of the conference was the foundation of a union of Acehnese *ulama*. Ismail Muhammad Syah, publicly well-known by the acronym Ismuha, the former rector of the State Institute for Islamic Studies (IAIN) of Banda Aceh, was the person responsible for this idea. He suggested that an organization of *ulama* was necessary to overcome the various problems in the public life of the Acehnese. One reason put forward to establish this exclusive organization was that the representation of *ulama* was important at the provincial level to overcome the difficulties of communication between the government and all *ulama* from different parts of the province. Ismuha further emphasized that the organization would not resemble the PUSA, the earlier organization of the Acehnese *ulama* led by Daud Beureu-eh. According to him, unlike the PUSA, where any individual *ulama* was welcome to join, this organization of *ulama* would have a management board at the level of province, cities or regencies, and districts, without open membership.[12] It seems that Ismuha ignored the PUSA as a model for this association of *ulama* because the military saw the PUSA as a rebellious organization.

Many *ulama* welcomed the idea of a union of the Acehnese *ulama* as suggested by Ismuha. The new union was called the Majelis Permusyawaratan *Ulama* Daerah

Istimewa Aceh [The Consultative Council of the Acehnese *Ulama* of the Special Region of Aceh]. Tgk. Abdullah Ujung Rimba, head of the committee of the conference, was appointed to lead this *ulama* council. Of the seven presidiums of the conference, five figures were given the task of setting up the management board. They were also in charge of recruiting *ulama,* as well as Muslim intellectuals, to occupy the positions within the structure of this council.[13]

The five presidiums were also assigned to prepare a draft Pedoman Dasar (basic guidance document) for the council. This draft, which was completed by 5 January 1966, contained a provision (Article 4) that the objective of the organization was to unite the *ulama* and the Muslim community (*umma*) in an attempt to implement the Jakarta Charter, as implied by the 1959 Presidential Decree, and to implement Islamic *shari'a* for Muslim citizens in the province of Aceh within the limits of the existing Indonesian laws.[14]

This particular article, however, provoked objection from members of the political elite of the province. In February 1966, the military commander in the region appointed a team to review and finalize the draft Pedoman Dasar prepared by the five presidiums. This team consisted of eleven people, of whom only four were *ulama* and the rest military and government officials.[15] The provincial legislature then passed this revised draft Pedoman Dasar as Perda (Peraturan Daerah or Regional Regulation) no. 1/1966. This regulation was very different from what had been produced by the five presidiums at the previous *ulama* conference, especially the wording of the provision for implementing *shari'a* in the province. In this regulation, the objective of the *ulama* council (Article 4) was changed to a phrase in which no direct reference was made to the implementation of the seven words of the Jakarta Charter. Above all, the regulation provided that *ulama*'s activities were generally to be directed at maintaining local security and political stability, rather than enhancing religious awareness among Muslims.

Co-opting the Acehnese *Ulama*

The upshot of the enactment of Perda 1/1966 on the council of *ulama* shows a dichotomy between the *ulama* appointed by the government and those who were informal religious leaders within the Muslim community. From then on, only those who were appointed (Article 7) could represent the Acehnese *ulama* in the council and become a member of the elite of local governments, be it provincial or district. Slowly but surely, the distance between both types of *ulama* became wider as local political developments marginalized the rural *ulama*. The urban *ulama*, on the other side, were closely engaged in and supported the agenda of the new regime.

As Ricklefs pointed out, it was in this way that the council of *ulama* was used to co-opt the Acehnese *ulama* during the New Order era and make them dependent on the political institutions of the state.[16] By the early 1970s, each district in Aceh had a council of *ulama*,[17] the name of which later changed from the Consultative Council of *Ulama* (MPU) to the Council of Indonesia Ulama (MUI) of Aceh province, following its subordination to the national structure of the MUI in 1975. Many senior *ulama* in rural areas were soon recruited into this co-opted religious institution. The members of the local legislature (DPRD) provided another approach to co-opting individual *ulama*. It took place not only through an Islamic party (the PPP), but also through the Union of Functional Groups (Golkar), the government party. Teungku Abdullah Ujong Rimba, chairman of the MPU, for example, was a Golkar candidate for the national legislature (DPR) in the 1971 election, although he failed to secure a seat.

The co-optation of the *ulama* council was possible partly because in the three decades after the establishment of the *ulama* council in Aceh (1966–1998), its chair was occupied by two former state officials, Abdullah Ujong Rimba[18] and Muhammad Ali Hasjmy.[19] Both were closely involved in the judicative and the executive branches of government before they took up leadership positions on the *ulama* council.

The co-optation was not only shown by the histories of the top figures of the MUI of Aceh, but was also seen through legal products issued by the Fatwa Commission (Komisi Fatwa) of the MUI.[20] The *fatwa* produced during the chairmanship of both individuals showed a tendency to co-optation in that many *fatwa* supported the agenda of national development. No one could deny that the government had benefited from *fatwa* on banking, ecology, transmigration, reproduction, gender, and economic enterprises.[21] Thus the impact of the co-optation policy of the New Order deeply compromised the *ulama* in Aceh and eliminated the independence they once possessed. The robust ideological stance on the local implementation of *shari'a* the *ulama* had expressed since the 1950s gradually faded away during the New Order period.

The foregoing discussion demonstrates that the struggle of the Acehnese *ulama* to regain political influence during the New Order period was fruitless. Initially, the *ulama* thought that the foundation of the regional MUI could be employed to progressively apply Islamic *shari'a* in Aceh. In reality, this expectation soon evaporated. Instead of transferring a special role to the *ulama* in the implementation of *shari'a*, the establishment of the Acehnese *ulama* council had been effective in persuading many religious leaders to abandon their ideals.

Furthermore, the central government pursued policies that undermined the expression of the Islamic identity of the Acehnese. The New Order regime not only co-opted the council of *ulama*, but it also refused to validate Regulation 6/1968 on the Implementation of Shari'a Law in Aceh, passed by the provincial legislature.[22] According to the central government, there was no law that allowed the decentralization of religious affairs to a provincial government. This rejection was a clear sign from the central government that any step that legitimized the pursuit by the *ulama* of an Islamic agenda in the region was undesirable. The failure of this regulation naturally furthered the drastic decline of the authority of Acehnese *ulama* in local political space.

It seems that the central government saw any expressions of Islamic identity as a dangerous threat to the unitary state of Indonesia that must be suppressed. According to Boland, the central government was afraid that Aceh could create a precedent that other regions (South Sulawesi for example) would be tempted to follow. For the central government, permitting such regional endeavors could lead to the end of the Indonesian unitary state.[23] Thus, it was not surprising that on the grounds of unity the New Order regime later issued Law 5/1974 on Local Government, which implied the abolition of the special status for the Acehnese province, even though its special status continued to appear in official documents.

Although the *ulama* helped eliminate the few PKI in Aceh and pave the way for the New Order regime to emerge there, they were not regarded as the ideal partner for implementing the political agenda of the new government. The relationship between the central government and Aceh was a crucial factor in the distinction between the visions of the technocrats and those of the *ulama*. For the regime, as Morris illustrates, the *ulama* were more concerned with religious autonomy under the special status of Aceh rather than the relationship between Aceh and the central government. The New Order regime, therefore, needed new *uleëbalang* as a natural local ally to counter the influence of the *ulama* in the region, and they saw technocrats as the ideal candidates for this role. The new *uleëbalang* holding local authority were thus a combination of academics, bureaucrats in the local government, and military officers.[24]

The technocrats' main objective was to break what they viewed as the marginalization of Aceh and fully incorporate Aceh both economically and politically into the national system designed by the New Order regime.[25] While the regime's economic agenda was modernization and development, its political agenda was to restrict political participation and to suspend any ideological mobilization, including the *ulama*'s efforts to implement a form of religious autonomy. The technocrats, therefore, made great endeavors to ensure victory for the Golkar and the defeat of PPP during each election under the New Order era. A victory for Golkar in the elections would keep the Acehnese on track to alignment with the regime's agenda of development. Any success by the PPP, in the eyes of the technocrats, was an indication that the Acehnese preferred to have their own way with special status, which would only further undermine development in the province.[26]

The Islamic factor, however, could not be underestimated in the regional political sphere. Although the technocrats viewed the *ulama*'s agenda as a stumbling block in the struggle to keep the province of Aceh in line with the national program of modernization and development, they were aware that Islamic symbols and figures of Acehnese *ulama* played important roles in legitimizing their claim for local leadership. As McGibbon puts it: "Daud Beureu-eh and older *ulama* figures were invoked symbolically by the technocrats to enhance their popularity while they also promoted Islamic culture and symbols in order to counter the charge that they were [merely] secularists."[27]

A major development in religious life was the governorship of Ibrahim Hasan (1987–1993). His provincial government not only helped with the construction or expansion of mosques, but also allocated more funds to build *dayah* (Islamic boarding schools) in many parts of the province. In addition, Governor Hasan issued Instruction no. 2/1990 requiring primary school graduates to be able to read the Qur'an and the restoration of the institution of *meunasah*[28] at the low levels of governance after a prolonged absence.[29] All these measures were obviously intended to demonstrate the technocrats' symbolic commitment to Islam. It is therefore no wonder that since the latter part of the 1980s, the *ulama*'s appeal to religious autonomy has become increasingly muted.[30] Indeed, one could say that the technocrats during the New Order era have almost taken over the role of *ulama* as the new agents in defining Aceh.

By the 1990s, the political influence of the Acehnese *ulama* had almost completely deteriorated and their social base had been fundamentally transformed. According to Kell, this had much to do with the emergence of a new middle class of professionals and businessmen after the late 1970s, as a result of the regime's policies of rapid modernization.[31] Another element that transformed the social base of the *ulama* was their deep involvement in the political arena, beginning with the foundation of PUSA in 1939 and continuing until the end of the rebellion in the early 1960s, which had made them less concerned with the nuances of education in the *madrasa* or *dayah*.[32]

Above all, what gave the technocrats more political authority than the *ulama* was that the technocrats were successful in subduing the *ulama* through a number of economic and political bargains. During the three decades of the New Order period, almost all religious figures in Aceh had been provided with a respectable social status and generous incomes by the New Order regime. The urban *ulama* were offered positions on the *ulama* council (MUI), as lecturers and professors at the IAIN of Banda Aceh, as judges in the religious courts, as teachers in the state or private *madrasa,* or as chiefs of the offices of religious affairs (Kantor Wilayah Departemen Agama) in each city or regency in Aceh.[33] These appointments led to the separation of the Acehnese *ulama* into those who were allied with the regime and those who withdrew from public life. Only a few *ulama* (rural ones in particular) could escape such political co-optation by concentrating their energies on religious education in their respective *dayah,* thus allowing them to maintain moral authority and integrity in specific regions within Aceh.[34]

Another factor that provided the rural *ulama* with more popular support than the urban *ulama* was the widespread *hadith* (Prophet's saying) among the Aceh-nese people implying that "the worst among the *ulama* are those who go and see the *umara* (the ruler)." Although this *hadith* was considered *da'if* (having weaknesses), many preachers at Friday sermons or at other religious meetings often quoted it to discredit the co-opted *ulama.*[35] So, for example, Rusydi Ali Muhammad, the former rector of IAIN Banda Aceh, often referred to this *hadith.* Quoting the teaching of al-Ghazali that there are two kinds of *ulama:* the profane *ulama* (*ulama dunia*) and the saintly *ulama* (*ulama akhirat*), Muhammad confirmed that both types of *ulama* were observable in Aceh under the New Order regime in particular.[36] The former type of *ulama* was condemned as they often supported the regime in exchange for material benefits, while the latter were praised because they challenged an authoritarian, secularist government.

Reinventing the *Ulama*'s Prerogatives

Political challenges to the local leadership of the technocrats increased from various groups of the Acehnese society in the post–New Order era. The technocrats' policies in economic affairs were condemned as having exploited the Acehnese natural resources mostly for the benefit of the central government rather than for the local people. Furthermore, the destructive excess of development was criticized because it had prompted many immoral (*maksiat*) acts, such as fraud, gambling, and prostitution, in many parts of the province. Even though the technocrats prudently maintained a nominal Islamic aura, they could not withstand accusations that they were merely implementing secular scenarios laid down by the central government.[37] Clearly, the collapse of the New Order regime in 1998 worsened the crisis of legitimacy for the technocrats.

As the local leadership of the technocrats weakened and, more importantly, because Aceh's nine-year status as a military zone (DOM) was revoked in August 1998, the Free Aceh Movement (GAM), NGO activists, and the groups took a greater political role. The GAM was able to consolidate its military power and strengthen its control over large areas of Aceh's territory, and the NGO activists— who were not necessarily allies of the GAM—managed to articulate internationally their complaints regarding the exploitation of Aceh's natural resources and the violation of human rights committed by the security forces.[38] In the meantime, following the referendum in East Timor, student groups such as the Information Center for Referendum of Aceh (SIRA), formed in January 1999, sought to advocate a referendum on Aceh's independence. Unlike the GAM, which saw armed confrontation as the most likely way to achieve Aceh's independence, the SIRA campaigned for self-determination through a referendum, which they regarded as non-violent and thus more internationally acceptable.[39]

Meanwhile, during the years of political transition (1998–1999), the voices of marginalized Muslim groups (the rural *ulama* and their students in *dayah*) began to be articulated. *Dayah* students were able to organize themselves under the Union of the Dayah Students of Aceh (RTA) in April 1999,[40] and the rural *ulama* agreed to establish a new organization, the Association of the Dayah Ulama of Aceh (HUDA), in September 1999. Both these organization had a similar mission: to restore the religious identity of the Acehnese.

In the view of the HUDA, Aceh's Islamic identity had been contaminated by government policies of the New Order era. The impact of this was observable not only in economic and in sociopolitical problems, but also in religion. The solution to this crisis, according to the HUDA, was the reinstatement of Islamic *shari'a* for the Acehnese.[41] Indeed, at the Aceh People's Congress, held in the front of the Baiturrahman Mosque, Banda Aceh, on 15 September 1999, the HUDA demanded a referendum.[42]

In the post-Soeharto era, the emergence of an organization of rural *ulama* (HUDA) created a clear boundary between the rural *ulama* and the urban *ulama*. If the HUDA wanted both the *shari'a* and a referendum, the urban *ulama*—who were mostly from the MUI—were cautious in response and preferred the introduction of Islamic *shari'a* under the auspices of a special autonomy. While the HUDA considered a referendum the best way to determine the preference of the Acehnese as between the options of special autonomy and independence,[43] the urban *ulama* put a high priority on the proposal for *shari'a* implementation rather than the idea of a referendum.[44] HUDA's preference for a referendum certainly contravened the advice of the urban *ulama* to the central government. The urban *ulama,* who were mostly recruited to the advisory board of President Habibie concerning Acehnese issues, advised that launching the implementation of *shari'a* would be an effective approach to solve the prolonged conflict in Aceh. According to Usman Hasan, the head of this advisory board, "the breakthrough to settle Aceh conflict is to declare the application of *shari'a* in Aceh. . . . In doing so, it would be clear whether the GAM is Islamic or not. If the GAM proved to be un-Islamic, the [Acehnese] people will not support it."[45]

Support of the HUDA for the referendum surprised many in Aceh, including the GAM.[46] In fact, the GAM was suspicious of the HUDA and saw it as a potential rival, which was understandable given that the *ulama* had controlled local politics in the past. Additionally, under a situation where the technocrats' leadership had been deteriorating, the *ulama* were more able to play an important role. Aware of the crucial position of *ulama,* the central government offered limited *shari'a* implementation as a strategy to help solve the conflict in Aceh, seeking to empower sympathetic *ulama* by providing them with a greater role in the local political administration. This offer from the central government not only benefited the *ulama,* but it also reinforced the political position of the technocrats against the resistance of GAM and other opposition groups in Aceh.

The enactment of Law 44/1999 on Aceh's special status was the confirmation of the *ulama*'s position in the political structure of local government. The provisions in this law (Article 9) state that there should be an organization of *ulama* to actively participate in the public life of Aceh. This *ulama* organization is to be located not only at the provincial level, but also at the district level. The main function of this *ulama* organization, according to Article 9, is to provide oral or written advice and religious considerations for making local policy in the various aspects of social, economic, and political life in Aceh.[47]

One may wonder why the *ulama*—again—won a significant role in the local political institutional structure of Aceh. The conventional explanation refers to the history of Aceh, where the *ulama* had had a crucial position at the top structure of Acehnese political culture for a long time.[48] Therefore, the reintroduction of a formal role for the *ulama* in Law 44/1999 was, according to Mukhtar Aziz, an Acehnese legislator, merely to reassert the unique role in sociopolitical life in Aceh they had enjoyed in the past.[49] A similar explanation comes from Muslim Ibrahim, chairman of the *ulama* council, and Al Yasa' Abubakar, the head of the Office of Shari'a in Aceh (DSI). They all took the view that the central government's offer to grant Aceh the three aspects of autonomy (religion, local custom, and education) inherently required that the *ulama* be active in power. In fact, the idea of the implementation of *shari'a* must implicitly entail handing over some authority to the *ulama*[50] because they are the only ones with appropriate knowledge of Islamic law.

These explanations, in my view, are not fully satisfactory since they do not go to the real motives for the offer. I would argue that the offer was primarily intended to cure the declining position of the technocrats in local politics. As the *ulama* were the only group that could counter the legitimacy of opposition groups in Aceh (the GAM, the NGOs, and student movements), preferring the *ulama* was an excellent strategy for Jakarta to combat its opponents in Aceh. The offer to the *ulama* to play a major role in the post-Soeharto era not only reinforced the political legitimacy of the technocrats in Aceh, but it also was a step toward countering the increasing popularity of the GAM, though this latter goal remained unachievable.

Giving the province of Aceh the right to regionally apply *shari'a* meant that the *ulama* were provided with the authority to supervise legal policy in the region. For the *ulama,* this offer was an opportunity to retrieve the political leadership they had enjoyed in the past, while the technocrats, on the other hand, saw opportunities in such a situation to consolidate their political legitimacy amid dramatic political transition. To this end, the technocrats not only endorsed the enactment of a great number of regulations that contained *shari'a* rules,[51] but also allocated considerable revenue for the successful implementation of *shari'a.* Among other things, the budget for the council of *ulama* (MPU) and the provincial Office of Shari'a in Aceh (DSI) increased dramatically from millions to billions of rupiahs during the years 2003 and 2004.[52] In doing so, the technocrats attempted to win the hearts of the Acehnese people and legitimize and restrengthen their position locally in the post-Soeharto era.

Needless to say, however, once the technocrats were successful in regaining their political legitimacy, the *ulama* were likely to be left behind. The technocrats, who are now mostly politicians as well, only need support from the *ulama* during political crises and do not hesitate to disregard them when the *ulama*'s assistance is no longer necessary. As Yusni Sabi (rector of IAIN of Banda Aceh) puts it, the *ulama*'s support is always sought to help the driver push his broken-down car, but when the car is running well, the driver usually does not allow the *ulama* into the car.[53] In fact, similar events recurred during the political crises of both 1945 and 1965. The Acehnese *ulama* helped the government expel the colonial Dutch in 1945 and fight the communists in 1965, but to this day they have never received what they see as a satisfactory reward from the government.

18

Ulama and *Qanun* Lawmaking

The downfall of Soeharto in 1998 offered a new chance for the return of the Aceh-nese *ulama* to power. The efforts of the central government to solve the conflict in Aceh gave advantages to both urban and rural *ulama*. As the New Order regime had been successful in co-opting the urban *ulama* through the *ulama* council (MUI), the government now attempted to subdue the rural *ulama* by offering them posi-tions in the council.[1] It was important for the government to subjugate the rural *ulama* and bring them back under its influence.

In June 2001, 180 *ulama* from across the province of Aceh attended a meeting of *ulama*. They comprised religious leaders of *dayah,* top figures of Islamic orga-nizations, heads of religious colleges, Muslim intellectuals, and individual Islamic leaders. This meeting was to form, or more precisely to transform the MUI into, the MPU. Instead of MUI, the title MPU was chosen because that had been the name of the first association of *ulama* established in Aceh in the mid-1960s.[2]

The government's preference to work more closely with the rural *ulama* was received enthusiastically, and the rural *ulama* sought to take up the leadership of the MPU. Two candidates from the rural *ulama* camp were able to secure high positions in the MPU leadership: Muslim Ibrahim[3] and Daud Zamzami,[4] who were elected as the chairman and vice chairman of MPU respectively, for the period from 2001 to 2006. Although the contender from the urban *ulama* camp, Al Yasa' Abubakar, failed in two consecutive elections for chairman and vice chair-man, he was offered a position as the second vice chair.[5] However, Abubakar with-drew from this position when he was appointed by the governor to lead the Office of Shari'a in Aceh (DSI) of the provincial government in February 2002. Ismail Yacob, an academic from the State Institute for Islamic Studies (IAIN) but with a strong rural *ulama* background, subsequently replaced Abubakar. In contrast to the MUI of Aceh under the New Order era, which was dominated by the urban *ulama,* the leadership of the MPU in the post–New Order period is now dominated by the rural *ulama*.

In addition to the structure of the MPU leadership, Articles 14 and 15 of Perda

3/2000 state that a highly prestigious and vital institution called the Plenary Board of *Ulama* (DPU) should be established as well. The main task of this board is "to monitor, to formulate suggestions and to offer opinions, guidance and advice to the executive and legislative branches of the provincial government in making local policy." [6] Additionally, the board has the power "to issue *fatwa* in the field of Islamic *shari'a* on issues related to development, governance and societal building." [7] This board consisted of twenty-seven prominent *ulama* across the province of Aceh, including the chairman of the MPU and the two vice chairmen. The twenty-seven members of this board were selected from 180 *ulama* who were recruited hierarchically from the lower level of the legal community, such as *gampong* (village) and *mukim* (several villages), to the middle level of the local government (district or city). Each *ulama* on the board receives a monthly allowance. [8] Above all, members of this board have political privileges including a type of immunity. [9] According to Kaoy Syah, a former legislative member from Aceh, the immunity means that members of the DPU are immune from prosecution for what they say in formal meetings within the MPU itself or in meetings with the legislature. [10]

Following the enactment of Law 18/2001 on the Special Autonomy of Nanggroe Aceh Darussalam, the Perda 3/2000 on the MPU was amended to include provisions that granted extensive rights to the DPU as follows: [11]

1. To obtain information from the executive and the legislative branches of the provincial government regarding policies that might be implemented.
2. To issue legal opinions, to offer considerations, and to present proposals of regional policies to the executive and the legislative branches of provincial government.
3. To supervise and to review the implementation of regional policy in accordance with Islamic *shari'a*.
4. To request an explanation from the executive and the legislative branches of provincial government, state officials, and other ordinary citizens regarding any urgent action of regional policy that is needed to be taken directly or indirectly.

It is clear that at least on paper, the MPU has much more authority than the New Order's council of *ulama* (the MUI). The MPU is independent in the sense that it has an equal status with, and is on the same level as, the executive and the legislative branches of provincial government. [12] In fact, unlike before, where a request was required, the MPU now is authorized to offer considerations and suggestions, with or without request, from any governmental institution in Aceh, such as the governor, the Provincial Legislature, the Regional Police Force, the Provincial Prosecutor Office, and the Regional Armed Force. All these provincial institutions are obliged to consult the MPU before any decision on regional policy is made.[13] The rationale behind these provisions, as explained in the elucidation, is to avoid contradictory policies between different provincial institutions, especially regarding the implementation of *shari'a* in this region. After all, it is believed that any policy produced with the consultation of the MPU would have a special legitimacy, thus making Acehnese Muslims more ready to follow its instructions. However, as will be discussed in the following section, the MPU is not really as powerful as these arrangements suggest.

The *Qanun*

Apart from issuing *fatwa*, the key role that the *ulama* could play in the implementation of *shari'a* in the modern nation-state is involvement in the codification of Islamic rules. By assisting in the development of Laws on the Special Status of Aceh, the MPU has largely participated in the legislative process at the provincial level, especially in producing regional regulation or *qanun* that are relevant to the implementation of *shari'a* in Aceh. Muslim Ibrahim has explained that there are two ways the MPU engages in the regional legislation. First, the MPU prepares a draft of *qanun* at the preparation stage. Second, the MPU takes part at the formal meetings conducted at the legislative chamber. In these meetings, along with the provincial legislature, the MPU discusses the draft *qanun* as proposed by the provincial government (DPRD).[14]

As far as the implementation of *shari'a* in Aceh is concerned, there are at least seventeen regulations or *qanun* that were enacted between the years 2000 and 2006. The MPU certainly has been a contributing institution to the production of those *qanun*, which can be classified into two categories. The first category relates to the institutions and procedures needed to apply *shari'a* in the region. Table 18.1 lists the first category of *perda/qanun*.

In addition to the *perda* and *qanun* on the institutions and procedures shown in Table 18.1, the governor of Aceh issued Decree 01/2004 on the Foundation and the Organization of Wilayatul Hisbah (A task force for implementing *qanun*).

The second category of *perda/qanun* relates to the rules of *shari'a* that are being implemented in Aceh, as shown in Table 18.2.

Any Muslim who lives in Aceh and violates a provision in the second category of *qanun* will be liable for punishment. The punishments specified in the *qanun* are generally regarded as *ta'zir* or discretionary punishment.[15] In addition to fines and imprisonment, one particular *ta'zir* punishment stated in the *qanun* is caning. The minimum and the maximum caning inflicted upon the offender are two lashes and forty lashes respectively, and the amount of caning imposed depends upon

TABLE 18.1. *Qanun* on institutions and procedures

No. and Year Issued	Subject matter of Perda/Qanun
Perda 3/2000	Foundation and Organization of the Consultative Council of *Ulama* (Majelis Permusyawaratan Ulama)
Perda 7/2000	Organizing Social Life Based on *Adat*
Perda 33/2001	Structure and Organization of the Department of Islamic *Shari'a* (Dinas Syariat Islam)
Qanun 10/2002	The *Mahkamah Syar'iyyah* (*Shari'a* Court)
Qanun 2/2003	Status and Authority of the District (*kabupaten*) or City (*kota*) Government in the Province of Nanggroe Aceh Darussalam
Qanun 3/2003	Status and Authority of the Sub district (*kecamatan*) Government in the Province of Nanggroe Aceh Darussalam
Qanun 4/2003	The *Mukim* Government in the Province of Nanggroe Aceh Darussalam
Qanun 5/2003	The *Gampong* (village) Government in the Province of Nanggroe Aceh Darussalam
Qanun 9/2003	The Functional Relationship between the Consultative Council of *Ulama* (MPU) and the Executive, the Legislative and other Institutions of Provincial Government
Qanun 3/2004	Foundation and Organization of the Aceh *Adat* Council
Qanun 11/2004	The Functional Tasks of the Regional Police of Nanggroe Aceh Darussalam
Qanun 12/2004	The Culture of Aceh

which offense is committed. Table 18.3 summarizes the amount of caning for each criminal offense mentioned in the *qanun*.

In assessing the punishments mentioned in the *qanun*, most of them (except for liquor consumption) fall under the category of *ta'zir*, the third category described in the Islamic penal system. The other two primary categories of punishments, *hudud* (fixed punishments for certain crimes such as adultery or fornication and theft) and *qisas* (just retaliation, mostly applied as the punishment for murder),[16] despite being prescribed explicitly in the Qur'an and Sunna, have not been enacted in any of Aceh's *qanun* to date.

As *ta'zir* is mainly a human discretionary punishment, there will often be no agreement on the particular kind of *ta'zir* punishment applicable in a given situa-

TABLE 18.2. *Qanun* on *Shari'a* Rules

No. and Year Issued	Subject matter of *Qanun*
Qanun 11/2002	Incorporation of some aspects of theology (*akidah*), rituals (*ibadah*) and activities that glorify Islam (*syiar Islam*) into the *qanun*
Qanun 12/2003	[Prohibition on] liquor (*khamar*)
Qanun 13/2003	[Prohibition on] gambling (*maisir*)
Qanun 14/2003	[Prohibition on] close proximity between unmarried or unrelated couples (*khalwat*)
Qanun 7/2004	Administration of *zakat* (alms)

TABLE 18.3. Amount of caning prescribed for offenders

Offenses	Amount of Caning	Source
The propagation of deviant sects or cults	12 lashes	Article 20 (1) Qanun 11/2002
Apostasy or disgracing the religion of Islam	Not yet arranged, as it will be enacted in particular *qanun*	Article 20 (2) Qanun 11/2002
Failure to observe Friday prayers three weeks consecutively without a religiously legitimate reason	3 lashes	Article 21 (1) Qanun 11/2002
To provide amenities that encourage Muslims to break fasting during the Ramadan month	6 lashes	Article 22 (1) Qanun 11/2002
To eat or drink publicly during the daylight hours in the Ramadan fasting month	2 lashes	Article 22 (2) Qanun 11/2002
To consume liquor and other similar things	40 lashes	Article 26 (1) Qanun 12/2003
To commit gambling	Max 12 lashes, and min 6 lashes	Article 23 (1) Qanun 13/2003
To commit *khalwat*	Max 9 lashes, and min 3 lashes	Article 22 (1) Qanun 14/2003

tion. In addition, the fact that the *ta'zir* penalties appear in a great number of *qanun* suggests that the human element as a source for the implementation of *shari'a* in Aceh are greater than the divine will of God. This implies that the Islamization by *qanun* in Aceh is subject to the criticism that instead of Islamization, it entails the practical secularization of *shari'a,* namely the penetration of non-divine aspects (such as parliamentary enactments) into the formulation of *shari'a* rules in the *qanun.* This could have been avoided if each *qanun* was declared to be 'inspired' by *shari'a* rather than merely 'codifying' *shari'a.* The different impact is clear. The former assumes that the *qanun* is man-made law, while the latter sees it as God's law itself, though it clearly is not.

Dissonance in *Qanun*

It was much easier to establish the caning penalty in the *qanun* than to put it in practice. As early as October 2002, the chairman of the MPU had announced that "caning will be introduced for Muslims who do not fast and are caught eating lunch in public places in the upcoming Ramadan." [17] But until Aceh was hit by a tsunami in December 2004, not a single person had been caned. This was not because nobody had violated the *qanun,* but rather because the legal infrastructure was not then present to support caning. But this is not the sole problem in implementing the *qanun* in pre-tsunami Aceh. Other problems stemmed from within the camps of the *ulama* themselves.

As pointed out by Hamid Sarong, the dean of faculty of syari'ah of the IAIN of Banda Aceh, many problems in implementing *qanun* have to do with a lack of basic knowledge of legal drafting. Sarong explains that as the legal drafting process was dominated by the *shari'a* jurists while the involvement of non-Islamic law experts with experience in legal drafting was very small (well under 10 percent), there were some provisions that were included in the *qanun* without any clear indication of how they could be carried out. [18] For example, how could one determine that an individual Muslim has failed, without a religiously legitimate excuse, to perform three Friday prayers consecutively? Should all Muslims become formally and exclusively attached to a particular mosque for the purpose of Friday prayers, or should each mosque list attendees at Friday prayers? This kind of provision is simply impracticable.

Furthermore, the way the rural *ulama* understood *shari'a* rules has led at times to problems in implementing the various *qanun.* Equally pertinent to the process was that when drafting a *qanun,* the rural *ulama* looked mostly at the Islamic concepts or teachings in the *fiqh* textbooks rather than taking into account the educational background and the understandings of the ordinary Acehnese of Islamic injunctions.[19] The rural *ulama* seemed to assess the appropriateness of a particular provision in a *qanun* based on their own personal attitudes or expectations, assuming that ordinary Muslims would behave as the *ulama* do. This is an unrealistic assumption, to say the least.

As far as the involvement of *ulama* in the legislation process is concerned, one of the most controversial issues related to the definition of acceptable *akidah* (Islamic creeds) in Aceh.[20] During drafting of the *qanun,* different positions emerged between the rural *ulama* and the urban *ulama,* who were mostly Muslim intellectuals, regarding what sort of *akidah* Muslims in Aceh could adhere to. The voice of the rural *ulama* was articulated by Teungku Daud Zamzami, the vice chairman of the MPU, while the standpoint of the urban *ulama* was presented by Al Yasa' Abubakar, the chairman of the DSI. The rural *ulama* sought to define the term *akidah* exclusively as a reference to *Ahlussunnah wal Jama'ah* (widely understood as Sunni), while for the urban *ulama,* there was no need to specify a single acceptable *akidah* for Aceh. According to the urban *ulama,* the explication of *akidah* in the *qanun* as such would ignore the plural reality of Muslims in Aceh. Additionally, to determine that there is only one kind of *akidah* acceptable in Aceh would contravene the spirit of the official name of the region, "Nanggroe Aceh Darussalam," which identifies Aceh as a "peaceful territory that protects everyone."[21]

Apparently, the rural *ulama*'s view that the *Ahlussunnah wal Jama'ah* was the only Islamic creed acceptable in Aceh was irresistible. Although the urban *ulama,* which comprised a number of IAIN intellectuals,[22] initially rejected the inclusion of the term *Ahlussunnah wal Jama'ah* in the provision, they finally succumbed, largely because of a warning sent by Teungku Muhibuddin Waly, one of the most well-known rural *ulama,* that the rural *ulama* would not be responsible for the implementation of such *qanun* if the creed of *Ahlussunnah wal Jama'ah* was not explicitly stated.[23] The provincial legislature itself did not formally take a side during this debate. Its approach was more pragmatic and it simply adopted the rural *ulama*'s proposal because it was seen as more acceptable to the Acehnese people in general.

The notion of an undefined Islamic creed as argued by the urban *ulama* was actually much more practical in light of the realities of legal drafting. As explained by Sarong, the inclusion of such specific *akidah* into the legal text is inappropriate because *akidah* is not an issue between humans. It is relevant to the relationship between God and his creatures, which is certainly beyond the competency of man-made law to regulate. According to Sarong, if the rural *ulama* want to prevent the Acehnese people from subscribing to non-Sunni creeds, the best way to achieve this is not by banning those creeds in a *qanun,* but by campaigning against them in sermons or through religious education. Above all, Sarong queried, how could a public prosecutor prove that an Acehnese Muslim had failed to adhere to the creed of *Ahlussunnah wal Jama'ah?* Would conversion from this particular creed to Ahmadiyya, for example, be considered analogous to apostasy, and hence a crime?[24] What would the punishment be for such crime? The *qanun* were silent on this issue.

The imposition of an exclusive Islamic creed as revealed in the 11/2002 *qanun* may violate individual rights in the 1945 constitution (Article 28E (2)) insofar as it is incompatible with ideological freedom.[25] Moreover, the *qanun* has also defined individual rights according to the *ulama*'s understanding of tolerable conduct and for the sake of communal identity. When asked whether this provision would infringe on the human rights provisions stated in the constitution, and hence whether it should be judicially reviewed by the Supreme Court, the chairman of the MPU, Muslim Ibrahim, answered by stating that given that the province of Aceh itself is exclusively administered under its special status as Nanggroe Aceh Darussalam, the *qanun* must be considered an exception within the territory of Indonesia. As a result, he argued, once a *qanun* is passed by the legislature, there is no other legal choice available for Muslims in Aceh but to carry it out. As far as the implementation of *qanun* in Aceh is concerned, as explained by Ibrahim, "the issue of human rights therefore must not be extensively taken into account. Otherwise, most *qanun* will be non-starters."[26] These comments conflict directly with the increasing demands in Aceh to investigate human rights abuses that have taken place since the status of Military Operation Zone (DOM) was applied to Aceh in the early 1990s.

The *qanun* in Aceh show that the transformation of *shari'a* doctrines or *fiqh* rules into positive law is not an easy task. Even a simple daily religious activity, such as a provision in Article 9 of Qanun 11/2002 that a driver of public transportation must stop his vehicle at prayer time to allow the passenger(s) to pray, cannot easily be upheld. This is not only because some aspects of *shari'a* cannot be codified (such as those related to creed and daily rituals), but also because most drafters of *qanun* did not have sufficient knowledge of legal drafting, which has led to a rigid formulation of the *qanun* provisions, which in turn has tended to make them unworkable.

In Sarong's view, the *ulama* are not necessarily legal drafters, but they could participate in the early stage of the process by selecting some Islamic teachings that may be appropriate and applicable to be enacted in the form of statute or *qanun.* Where doctrines cannot be legislated, the *ulama* should put them aside. Selected teachings should, however, be sent to experts on legal drafting who can transform them into the legal texts in accordance with the science of jurisprudence.[27]

Finally, it is the legislature (DPRD), and not the *ulama,* that still holds the final word on *qanun* lawmaking in Aceh. Although the MPU has a full right to initiate draft *qanun,* the legislative function is nonetheless still in the hands of the DPRD members. Unlike the Shi'ite *ulama* in Iran, the Acehnese *ulama* have never secured a real authority in the legislature, let alone sufficient powers to veto a *qanun* passed by the provincial legislature. This situation shows the tension of legal authority between the provincial legislature and the *ulama,* with a result that the *ulama* have to give way.

The power of MPU, as granted by several *qanun,* remains at present mostly on paper. The MPU's authority in Aceh perhaps is little more than the role formerly played by the Supreme Advisory Council (DPA) at the national level. This was a governmental institution that was abolished by the Fourth Amendment to the constitution, but which had formally existed since independence. Advice issued by this institution was not effective unless there was another party willing to carry out the advice. However, unlike the static DPA, the MPU is more active and is more involved in a number of various crucial issues, albeit without a decisive role. The discussion on the role of *ulama* in post-tsunami Aceh in the next chapter will further clarify this contention.

19
After the Tsunami

As mentioned, by the end of 2004, no criminal (*jinaya*) case had been brought to the *shari'a* court (*Mahkamah Syar'iyyah*). All related cases, gambling in particular, were dealt with in the state court. However, the tsunami severely damaged most coastal areas of Aceh on 26 December 2004 and unexpectedly created a momentum for further pushing the implementation of *shari'a* in the region. In fact, in the post-tsunami period, the *shari'a* court of the Bireuen District had sentenced more than twenty people for gambling offenses, and fifteen of them were publicly caned in the mosque yard in Bireuen on 24 June 2005.[1]

Whether or not the tsunami was the decisive factor in speeding up the application of *shari'a* in Aceh depends much on the way the people conceived the catastrophe itself. Many Acehnese saw it as a spiritual test or even a punishment from God and saw it as creating an opportunity for accelerating the application of *shari'a* in Aceh. For them, the tsunami was not merely a coincidence, but the will of God. There is a belief that through the tsunami, God told the Acehnese to stop committing sinful deeds, to reconcile with each other, and to return to religion as a way of salvation. In short, the tsunami brought a message that the Acehnese people should comply with *shari'a* rules and the provincial governments should enforce them in earnest.

Some other Acehnese, however, perceived the tsunami merely as a natural process (*sunnatullah*), a geological shift under the earth.[2] For them, the tsunami has nothing to do with the implementation of *shari'a*. They argued that even if *shari'a* were fully implemented in Aceh, there is no guarantee that another tsunami would not hit Aceh in the future. Since Aceh unfortunately is located where earthquakes often occur, the tsunami is one occurrence and the application of *shari'a* is another matter. This sort of argument was in line with the views of Al Yasa' Abubakar, the head of the Office of Shari'a in Aceh (DSI). He claims, in fact, that the tsunami was not an escalating factor for the implementation of *shari'a* in Aceh. The caning punishment held in Bireuen District on 24 June 2005 was a result of the ongoing process of the implementation of special autonomy granted to Aceh. Al Yasa' has described the process chronologically.

The year 2001 watched the formal establishment of Mahkamah Syar'iyyah (*shari'a* court) through Law 18/2001 on the Special Autonomy for Nanggroe Aceh Darussalam; the year 2002 witnessed the enactment of the Qanun of the Mahkamah Syar'iyyah by the provincial parliament; the year 2003 saw the formal inauguration of the Mahkamah Syar'iyyah, which was transformed from the existing religious court by the presidential decree; the year 2004 saw the formal transfer of some criminal jurisdiction (*jinaya*) from the state court to the Mahkamah Syar'iyyah by the decree of chairman of the Supreme Court; and the year 2005 is seeing the operation of the Mahkamah Syar'iyyah and the execution of its verdicts.[3]

This latter argument sounds much more logical than the interpretation that the tsunami was God's will, as described above. However, in my view, to deny any significance to the tsunami would be too hasty. The post-tsunami situation had created a context for the proponents of *shari'a* to emotionally pressure the provincial government and the central government to more earnestly apply *shari'a* in Aceh. In fact, the caning in Bireuen could never have happened without support from the acting governor of Aceh, Azwar Abubakar,[4] and the attorney general's consent.

The approval of the attorney general, Abdul Rahman Saleh, was needed since both the provincial and the district public prosecutor had doubts. For this reason, some proponents of the formal implementation of *shari'a* sought to meet the attorney general in Jakarta to request his support for the caning punishment in Aceh. As described by Muslim Ibrahim, some leading provincial figures on their return trip to Aceh from Semarang, where a conference on the tsunami devastation was held, met the attorney general in an unscheduled meeting on 3 June 2005 at his office in Jakarta.[5] Initially the attorney general had no time to meet, as he was very busy that week. It was only with the help of the National Development Planning Agency (Bappenas) officials, whose institution is responsible for rebuilding and reconstructing Aceh, that the meeting was facilitated. After persistent efforts, they finally secured the attorney general's approval.[6]

The *Shari'a* Court

Moreover, the tsunami had created many cases that needed to be decided by the *shari'a* court. Most of these related to inheritance, remarriage for people who had lost their spouses, orphaned children, and the status of properties whose owners were missing. However, due to the tsunami, the *shari'a* court in Banda Aceh, Meulaboh, and Calang lacked appropriate human resources and infrastructure. Thus, existing judicial institutions could not promptly adjudicate current cases. In the one-year period after the tsunami, the *shari'a* court dealt largely with inheritance issues, a topic traditionally within the *shari'a* court's jurisdiction everywhere in the Muslim world.

Until 13 June 2005, the Mahkamah Syar'iyyah of Banda Aceh, for instance, had issued 4,053 letters declaring the lawful heirs of the tsunami victims.[7] The estimate at the end of 2005 stated that roughly nine thousand inheritance cases had been reviewed by the Mahkamah Syar'iyyah.[8] This amount, however, remains a small proportion of the dead, who numbered more than one hundred thousand. Above all, the type of property dealt with by the *shari'a* court in Aceh was mostly limited to bank deposits or savings of the deceased owners and did not include other assets such as land.

Other informal institutions outside the *shari'a* court, such as *adat* or local practice, have appeared to help many Acehnese people manage their own legal problems in post-tsunami Aceh. Although the *ulama* council (MPU) issued *fatwa* regarding the judicial authority of the *shari'a* court over various legal issues arising in the aftermath of the tsunami,[9] many cases of remarriage were not brought to the *shari'a* court, which was authorized to issue an order that a previous spouse of an applicant was missing (*mafqud*) and that the applicant was free to remarry.[10]

As a matter of fact, a number of remarriages between those whose spouses were lost took place without judicial declaration from the *shari'a* court. These remarriages mostly occurred after the waiting period (*'idda*) of the women whose husbands had died elapsed, which is after four months and ten days, or 130 days. Such religious knowledge has long been commonly applied in local practice, therefore neither partner went to obtain a judicial declaration from the *shari'a* court that their previous spouse was missing. It is interesting to note here that there was a case in the district of Aceh Besar where a missing husband appeared and found his wife already married to another man. This case, however, was not brought to the Mahkamah Syar'iyyah since local practice provides the solution, which is also Islamic in nature. The first husband (who had been missing) was offered the choice of having his wife back or to accept her new marriage and receive from her the *mahar* (dowry) handed over at the time of his marriage to her. The first husband chose the former option.[11] This case suggests that although the Acehnese were keen to implement a form of religious injunction in their daily lives, they did not necessarily see a need to go to the formal institution (the *shari'a* court) to carry it out.

The Role of *Ulama*

The role of the *ulama* in post-tsunami Aceh was also marginal, since they were unable to rebuild Aceh without widespread institutional influence. This became more obvious when the process of rebuilding and reconstructing the devastated areas of Aceh commenced. If the MPU were a powerful institution, they would surely have been involved at least in formulating the blueprint for the rebuilding and the reconstruction of Aceh.[12] Although the MPU had strongly advocated that the voice of *ulama* must be heard, it was the Bappenas that formulated the official blueprint, largely without *ulama* input.[13]

For this reason, the *ulama* were mostly unhappy with the blueprint. The rural *ulama*, who come mostly from *dayah* backgrounds, organized a meeting, which was partly steered and sponsored by figures in the MPU leadership, to criticize the blueprint for lacking sufficient religiosity.[14] Also in this meeting, the *ulama* insisted that consultation with the *ulama* is a must (*harus*) for any policy to redevelop Aceh. Similar consultation should also be carried out by national or international funding agencies seeking to support the redevelopment of Aceh.[15] These *ulama*'s demands, however, have not had much impact.

Additionally, the recruitment of personnel for the BRR (Body for Rehabilitation and Reconstruction of Aceh and Nias) is perhaps a good example of the institutional weakness of the *ulama*. The BRR personnel were appointed by Presidential Decree 63/2005, and most did not meet the expectations of the *ulama*. Although Muslim Ibrahim, the chairman of the MPU, was included as a member of the steering board of the BRR, he could not conceal his dissatisfaction that his personal nominee was not appointed chairman of its executive board.[16] If the MPU were an influential institution, the chairman of the MPU would have surely been able, at least, to notify President Soesilo Bambang Yudhoyono of the *ulama* candidate to chair the BRR. When I asked Muslim Ibrahim why he did not proactively submit his nominee to the president, he replied that the president did not request a name from him.[17] This event shows the absence of a strong leader among the current Acehnese *ulama*. Certainly, the political power of Muslim Ibrahim is still far behind that enjoyed by his charismatic Acehnese *ulama* predecessor, Daud Beureu-eh. This suggests that the *ulama*'s influence remains relatively weak and that accordingly their role remains mainly symbolic in the current sociopolitical climate in Aceh.

In conclusion, my examination of the position of the *ulama* and *shari'a* in post-tsunami Aceh above shows that the nation-state of Indonesia is still influential in that province and that there is not much difference between what the MPU had achieved before and after the tsunami. The ascent of Acehnese *ulama* to local power was not a guarantee that they could direct the reconstruction in post-tsunami Aceh, which has, in fact, been tightly controlled by the central government. The same is true for the punishment imposed by the *shari'a* court on gamblers in the Bireuen District. Their caning would not have taken place without authorization by the nation-state—in this case by the attorney general in Jakarta. The new additional jurisdiction won by the *shariʻa* court does not necessarily imply that the *shariʻa* will instantly apply in Aceh. Indeed, as both the police and the public prosecutor are not decentralized but remain Jakarta-based, nationwide institutions, the actual implementation of *shariʻa* in Aceh remains more or less entirely under the control of the nation-state of the Republic of Indonesia. As both the *ulama* and the *shariʻa* are, in this case, once again in a subordinate position vis-à-vis the nation-state, there is surely legal and political dissonance in the regional implementation of *shariʻa* in Indonesia.

Conclusion

The relationship between law and religion in the era of the modern nation-state is a complicated issue. While a distinction between law and religion is observable in many Western secular countries, a greater unity of law and religion is more commonly found in the legal systems of many Muslim-majority countries. For many devout Muslims, to distinguish between law as a branch of religion and law as a secular product of the state is an odd practice. In their view, the state laws that largely affect Muslim daily life, such as family and penal law, have to take religious rules into account or, at least, comply with *shari'a* norms. As the legal sovereignty of the state and the legal authority of religion are often incongruent in the modern period, Muslim leaders in some countries, such as Sudan, Egypt, Pakistan, Iran, and Afghanistan, have sought to resolve this tension by seeking to make Islamic *shari'a* the law of the land, or more precisely to religionize the legal political system of a state.

This book has demonstrated that re-emerging calls for the official implementation of *shari'a* in Indonesia are efforts to religionize the legal political system of a modern state. In Indonesia, these efforts have been observable at least since independence and have continued throughout modern Indonesia's history, with Islamic *shari'a* remaining the central issue. Through three case studies (constitutionalization of *shari'a*, nationalization of *shari'a* and localization of *shari'a* in Aceh), this study has found that there has been an intensive and ongoing attempt to Islamize Indonesian laws over the past three decades.

In this book, I have set out to test the hypothesis that the formal implementation of *shari'a* in Indonesia is dissonant, in the sense that it has been characterized by a continuum between tensions in meanings and direct contradictions in terms. I have identified a large range of examples of this dissonance at the constitutional level, at the level of political ideology, and at the level of subordinate regulations. These dissonances essentially arise because of the difficulty in reconciling the centrality of *shari'a* for pious Muslims with the fundamental importance of the plural religious system that is at the heart of Indonesia as a secular state. To highlight this concern, the following section will present the key findings of this study and will seek to demonstrate the complexity of legal and political dissonance in the implementation of *shari'a* in Indonesia.

Dissonant Implementation of *Shari'a*

The Islamization of laws under the frame of national law or religious autonomy remains legally and politically dissonant. I demonstrate in part III, especially chapter 11, that both proposals (Alternatives Two and Three) of the Islamic faction to amend Article 29 of the 1945 constitution were dissonant. Both were intended to restrict the list of specific liberties mentioned in Article 28 on Human Rights in the constitution, which had been decided earlier. The dissonance stems from the fact that Islamic parties' proposals gave emphasis to (religious) duties over rights, despite their being expressed in terms of rights. More direct dissonance is discernible between the aspiration for the formal implementation of *shari'a* and constitutional rights of religious freedom. If successful, the proposal for *shari'a* implementation would restrict religious freedom of individuals in the name of communal religious obligations. Indonesian nationals would be treated not as autonomous individual citizens but as members of a religious community—a fundamental contradiction with the concept of a nation-state. This would likely alienate and coerce citizens who do not subscribe to the official or dominant religious interpretation and would foster political divisiveness among citizens of different religious affiliations.[1] As the constitutional principle of equal citizenship in Article 28I (2) mandates that all citizens have equal rights regardless of their ethnicity, gender, or religion,[2] lawmaking that is solely based on, and for the interest of, one particular religion may breach this provision of the constitution.

Part IV has discussed the enactment of Zakat Administration Law 38/1999 and showed that citizens' basic rights to equality without regard to their religious background were violated. The law provided that Muslims who pay *zakat* may be entitled to a deduction from their taxable income, a provision available only to Muslim citizens and not to other religious believers.

Part V has revealed dissonance in the local implementation of *shari'a* in Aceh, where individual freedoms were restricted by the introduction of a number of rules, not necessarily *shari'a*-based, through *qanuns* or Acehnese Regional Regulations. To give an example, the inclusion of a *qanun* provision that only the Islamic creed of *Ahlussunnah wal Jama'ah* is acceptable in Aceh infringed the individual rights guaranteed by Article 28E (2) of the 1945 constitution, which guaranteed the freedom of all citizens "to posses convictions and beliefs, and to express his or her thoughts and attitudes in accordance with his or her conscience." The case of Islamic lawmaking in Aceh shows that while constitutional provisions at the national level guarantee individual rights of all citizens, lower regulations at the local level (*qanun*) deny those rights for certain groups of citizens. As a result, Indonesian Muslims living in Aceh do not enjoy the same rights as other Indonesian Muslims.

The Impact of Islamization

The following paragraphs will assess to what extent attempts at the Islamization have influenced social political transformation in Indonesia. I suggest that there are four salient features of the Islamization of Indonesian laws: (1) the decline of *ulama* authority; (2) the rise of the religious bureaucracy; (3) increasing calls for a return to the approach of the colonial state; and (4) calls for greater regional influence as a new path toward implementing *shari'a*.

The Decline of *Ulama* Authority
In the preceding chapters, I note that currently there is an increasing trend toward creating a 'fragmentary' state, which offers degrees of autonomy to certain people or areas based on religion. The idea of the fragmentary state, as I argue in chapter 7, reflects the Ottoman millet system, which lasted from the mid 1400s to the early decades of the 1900s. This millet system became untenable due to shifts in the world political order and a change in world values after the late eighteenth century. This shift was a result of the change away from national boundaries based on distinct religious lines and because of a movement away from discrimination and social segregation toward more universal values of equality and pluralism. All these new trends led to the rise of an Ottoman 'nationality' over and above separate identities of religious community and ethnic groups. This late period of the Ottoman Empire is important to understand the decline of authority of religious leaders, and it also helps explain the context of the events, ideas, and actions that led to the rise of calls for the formal implementation of *shari'a*.

As the transition from a dynastic empire, or from colonial rule, to the formation of an independent nation-state implied the upholding in principle of equality before the law, resentment was observable among many religious leaders. This principle weakened their legal authority over their followers and indeed eliminated many of the political privileges enjoyed by Muslim citizens in the previous millet system. The character of the nation-state was not well-understood by these religious leaders. Yet the reality of the nation-state was unavoidable, and the option available to religious leaders in many Muslim countries, including Indonesia, was to deal with it either by invoking ideas of an Islamic state and a constitutional status for *shari'a* (see chapters 7, 10, and 11), by legislating some aspects of *shari'a* (see chapter 15), or by inventing a political role for *ulama* in the public sphere (see chapter 17).

How then have conceptions of the modern nation-state and religious law interacted in the minds of many Muslim leaders to result in the emerging calls for the implementation of religious law in a modern state? Religious leaders or *ulama* were unlikely to have envisaged that the positions they held before in the pre–nation-state era, where they functioned autonomously from the authority of a specific ruler, would quickly disappear. In the precolonial period, it was the *ulama*, especially the *fukaha* (legal scholars), who were actively engaged in the process of the elaboration of *shari'a*. They not only issued *fatwa*, but also wrote books of *fiqh* that often were used by the Islamic judges (*qadi*) in the *shari'a* court. However, since colonial rule, the *ulama* have lost most of their authority over *shari'a* across the world. In the modern world, the codification of *shari'a* is mostly the work of the legislatures and executives of nation-states.[3]

Looking at the fate of *shari'a* in the legal system of modern nation-states, Sami Zubaida has aptly described how the role of *ulama* was affected.

> [The] incorporation of *shari'a* into the state has separated *shari'a* from its religious locations, from the books and traditions of *fiqh* and into state manuals, from the custody of scholars to that of bureaucrats and legislators. . . . Legislation and judgment are now subject to bureaucratic and political logic and not to the ratio[nality] of *fiqh* tradition and method. The judge rules in accordance with law codes, and not the books of *fiqh*.[4]

In light of this, it is perhaps fair to say that the rising calls for the implementation of *shari'a* in a modern state have partly to do with efforts to reconsolidate the weakening authority of the *ulama*. Seeking to retain lawmaking power, the *ulama* attempted to occupy vital positions in the religious bureaucracy as well as in the legislatures. Yet these attempts have more often than not failed.

The Rise of Religious Bureaucracy

In order to obtain legitimacy, the state, through its religious bureaucracy, sought to appropriate *shari'a* from the *ulama* classes. The religious bureaucracy in Indonesia (the Ministry of Religious Affairs or MORA) has been an important institution in accelerating the development of Islam since the early years of independence. The MORA has largely spearheaded the government-led campaign of Islamization, nationally directing, regulating, and promoting all kinds of religious activities, especially Islamic ones.[5] Legislative efforts were an important means employed by this ministry to nationalize *shari'a* in Indonesia. As a result, some legal aspects of *shari'a* have been incorporated into the national legal system and become standardized.

With regard to the implementation of *shari'a* in Aceh, the religious bureaucracy (*Dinas Syariat Islam* or the provincial Office of Islamic Shari'a) has played a more important role than the *ulama* council (MPU). The provincial religious bureaucracy has been engaged in numerous tasks: planning future activities, recruiting members of the *shari'a* law enforcement authority (*wilayatul hisbah*), preparing manuals, disseminating information and guidelines, coordinating the meetings of all relevant provincial institutions, and supervising the application of *shari'a* in Aceh.[6] Moreover, the share of the regional budget allocated to this office of *shari'a* is greater than that allocated to the *ulama* council.[7] All this suggests that in the modern state, the religious bureaucracy appears to have wider job scope, and hence is more functionally significant, than the *ulama* in the implementation of *shari'a*. This is because the *ulama* focus mostly on the content of *shari'a*, while the religious bureaucracy has to deal with both the content of *shari'a* and the procedural matters necessary for its application.

The Return to the Colonial State's Approach

Although some Muslim governments have been keen to formally facilitate the implementation of *shari'a*, this is frequently rejected by Islamic groups advocating what they term the 'real *shari'a*.' What the proponents of the formal implementation of *shari'a* often want is to go back to the authentic application of *shari'a*, although it is not clear what they mean by this. In fact, as Kozlowski points out, when religious actors or Muslim politicians call for the implementation of *shari'a* in many Muslim countries, they actually advocate a return to the period of colonial states, where *shari'a* had an organizational structure compatible with the modern nation-state, and not to the time of the Prophet or the era of the caliphate.[8]

Part IV of this book, chapter 16 in particular, points out the truth of this claim. It shows that the provision for tax deductibility of the *zakat* payment in the current Zakat Administration Law originated from the colonial tax ordinances. It must be noted here, however, that both the religious bureaucracy of the colonial state and that of the Indonesian state have different motives in the administration of *zakat*. While the colonial bureaucracy was mainly concerned with the misuse of *zakat* funds by its appointed native officials, the religious bureaucracy in contemporary Indonesia has been expected to promote *zakat* and even make it obligatory for

Muslim citizens. Nevertheless, the religious bureaucracies in both times have the same objective, which is to keep the state in control of religious practices.[9]

Efforts to return to the colonial state's approach have also been observable in the emerging idea of legal pluralism. While the Dutch colonial administration treated diverse groups of the population differently based on their racial classification, the religious bureaucracy of Indonesia modified this practice by substituting religious identity as the key criterion for classification, thus building walls between people of different religions. This was demonstrated by the fact that the MORA initiated and shaped most of the legislation in terms of religious categories. As a result, if the colonial legal policy led to racial discrimination, the Indonesian legal system has been equally prone to discriminate against citizens based on religion.

This notion of religious legal pluralism was also articulated in the Islamic parties' effort in the MPR Annual Session in 2000–2002 to amend Article 29 of the 1945 constitution by including a constitutional obligation on Muslims to practice *shari'a* (see chapters 10 and 11). Although the Islamic parties' proposals (the so-called Jakarta Charter and the Medina Charter) were rejected, it is worth noting here that both proposals, which imply the implementation of religious legal polycentrism, enjoyed—and presumably still do enjoy—considerable currency among many Muslim people in Indonesia. This was demonstrated by a poll conducted by *Kompas* (the biggest popular daily newspaper in Indonesia) during the MPR Annual Session in August 2002, in which most respondents supported a proposal to enforce religious legal polycentrism (the Medina Charter). This proposal, which would create a system barely distinguishable from the Ottoman millet system, was advocated by 49.2 percent of the respondents, while the proposal to enforce the Jakarta Charter was supported by only 8.2 percent.[10] As both proposals (the Jakarta Charter and the Medina Charter) imply similar things, this suggests that if the responses are taken together (57.4 percent) and compared to the number of respondents who preferred the original text of Article 29 on Religion (38.2 percent), there would be considerable support for implementing religious legal polycentrism in Indonesia.

One of the major advocates for the Medina Charter, or the idea of religious legal polycentrism in Indonesia, was the PK (now the PKS or Prosperous Justice Party), a leading Islamic party in the 2004 election. Hidayat Nur Wahid, a former president of this party and chairman of the MPR (2004–2009), openly supported it.[11] Other parties, such as the PBB (Crescent Moon Star Party), seemed to share the idea, although there was no clear reference made to the Medina Charter. According to Hamdan Zoelva, a leader of the PBB, this idea would not be problematic since it existed during Dutch colonial times, when different laws were applied for different people in the East Indies. For this reason, Zoelva argued, the state must allow each of the various subnational legal systems to operate.[12] This once again demonstrates that what Muslim politicians are currently seeking with regard to the formal implementation of *shari'a* is a return to the pluralistic legal approach of the colonial state—a de facto millet system.

Calls for Greater Religious Autonomy

We have seen in previous chapters (7, 10, and 11) that advocates of the formal implementation of *shari'a* have failed to give *shari'a* a constitutional status, thus *officially* preventing Indonesia from building a legal system that differentiates between citizens based on their religion. However, some of their demands have been partly accommodated. Given that the constitutional effort failed and that national legislation to apply *shari'a* has only achieved a limited success, the proponents of the formal implementation of *shari'a* have sought a new strategy, namely Islamization through the enactment of regional regulations (*perda*).

The increasing call for *shari'a* rules at the local level has been encouraged by the democratization process, a rapidly weakening central authority, and a national program of administrative decentralization. Although religious affairs were not decentralized, the local application of *shari'a* often received a free ride on the revival of local authenticity and its distinct identity. In light of this, some heads of districts (*bupati*) in cooperation with the local legislatures have passed regulations (*perda* and instruction letters of district heads) that order people to do things either in accordance with, or to refrain from doing anything against, Islamic tenets, such as the required use of a headscarf for Muslim females or the banning of liquor consumption. Moreover, as a result of the 2004 general election and the election of regional leaders (*pilkada*) in 2005, support for the formal implementation of *shari'a* has become greater in certain districts, especially those inhabited predominantly by Muslims. This support came not only from advocates of *shari'a* rules who have secured seats in the legislatures, but also from local bureaucracies.

This reveals that while the process of Islamization of laws has largely failed at the national level, it has been doing comparatively well at the regional level. The relatively successful Islamization of laws at the lower level has led the proponents of *shari'a* to strive for their goals from below. What becomes important now is not exclusively a constitutional status for *shari'a*, but religious autonomy by which the proponents of *shari'a* would be able to freely implement *shari'a* rules in a particular territory. This suggests that a decentralized state or a country run by a federal system is much more favorable to the formal application of *shari'a* than a centralized unitary state. Moreover, a transition in political power, where the central state often becomes weak while the society at the periphery becomes stronger, has often been a critical factor in the local implementation of *shari'a*, as in Aceh. Accordingly, the decline of central authority following the downfall of the Soeharto regime in 1998 must be taken into account when assessing the underlying factors of this limited success of the application of *shariʿa* in Aceh.

The relatively successful implementation of *shariʿa* in Aceh is not a unique phenomenon, as similar cases can be found elsewhere in the Muslim world. There are two comparable examples (Nigeria and Malaysia) that demonstrate how both the status of autonomy and the situation of political transition are contributing factors to the local application of *shariʿa,* its penal rules in particular. In Nigeria, there are at least twelve states that have passed controversial Islamic criminal laws allowing the use of caning and stoning as punishments.[13] It was the transition from a military to a civilian government through the electoral contest in 1999 that provided a chance for Islamization of the legal systems of some of the Nigerian states. In a country where Muslims constitute nearly half of the citizenry and where all three previous elected heads of governments were Muslim, Muslim support has been an important factor for the elected Nigerian president, Olusegun Obasanjo, a Christian. The regional implementation of Islamic criminal law in some northern states of Nigeria that followed the 1999 election can therefore be seen as a tradeoff between President Obasanjo and his Muslim constituencies.[14] It can be also viewed as reflecting the emerging strength of the periphery on the one hand and the weakened authority of the center on the other hand, as in Indonesia.

The second case is Malaysia, where the states in this federal country are given constitutional power to make laws on matters of Islam. Islamic criminal law nevertheless does not have a part in this legal autonomy, as the matter of the death penalty remains a constitutional issue. The state legislature of the Kelantan state had ratified the Hudud Bill in 1993, but for it to be implemented by the state certain provisions of the federal constitution would have to have been amended. The bill, however, was rejected by the Malaysian federal government on the grounds that it clashed with the federal constitution.[15] Regardless of the question of constitutionality, the failure of Kelantan to implement the *hudud* law has in part to do with the absence of political transition in Malaysia, which might weaken the federal government and give the states opportunities to commence new legal political initiatives, as in the case of some Nigerian states. The power of the federal government in Malaysia was still too strong for the Kelantan state to confront. This absence of political transition has prevented Kelantan from implementing its *hudud* law.

As far as the local implementation of *shariʿa* in Indonesia is concerned, Aceh has been the only region that has applied *shariʿa* rigorously. Law 11/2006 on the Governance of Aceh, passed in July 2006 by the legislature, has filled gaps and eliminated ambiguities in the previous regulations in relation to the application of *shariʿa* in Aceh.[16] Aceh's *qanuns* on *shariʿa* rules and institutions, and the status of *shari'a* court in particular, therefore, have a strengthened legitimacy. However, it remains to be seen whether the implementation of this new law will provide more opportunities to further the regional application of *shari'a.*

Islamization or Indonesianization?

Finally, seen within the context of the competing visions of the Islamic and nationalist camps regarding the shape of modern Indonesia, it appears that the former has recently been partly able to overcome the latter, despite a long history of defeats in the past. It is obvious that some attempts at Islamizing Indonesian laws have finally enjoyed limited success. Compared to the period from the 1950s to the 1980s, the influence of Islam in the Indonesian legal system has increased significantly since the 1990s. Pure secularization, in the sense of a full separation of religion and the state, is not entirely present, as state functions now often overlap with religious functions in Indonesia. However, a secularization of *shari'a* law in terms of the penetration of non-divine aspects into religious lawmaking has been evident in many cases, such as the enactment of the Zakat Administration Law and the introduction of the *qanun* in Aceh.

The Islamization of laws in Indonesia, therefore, is not a real or complete introduction of *shari'a.* What on the surface appears to be the Islamization of laws in Indonesia is in reality a symbolic token for the most part. Although provisions refer formally to *shari'a,* the procedure that carries it out seems an almost irreligious activity. It may therefore be said that both Islamization and secularization have been unable to entirely achieve their respective goals. For this reason, instead of perceiving the issue solely as an Islamization of the Indonesian legal system, I would argue that it is also an Indonesianization of *shari'a* law that is currently taking place. This means that Islamization of laws in Indonesia entails in part practical secularization of *shari'a,* namely human interference through parliamentary enactment in creating religious obligations that have non-divine character. What are purportedly considered sacred in the national legal system in fact are mostly man-made law, and not necessarily God's law.

Notes

Introduction

1. See Edwin B. Firmage et al., eds., "Editors' Introduction," in *Religion and Law: Biblical, Judaic and Islamic Perspectives* (Winona Lake, Ind.: Eisenbrauns, 1990), pp. vii–viii.

2. Further details on the Jakarta Charter debate appear in chapters 7, 10, and 11.

3. Safiya Safwat, "Islamic Laws in the Sudan," in *Islamic Law: Social and Historical Contexts,* ed. Aziz al-Azmeh (London & New York: Routledge, 1988); Abdel Salam Sidahmed, *Politics and Islam in Contemporary Sudan* (New York: St. Martin's Press, 1996), pp. 175–187.

4. Bassam Tibi, *Islam Between Culture and Politics* (New York: Palgrave, 2001).

5. See for instance Daniel Pipes, "Oil Wealth and Islamic Resurgence," in *Islamic Resurgence in the Arab World,* ed. Ali E. Hillal Dessouki (New York: Praeger, 1982); Richard T. Antoun and Mary Elaine Hegland, eds., *Religious Resurgence: Contemporary Cases in Islam, Christianity and Judaism* (New York: Syracuse University Press, 1987); Emile Sahliyeh, ed., *Religious Resurgence and Politics in the Contemporary World* (Albany: State University of New York Press, 1990).

6. See Emmanuel Sivan and Menachem Friedman, eds., *Religious Radicalism and Politics in the Middle East* (Albany: State University of New York Press, 1990).

7. See Mark Tessler, "Religion and Politics in the Jewish State of Israel," in Sahliyeh, *Religious Resurgence and Politics in the Contemporary World.*

8. See for instance W. F. Wertheim, "Religious Reform Movements in South and South-East Asia," *Archives de Sociologie des Religions* 12 (1961): pp. 53–62.

9. See for instance Julia D. Howell, M. A. Subandi, and Peter L. Nelson, "Indonesian Sufism: Signs of Resurgence," in *New Trends and Development in the World of Islam,* ed. Peter B. Clarke, pp. 277–297 (London: Luzac Oriental, 1997); Cf. also Julia D. Howell, "Sufism and the Indonesian Islamic Revival," *Journal of Asian Studies* 60, no. 3 (2001): pp. 701–729.

10. See for instance Karen Armstrong, *The Battle for God: Fundamentalism in Judaism, Christianity and Islam* (New York: Alfred A. Knopf, 2000); Charles S. Liebman, "Jewish Fundamentalism and the Israeli Polity," in *Fundamentalism and The State: Remaking Politics, Economies and Militance,* ed. Martin E. Marty and R. Scott Appleby (Chicago and London: The University of Chicago Press, 1993); Abdel Azim Ramadan, "Fundamentalist Influence in Egypt: The Strategies of the Muslim Brotherhood and the Takfir Groups," in

Fundamentalism and The State: Remaking Polities, Economies and Militance, ed. Martin E. Marty and R. Scott Appleby (Chicago and London: The University of Chicago Press, 1993); Krishna Kumar, "Religious Fundamentalism in India and Beyond," *Parameters* 32 (2002).

11. Bruce B. Lawrence, *Defenders of God: The Fundamentalist Revolt Against the Modern Age* (New York: Harper and Row, 1989).

12. Ann Elizabeth Mayer, "The Fundamentalist Impact on Law, Politics and Constitutions in Iran, Pakistan and the Sudan," in *Fundamentalism and The State: Remaking Polities, Economies and Militance,* ed. Martin E. Marty and R. Scott Appleby (Chicago and London: The University of Chicago Press, 1993).

13. Anita M. Weiss, ed., *Islamic Reassertion in Pakistan: The Application of Islamic Laws in a Modern State* (New York: Syracuse University Press, 1986); A. Y. Noori and S. H. Amin, *Legal and Political Structure of An Islamic State: The Implication for Iran and Pakistan* (Glasgow: Royson Limited, 1987); Rav Yaacov Ariel and Rosh Yeshiva-Yamit, "Secular Courts in the State of Israel," *Jewish Law: Examining Halacha, Jewish Issues and Secular Law.* http://www.jlaw.com/Articles/SecularCourts.html (accessed 8 August 2002).

14. N. Rakover, "Jewish Law and the State of Israel: Jewish Elements in Israeli Legislation," in *Law in Multicultural Societies: Proceedings of the IALL Meeting,* ed. E. I. Cuomo (Jerusalem: International Association of Law Libraries, 1989); Michael King, "Religion into Law, Law into Religion: The Construction of a Secular Identity for Islam," in *Nationalism, Racism and the Rule of Law,* ed. Peter Fitzpatrick (Aldershot: Dartmouth, 1995); Jorgen S. Nielsen, *Towards a European Islam* (London: Macmillan Press Ltd., 1999).

15. Soliman M. Santos Jr., *The Moro Islamic Challenge: Constitutional Rethinking for the Mindanao Peace Process* (Quezon: University of the Philippines Press, 2001); Abdullahi A. Na'im, "Political Islam in National Politics and International Relations," in *The Desecularization of the World: Resurgent Religion and World Politics,* ed. Peter L. Berger (Washington, D.C.: Ethics and Public Policy Center, 1999).

16. Sherman Jackson, *Islamic Law and the State: The Constitutional Jurisprudence of Shihab al-Din Qarafi* (Leiden: Brill, 1996); Faraj Fuda, *al-Haqiqa al-ghaiba* (Casablanca, 1989), as quoted in Ibrahim M.Abu-Rabi', *Intellectual Origins of Islamic Resurgence in the Modern Arab World* (New York: State University of New York Press, 1996).

17. Suha Taji-Farouki, "Islamic State Theories and Contemporary Realities," in *Islamic Fundamentalism,* ed. A. S. Sidahmed and A. Ehteshani (Boulder, Colo.: Westview Press, 1996).

18. See for example Harry J. Benda, *The Crescent and the Rising Sun: Indonesia Under the Japanese Occupation 1942–1945* (The Hague/Bandung: Van Hoeve, 1958); M. C. Ricklefs, *History of Modern Indonesia Since c. 1200* (Stanford, Calif.: Stanford University Press, 2001); Robert W. Hefner, "The Political Economy of Islamic Conversion in Modern East Java," in *Islam and the Political Economy of Meaning: Comparative Studies of Muslim Discourse,* ed. William R. Roff (Berkeley: University of California Press, 1987); Azyumardi

Azra, *Renaisans Islam Asia Tenggara: Sejarah Wacana dan Kekuasaan* (Bandung: Remaja Rosdakarya, 1999).

19. See R. Isaac Halevi Herzog, "The Authority of the Torah in the State of Israel," *Legislation According to Torah Law* (Beth Midrash for Torah Law, Legislation Department, Jerusalem, 1950, in Hebrew), as quoted by Eliav Shochetman, "Israeli Law and Jewish Law—Interaction and Independence: A Commentary," *Israel Law Review* 24, no. 3–4 (1990).

Chapter 1. The Notion of *Shari'a*

1. See Nathan J. Brown, "*Shari'a* and State in the Modern Muslim Middle East," *International Journal of Middle East* 29 (1997).

2. See for example Yusuf Al-Qaradawi, *Madkhal Li Dirasah al-Shari'a al-Islamiyya* (n.p., n.d.), pp. 7, 21; Manna' Khalil al-Qattan, *Wujub Tahkim al-Shari'a al-Islamiyya* (Cairo: Dar al-Tawzi' wa al-Nashr al-Islamiyya, 1987), pp. 8–9. The words that have been used in their definitions are *hukm* or *ahkam* to characterize *shari'a* as a legal subject matter.

3. See for example Abu al-A'la al-Mawdudi, *The Islamic Law and Constitution,* trans. and ed. Khursyid Ahmad (Lahore: Islamic Publications, 1977); Muhammad Qutb, *Hawla Tatbiq al-Shari'a* (n.p. Maktaba al-Sunna, n.d.).

4. See for example Abdul Qadim Zallum, *al-Afkar al-Siyasiyya* (Beirut: Dar al-Ummah, 1994).

5. See Joseph Schacht, *An Introduction to Islamic Law* (Oxford: Clarendon Press, 1964), p. 201; Cf. Asaf A. A. Fyzee, *A Modern Approach to Islam* (Bombay: Asia Publishing House, 1963), pp. 25–56.

6. Al-Qaradawi, *Madkhal Li Dirasah,* p. 10.

7. Tahir Mahmood, "Law in the Qur'an—A Draft Code," *Islamic and Comparative Law Quarterly* 7, no. 1 (1987): p. 1.

8. Noel J. Coulson, *Conflicts and Tensions in Islamic Jurisprudence* (Chicago and London: The University of Chicago Press, 1969).

9. See for example Mohammad Hashim Kamali, "Law and Society: The Interplay of Revelation and Reason in the Shariah," in *The Oxford History of Islam,* ed. John L. Esposito, pp. 107–110 (Oxford: Oxford University Press, 1999); Ibrahim Hosen, *Bunga Rampai dari Percikan Filsafat Hukum Islam* (Jakarta: YIIQ, 1997), pp. 1–2.

10. Ibn Qayyim al-Jawziyya, *al-Turuq al-Hukmiyya fi al-Siyasa al-Shar'iyya aw al-Firasat al-Mardiyya fi Ahkam al-Siyasa al-Shar'iyya* (Bayrut: Dar al-Kutub al-'Ilmiyya, 1995), p. 11.

11. See Knut S. Vikør, "The *Shari'a* and the Nation State: Who Can Codify the Divine Law?" in *The Middle East in a Globalized World,* ed. Bjørn Olav Utvik and Knut S. Vikør (Bergen: Nordic Society for Middle Eastern Studies, 2000), p. 232.

12. See Article 39 of Law 1/1974 on marriage.

13. See Muhammad ibn Yazid ibn Majah, *Sahih Sunan ibn Majah* (al-Riyad: Maktaba al-Ma'arif li al-Nashr wa-al-Tawzi', 1417 [1997]), chapter on divorce, *hadith* no. 2008.

14. See Brown, "Shari'a and State"; Muhammad S. Ashmawi, *Against Islamic Extremism,* trans. and ed. C. Fluehr-Lobban (Gainesville: University Press of Florida, 1998).

15. Ashmawi, *Against Islamic Extremism,* pp. 97–98.

16. Michael King, "Religion into Law, Law into Religion: The Construction of a Secular Identity for Islam," in *Nationalism, Racism and the Rule of Law,* ed. Peter Fitzpatrick (Aldershot: Dartmouth, 1995).

17. See Aharon Layish, "The Contribution of the Modernists to the Secularization of Islamic Law," *Middle Eastern Studies* 24 (1978): pp. 263–277; Haim Gerber, *Islamic Law and Culture 1600–1840* (Leiden, Boston, and Köln: Brill, 1999), pp. 105–115.

Chapter 2. Is There Unity of Islam and the State?

1. See Munawir Sjadzali, *Islam dan Tata Negara: Ajaran Sejarah dan Pemikiran* (Jakarta: UI Press, 1993).

2. See Ibn Taymiyya, *al-Siyasa al-Shar'iyya fi Islah al-Ra'i wa al-Ra'iyyah* (Egypt: Dar al-Katib al-'Arabi, 1969), p. 161. This *hadith* from Abu Dawud.

3. Nazih Ayubi, *Political Islam: Religion and Politics in the Arab World* (London and New York: Routledge, 1991), p. 7.

4. Ayubi, *Political Islam,* p. 8.

5. See Ayubi, *Political Islam,* p. 22. Erwin I. J. Rosenthal, *Islam in the Modern National State* (Cambridge: Cambridge University Press, 1965); P. J. Vatikiotis, *Islam and the State* (London, New York, and Sydney: Croom Helm, 1987); Mohammad Hashim Kamali, "The Islamic State and its Constitution," in *Shari'a Law and the Modern Nation-State,* ed. Norani Othman, pp. 45–66 (Kuala Lumpur: Sisters in Islam, 1994).

6. For an example, see S. Taji-Farouki, *A Fundamental Quest: Hizb al-Tahrir and the Search for the Islamic Caliphate* (London: Grey Seal, 1996).

7. See James P. Piscatori, *Islam in a World of Nation-States* (Cambridge: Cambridge University Press, 1986), p. 11.

8. Frederick Denny, "The Meaning of Ummah in the Qur'an," *History of Religions* 15, no. 1 (1975).

9. The Constitution of Medina is an agreement between Prophet Muhammad and the people of Medina at the beginning of Muhammad's residence in Medina. See W. Montgomery Watt, *Muhammad at Medina* (London: Oxford University Press, 1956).

10. See Riaz Hassan, *Faithlines: Muslim Conceptions of Islam and Society* (Oxford: Oxford University Press, 2002); Frederick Denny, "Ummah in the Constitution of Medina,"

Journal of Near Eastern Studies 36 (1977); Abdullah Al-Ahsan, *Ummah or Nation? Identity Crisis in Contemporary Muslim Society* (London: The Islamic Foundation, 1992).

11. See Muhamad Ali, "The Concept of Umma and the Reality of the Nation-State: A Western and Muslim Discourse," *Kultur* 2, no. 1 (2002).

12. See Hassan, *Faithlines,* pp. 86–87.

13. The term *khalifa* is a Qur'anic word that refers to the vicegerency of man as the trustee of Allah on earth. See Q. 2:30.

14. Rosenthal, *Islam,* p. 13.

15. See for example Al-Mawardi, *al-Ahkam al-Sultaniyya* (Bayrut: al-Maktab al-Islami, 1996).

16. Ira M. Lapidus, "State and Religion in Islamic Societies," *Past and Present* 151 (May 1996): p. 6.

17. See Ibn Qayyim al-Jawziyya, *al-Turuq al-Hukmiyya fi al-Siyasa al-Shar'iyya aw al-Firasat al-Mardiyya fi Ahkam al-Siyasa al-Shar'iyya* (Bayrut: Dar al-Kutub al-'Ilmiyya, 1995), pp. 10–11.

18. See John Esposito, *Islam and Politics,* Revised Second Edition (New York: Syracuse University Press, 1987), pp. 5–6.

19. Sami Zubaida, *Islam, the People and the State: Essays on Political Ideas and Movements in the Middle East* (London and New York: Routledge, 1989), pp. 5–6.

20. Rosenthal, *Islam,* p. 13; Ayubi, *Political Islam,* p. 14.

21. Rosenthal, *Islam,* p. 15; Cf. Ibn Taymiyya, *al-Hisba fi al-Islam aw Wazifa al-Hukuma al-Islamiyya* (Dar al-Katib al-'Arabi, n.d.), pp. 2, 6.

22. Ayubi, *Political Islam,* p. 14.

23. Those four immediate successors were Abu Bakr, 'Umar b. Khattab, 'Uthman b. 'Affan and 'Ali b. Abu Talib. The period of rule of these four caliphs lasted almost thirty years, from 632 to 661 CE.

24. Ira M. Lapidus, "The Separation of State and Religion in the Development of Early Islamic Society," *International Journal of Middle East Studies* 6 (1975).

25. Lapidus, "The Separation," p. 366.

26. The four major Sunni *madhhabs* emerged in this period: Hanafi, Maliki, Shafi'i, and Hanbali. These *madhhabs* refer to their founding fathers: Abu Hanifa (d. 767), Anas b. Malik (d. 795), Muhammad Idris al-Shafi'i (d. 820), and Ahmad b. Hanbal (d. 855).

27. Lapidus, "The Separation," p. 369.

28. Lapidus, "The Separation," p. 370, 382–383.

29. See Knut S. Vikør, "The Shari'a and the Nation State: Who Can Codify the Divine Law?" in *The Middle East in A Globalized World,* ed. Bjørn Olav Utvik and Knut S. Vikør, p. 224 (Bergen: Nordic Society for Middle Eastern Studies, 2000).

30. Lapidus, "State and Religion," pp. 13–14.

31. See Ibn Taymiyya, *al-Hisba,* pp. 3, 81.

32. Ibn Taymiyya, *al-Siyasa,* p. 166; Also cf. Arskal Salim, *Etika Intervensi Negara: Perspektif Etika Politik Ibnu Taimiyah* (Jakarta: Logos, 1998), p. 51.

33. Salim, *Etika Intervensi,* p. 52.

34. Lapidus, "State and Religion," p. 23.

35. Zubaida, *Islam, The People,* p. 34.

36. Lapidus, "State and Religion," p. 24; Hassan, *Faithlines,* p. 16; Bahtiar Effendy, *Islam dan Negara: Transformasi Pemikiran dan Praktik Politik Islam di Indonesia* (Jakarta: Paramadina, 1998), pp. 6–16.

37. M. Din Syamsuddin, "Usaha Pencarian Konsep Negara dalam Sejarah Pemikiran Politik Islam," *Jurnal Ulumul Qur'an* 4, no. 2 (1993); See also Sjadzali, *Islam dan Tata Negara,* pp. 5–6.

Chapter 3. Dissonant Implementation of *Shari'a*

1. Theda Skocpol, "Bringing the State Back In: Strategies of Analysis in Current Research," in *Bringing the State Back In,* ed. Peter B. Evans, Dietrich Rueschemeyer, and Theda Skocpol, p. 22 (Cambridge: Cambridge University Press, 1985).

2. I. England, "Law and Cultural Heritage in Multicultural Societies," in *Law and Multicultural Societies: Proceedings of the IALL Meeting,* ed. E. I. Cuomo, p. 7 (Jerusalem, International Association of Law Libraries, 1989).

3. See Martin van Creveld, *The Rise and Decline of the State* (Cambridge: Cambridge University Press, 1999), p. 86.

4. See John Esposito, *Islam and Politics,* Revised Second Edition (New York: Syracuse University Press, 1987); Erwin I. J. Rosenthal, *Islam in the Modern National State* (Cambridge: Cambridge University Press, 1965); James P. Piscatori, *Islam in a World of Nation-States* (Cambridge: Cambridge University Press, 1986), pp. 82–89.

5. See Piscatori, *Islam in a World,* pp. 82–89.

6. Sami Zubaida, *Islam, the People and the State: Essays on Political Ideas and Movements in the Middle East* (London and New York: Routledge, 1989), p. 121.

7. Ann E. Mayer, "Islam and the State: Religious Law and Legal Pluralism," *Cardozo Law Review,* February/March 1991, p. 1015.

8. Mark Cammack, "Islam, Nationalism, and the State in Suharto's Indonesia," *Wisconsin International Law Journal* 17, no. 1 (1999), p. 30; Cf. Sherman Jackson, *Islamic Law and the State: The Constitutional Jurisprudence of Shihab al-Din Qarafi* (Leiden: Brill, 1996), pp. xiv–xv.

9. Cammack, "Islam, Nationalism," p. 30.

10. Cammack, "Islam, Nationalism," p. 30.

11. Cammack, "Islam, Nationalism," pp. 39–40.

12. Cammack, "Islam, Nationalism," pp. 40–41.

13. Wael B. Hallaq, "Juristic Authority vs. State Power: The Legal Crises of Modern Islam," *Journal of Law and Religion* 19 (2003–2004): p. 243.

14. See Farouk A. Sankari, "Islam and Politics in Saudi Arabia," in *Islamic Resurgence in the Arab World,* ed. Ali E. Hillal Dessouki, p. 179 (New York: Praeger, 1982); Ayman al-Yassini, *Religion and State in the Kingdom of Saudi Arabia* (Boulder, Colo., and London: Westview Press, 1985), pp. 25–26, 30, 32; Joseph A. Kechichian, "The Role of the Ulama in the Politics of an Islamic State: The Case of Saudi Arabia," *International Journal of Middle East Studies* 18 (1986): pp. 53–54.

15. Al-Yassini, *Religion and State,* p. 30.

16. For further details, please see Albert Hourani, "The Changing Face of the Fertile Crescent in the XVIIIth Century," *Studia Islamica* 8 (1957): pp. 89–122.

17. Al-Yassini, *Religion and State,* pp. 59–79.

18. See Frank E. Vogel, *Islamic Law and Legal System: Studies of Saudi Arabia* (Leiden, Boston, and Köln: Brill, 2000); Piscatori, *Islam in a World,* p. 123.

19. Vogel, *Islamic Law,* pp. 173–174.

20. See Al-Yassini, *Religion and State,* pp. 133–136.

21. For details of the doctrine of *wilaya al-faqih,* see, among other things, Gregory Rose, "*Velayat e-Faqih* and the Recovery of Islamic Identity in the Thought of Ayatollah Khomeini," in *Religion and Politics in Iran,* ed. Nikki R. Keddie (New Haven, Conn.: Yale University Press, 1983); Mehdi Mozaffari, *Authority in Islam: From Muhammad to Khomeini* (London: M. E. Sharpe, 1987); Mehran Tamadonfar, *The Islamic Polity and Political Leadership, Fundamentalism, Sectarianism and Pragmatism* (Boulder, Colo.: Westview Press, 1989); Mohsen M. Milani, "The Transformation of the Velayat-e Faqih Institution: From Khomeini to Khamenei," *The Muslim World* 82 (July–October 1991): pp. 175–190; Hamid Enayat, "Iran: Khumayni's Concept of the Guardianship of the Jurisconsult," in *Islam in the Political Process,* ed. James P. Piscatori (Cambridge: Cambridge University Press, 1993).

22. Said Amir Arjomand, *The Turban for the Crown: The Islamic Revolution in Iran* (New York: Oxford University Press, 1988), p. 179.

23. Ann E. Mayer, "Law and Religion in Muslim Middle East," *The American Journal of Comparative Law* 35 (1987): pp. 158–159; Nikki R. Keddie, "Iran: Change in Islam: Islam and Change," *International Journal of Middle East Studies* 11 (1980).

24. See Zubaida, *Islam, The People,* p. 15.

25. Enayat, "Iran: Khumayni's Concept," pp. 164–165.

26. Said A. Arjomand, "Shi'ite Jurisprudence and Constitution Making in the Islamic Republic of Iran," in *Fundamentalism and The State: Remaking Polities, Economies and Militance,* ed. Martin E. Marty and R. Scott Appleby, p. 89 (Chicago and London: The University of Chicago Press, 1993).

27. Mehran Tamadonfar, "Islam, Law, and Political Control in Contemporary Iran,"

Journal for the Scientific Study of Religion 40, no. 2 (2001): pp. 206–208; Mayer, "Law and Religion," p. 159.

28. Enayat, "Iran: Khumayni's Concept," p. 166.

29. Tamadonfar, "Islam, Law," pp. 210–211.

30. Tamadonfar, "Islam, Law," pp. 213–215, 218.

31. Tamadonfar, "Islam, Law," pp. 207, 209.

32. Frank E. Vogel, "Islamic Governance in the Gulf: A Framework for Analysis, Comparison, and Prediction," in *The Persian Gulf at The Millennium: Essays in Politics, Economy, Security, and Religion,* ed. Gary G. Sick and Lawrence G. Potter, p. 281 (New York: St. Martin's Press, 1997).

33. Vogel, "Islamic Governance," p. 282.

34. Said Amir Arjomand, "Constitution-Making in Islamic Iran: The Impact of Theocracy on the Legal Order of a Nation-State," in *History and Power in the Study of Law: New Directions in Legal Anthropology,* ed. June Starr and Jane F. Collier, p. 125 (Ithaca, N.Y., and London: Cornell University Press, 1989).

35. See Article 45 of the 1992 Basic Law of Saudi Arabia; Article 4 of the 1979 Iranian constitution.

36. A clause in the Pakistani constitution (Article 227) states that no law should be enacted which is repugnant to the Holy Qur'an and Sunna.

37. Arjomand, "Constitution-Making," p. 125.

38. See Article 203D of the Pakistani constitution.

39. Ann E. Mayer, "The Fundamentalist Impact on Law, Politics and Constitutions in Iran, Pakistan and the Sudan," in *Fundamentalism and The State: Remaking Polities, Economies and Militance,* ed. Martin E. Marty and R. Scott Appleby, pp. 124–126 (Chicago and London: the University of Chicago Press, 1993); See also her other work, "Islam and the State," p. 1047.

40. Sami Zubaida, *Law and Power in the Islamic World* (London; New York: I. B. Tauris, 2003), p. 219.

Chapter 4. Between Nation and Millet

1. Kemal H. Karpat, "Millets and Nationality: The Roots of the Incongruity of Nation and State in the Post-Ottoman Era," in *Christian and Jews in the Ottoman Empire: The Functioning of a Plural Society,* Volume I, ed. Benyamin Braude and Bernard Lewis, p. 141 (New York and London: Holmes & Meier Publishers, 1982).

2. Karpat, "Millets and Nationality," p. 141.

3. As quoted in Bassam Tibi, *Arab Nationalism: Between Islam and the Nation-State,* Third Edition (New York: St. Martin's Press, 1997), p. 29.

4. Montserrat Guibernau, *The Nation-State and Nationalism in the Twentieth Century* (Cambridge: Polity Press, 1996).

5. Guibernau, *The Nation-State,* pp. 1–3.

6. Guibernau attaches this notion to Herder, *On Social and Political Culture,* as cited in Guibernau, *The Nation-State,* pp. 1–2.

7. Ernest Gellner, *Nation and Nationalism* (Oxford: Basil Blackwell, 1983).

8. Anthony Smith, *National Identity* (London: Penguin Books, 1991); Benedict G. Anderson, *Imagined Communities: Reflections on the Origin and Spread of Nationalism* (London: Verso, 1983).

9. Guibernau, *The Nation-State,* p. 47.

10. Guibernau, *The Nation-State,* p. 47.

11. Benedict G. Anderson, "Indonesian Nationalism Today and in the Future," *Indonesia* 67 (1999): p. 3.

12. Anthony Giddens, *The Nation-State and Violence* (Cambridge: Polity Press, 1985), pp. 215–216.

13. Guibernau, *The Nation-State,* p. 47.

14. Guibernau, *The Nation-State,* p. 47.

15. See Giddens, *The Nation-State.*

16. Giddens, *The Nation-State,* p. 189.

17. On this issue, please see for instance Edward S. Herman and Noam Chomsky, *Manufacturing Consent: The Political Economy of the Mass Media* (New York: Pantheon Books, 2002); Noam Chomsky, *Media Control: The Spectacular Achievements of Propaganda,* Second Edition (New York: Seven Stories Press, 2002).

18. Q. 2:130,135; Q. 3:95; and Q. 16:123.

19. W. Montgomery Watt, *Muhammad: Prophet and Statesman* (London and New York: Oxford University Press, 1974), pp. 93–96.

20. Benyamin Braude, "Foundation Myths of the Millet System," in *Christian and Jews in the Ottoman Empire: The Functioning of a Plural Society,* Volume I, ed. Benyamin Braude and Bernard Lewis, pp. 70–71 (New York and London: Holmes & Meier Publishers, 1982).

21. Karpat, "Millets and Nationality," p. 145; Braude, "Foundation Myths," p. 82.

22. Karpat, "Millets and Nationality," p. 148.

23. See Stanford J. Shaw, *The Jews of the Ottoman Empire and the Turkish Republic* (London: Macmillan, 1991), pp. 27–28; Robert Mantran, "Foreign Merchants and the Minorities in Istanbul during the Sixteenth and Seventeenth Centuries," in *Christian and Jews in the Ottoman Empire: The Functioning of a Plural Society,* Volume I, ed. Benyamin Braude and Bernard Lewis, pp. 127–128 (New York and London: Holmes & Meier Publishers, 1982).

24. Karpat, "Millets and Nationality," pp. 145–146.

25. Braude, "Foundation Myths," pp. 79–81.

26. Braude, "Foundation Myths," p. 81; Karpat, "Millets and Nationality," p. 146.

27. Albert H. Hourani, *A Vision of History: Near Eastern and Other Essays* (Beirut: Khayats, 1961), pp. 73–74, 76.

28. Michael M. Pixley, "The Development and Role of the Seyhulislam in Early Ottoman History," *Journal of the American Oriental Society* 96 (1976): pp. 92–95.

29. Stanford J. Shaw, *History of the Ottoman Empire and Modern Turkey,* Volume I (Cambridge and New York: Cambridge University Press, 1976), p. 151.

30. Karpat, "Millets and Nationality," p. 141; Braude, "Foundation Myths," p. 69.

31. Donald Quataert, *The Ottoman Empire, 1700–1922, New Approaches to European History* (Cambridge: Cambridge University Press, 2000), p. 175.

32. Shaw, *History,* p. 152.

33. Bruce Masters, "Ottoman Policies Toward Syria in the 17th and 18th Centuries," in *The Syrian Land in the 18th and 19th Century,* ed. Thomas Philip, pp. 11–26 (Stuttgart: Franz Steiner Verlag, 1992), as cited in Haim Gerber, *Islamic Law and Culture 1600–1840* (Leiden: Brill, 1999), p. 68.

34. John Voll, "Old Ulama Families and Ottoman Influence in Eighteenth Century Damascus," *American Journal of Arabic Studies* 3 (1975): pp. 48–59, as cited in Haim Gerber, *Islamic Law and Culture 1600–1840* (Leiden: Brill, 1999), p. 69.

35. Quataert, *The Ottoman Empire,* pp. 67, 77–78.

36. See Mantran, "Foreign Merchants," p. 127; Carter V. Findley, *Bureaucratic Reform in the Ottoman Empire: The Sublime Porte, 1789–1922, Princeton Studies on the Near East* (Princeton, N.J.: Princeton University Press, 1980), p. 22; Shaw, History, p. 97.

37. See Quataert, *The Ottoman Empire,* pp. 77–78.

38. Joseph Maila, "The Arab Christians: From the Eastern Question to the Recent Political Situation of the Minorities," in *Christian Communities in the Arab Middle East,* ed. Andrea Pacini, pp. 34–35 (Oxford: Clarendon Press, 1998); James P. Piscatori, *Islam in a World of Nation-States* (Cambridge: Cambridge University Press, 1986), p. 51.

39. Shaw, *The Jews,* p. 115.

40. See Roderick H. Davison, *Reform in the Ottoman Empire, 1856–1876* (Princeton, N.J.: Princeton University Press, 1963), pp. 260–262.

41. See Karpat, "Millets and Nationality," p. 162.

42. See Kemal H. Karpat, *The Politicization of Islam: Reconstructing Identity, State, Faith, and Community in the Late Ottoman State, Studies in Middle Eastern History* (New York: Oxford University Press, 2000), p. 9.

43. Quataert, *The Ottoman Empire,* p. 176.

44. Noel J. Coulson, *A History of Islamic Law* (Edinburgh: Edinburgh University Press, 1964), pp. 150–151.

45. Benyamin Braude and Bernard Lewis, "Introduction," in *Christian and Jews in the Ottoman Empire: The Functioning of a Plural Society,* Volume I, ed. Benyamin Braude and

Bernard Lewis, p. 30 (New York and London: Holmes & Meier Publishers, 1982); Karpat, "Millets and Nationality," p. 165; Shaw, *The Jews*, p. 158.

46. Feroz Ahmad, "Unionist Relations with the Greek, Armenian, and Jewish Communities of the Ottoman Empire, 1908–1914," in *Christian and Jews in the Ottoman Empire: The Functioning of a Plural Society*, Volume I, ed. Benyamin Braude and Bernard Lewis, p. 407 (New York and London: Holmes & Meier Publishers, 1982).

47. Karpat, "Millets and Nationality," pp. 165–166.

48. See for example Dwi Purwoko et al., *Negara Islam: Percikan Pemikiran H. Agus Salim, K.H. Mas Mansyur, K.H. Hasjim Asy'ari, Dan Mohammad Natsir* (Jakarta: Permata Artistika Kreasi, 2001).

Chapter 5. Islamization in Indonesia

1. Cf. Ann E. Mayer, "Law and Religion in Muslim Middle East," *The American Journal of Comparative Law* 35 (1987): p. 129. In her words, Islamization refers to "the various agendas of reforms that are being presented as necessary to make societies and law more 'Islamic'." [It] "call[s] at a minimum for the reinstatement of Islamic law as the law of the land and making Islam a more prominent component of political life and social organization."

2. See Ja'far Sheikh Idris, *The Process of Islamization*, The Muslim Students' Association of the US and Canada, 1977 (4th Printing January 1983), Part 1.

3. Suha Taji-Farouki, "Islamic State Theories and Contemporary Realities," in *Islamic Fundamentalism*, ed. A. S. Sidahmed and A. Ehteshani, p. 36 (Boulder, Colo.: Westview Press, 1996).

4. Taji-Farouki, "Islamic State," p. 37.

5. See Arskal Salim and Azyumardi Azra, "Introduction: The State and *Shari'a* in the Perspective of Indonesian Legal Politics," in *Shari'a and Politics in Modern Indonesia*, ed. Arskal Salim and Azyumardi Azra (Singapore: ISEAS, 2003).

6. M. C. Ricklefs, "Six Centuries of Islamization in Java," in *Conversion to Islam*, ed. N. Levtzion (New York: Holmes and Meir, 1979).

7. See for instance, S. M. N. Al-Attas, *Preliminary Statement on a General Theory of Islamization of the Malay-Indonesian Archipelago* (Kuala Lumpur: Dewan Bahasa dan Pustaka, 1969); G. W. J. Drewes, "New Light on the Coming of Islam to Indonesia?" *Bijdragen tot de Taal-, Land-en Volkenkunde* 124 (1968); Christian Pelras, "Religion, Tradition and the Dynamics of Islamization in South Sulawesi," *Archipel* 29, no. I (1985): pp. 107–135; J. Noorduyn, "Makasar and the Islamization of Bima," *Bijdragen tot de Taal-, Land-en Volkenkunde* 143 (1987): pp. 312–342.

8. See Clifford Geertz, *Islam Observed: Religious Development in Morocco and Indone-*

sia (Chicago: The University of Chicago Press, 1968); Mark R. Woodward, *Islam in Java: Normative Piety and Mysticism in Sultanate of Yogyakarta* (Tucson: The University of Arizona Press, 1989); A. C. Milner, "Islam and the Muslim State," in *Islam in South-East Asia,* ed. M. B. Hooker (Leiden: E. J. Brill, 1983); G. W. J. Drewes, *An Early Javanese Code of Muslim Ethics* (The Hague: Martinus Nijhoff, 1978); M. B. Hooker, "The Translation of Islam into South-East Asia," in *Islam in South-East Asia,* ed. M. B. Hooker (Leiden: E. J. Brill, 1983); W. Cummings, "Scripting Islamization: Arabic Texts in Early Modern Makassar," *Ethnohistory* 48, no. 4 (2001): pp. 559–586; Eldar Braten, "To Colour, Not Oppose: Spreading Islam in Rural Java," in *Muslim Diversity: Local Islam in Global Context,* ed. Leif Manger (Surrey: Curzon Press, 1999).

9. For example, the spread of Islam in South Sulawesi in the early seventeenth century was conducted by war from 1608 to 1611 led by the king of Gowa Sultan Alauddin Tumenanga ri Gaukanna. See M. C. Ricklefs, *History of Modern Indonesia since c. 1200.* Third Edition (Stanford, Calif.: Stanford University Press, 2001), p. 57.

10. For further description, see M. C. Ricklefs, *Mystic Synthesis in Java: A History of Islamization from the Fourteenth to the Early Nineteenth Centuries* (Norwalk: Eastbridge, 2006).

11. M. C. Ricklefs, *Polarising Javanese Society: Islamic and Other Visions c. 1830–1930* (Singapore: Singapore University Press; Honolulu: University of Hawai'i Press; Leiden: KITLV Press, 2007); Cf. Ricklefs, "Six Centuries," pp. 112–117.

12. Ricklefs, *Polarising Javanese Society,* p. 99; M. C. Ricklefs, "Religion, Politics and Social Dynamics in Java: Historical and Contemporary Rhymes," paper presented at the 2007 Indonesia Update Conference, Canberra, 7 September 2007, p. 2.

13. Ricklefs, *History,* p. 169; Ricklefs, "Six Centuries," p. 101.

14. Ricklefs, "Religion, Politics," p. 2; for a full account, see Ricklefs, *Polarising Javanese Society.*

15. Ricklefs, "Six Centuries," pp. 112–117; Cf. Azyumardi Azra, *Jaringan Ulama Timur Tengah dan Kepulauan Nusantara Abad XVII dan XVIII: Melacak Akar-Akar Pembaruan Pemikiran Islam di Indonesia* (Bandung: Mizan, 1994), pp. 291–292.

16. Azra, *Jaringan Ulama,* p. 292.

17. Concerning the rise of Islamic reformist movements, see Deliar Noer, *Gerakan Modern Islam di Indonesia 1900–1942* (Jakarta: LP3ES, 1980).

18. For further discussion, see J. L. Peacock, *Purifying the Faith: The Muhammadiyah Movement in Indonesian Islam* (San Francisco: Cummings Publishing Company, 1978); H. M. Federspiel, *Persatuan Islam: Islamic Reform in Twentieth Century Indonesia* (Ithaca, N.Y.: Cornell University, Modern Indonesia Project, 1970).

19. Ricklefs, "Religion, Politics," p. 6.

20. Education and information (*da'wa*) were considered the most effective means of advancing this type of Islamization. See B. J. Boland, *The Struggle of Islam in Modern Indonesia* (The Hague: Martinus Nijhoff, 1982), p. 191.

21. Ricklefs, "Six Centuries," p. 101; Cf. Ricklefs, "Religion, Politics," pp. 7–21.

22. Chandra Muzaffar, "Islamization of State and Society: Some Further Critical Remarks," in *Shari'a Law and the Modern Nation-State*, ed. Norani Othman, pp. 113–114 (Kuala Lumpur: Sisters in Islam, 1994).

23. Debates between the leading figures of Persis and Soekarno appear in chapter 6. For a comprehensive study on Persis, please see Federspiel, *Persatuan Islam*.

24. On this account, please see Boland, *The Struggle*, pp. 7–89, 144–156; Endang Saefuddin Anshari, *Piagam Jakarta 22 Juni 1945* (Jakarta: Gema Insani Press, 1997); C. van Dijk, *Rebellion under the Banner of Islam: The Darul Islam in Indonesia* (The Hague: Martinus Nijhoff, 1981); Syafi'i Ma'arif, *Islam dan Masalah Kenegaraan: Studi Tentang Percaturan dalam Konstituante* (Jakarta: LP3ES, 1985); Adnan Buyung Nasution, *The Aspiration for Constitutional Government in Indonesia: A Socio-legal Study of the Indonesian Konstituante 1956–1959* (Jakarta: Pustaka Sinar Harapan, 1992); Andi Faisal Bakti, *Islam and Nation Formation in Indonesia: From Communitarian to Organizational Communications* (Jakarta: Logos, 2000).

25. Muhammad Syukri Salleh, "Islamization of State and Society: A Critical Comment," in *Shari'a Law and the Modern Nation-State*, ed. Norani Othman, p. 108 (Kuala Lumpur: Sisters in Islam, 1994).

26. For example, see Martin Rossler, "Islamization and the Reshaping of Identities in Rural South Sulawesi," in *Islam in an Era of Nation-States: Politics and Religious Renewal in Muslim Southeast Asia*, ed. Robert W. Hefner and Patricia Horvatich (Honolulu: Hawai'i University Press, 1997).

27. For example, see Robert W. Hefner, "Islamizing Capitalism: On the Founding of Indonesia's First Islamic Bank," in *Towards a New Paradigm: Recent Developments in Indonesian Islamic Thought*, ed. Mark Woodward and J. Rush (Tempe: Arizona State University Program of Southeast Asian Studies, 1995).

28. See Boland, *The Struggle*, pp. 164, 192–204.

29. See Martin van Bruinessen, "Genealogies of Islamic Radicalism in Post-Suharto Indonesia," *South East Asia Research* 10, no. 2 (2002): pp. 117–154.

30. See Arskal Salim, "*Shari'a* in Indonesia's Current Transition: An Update," in *Shari'a and Politics in Modern Indonesia*, ed. Arskal Salim and Azyumardi Azra, pp. 213–232 (Singapore: ISEAS, 2003).

31. For more details on these political accommodations, see Bahtiar Effendy, *Islam dan Negara: Transformasi Pemikiran dan Praktik Politik Islam di Indonesia* (Jakarta: Paramadina, 1998).

32. See for instance Robert W. Hefner, "Islamizing Java? Religion and Politics in Rural East Java," The *Journal of Asian Studies* 46, no. 3 (1987): pp. 533–554; Abdul Azis Thaba, *Islam dan Negara dalam Politik Orde Baru* (Jakarta: Gema Insani Press, 1996); Aminuddin, *Kekuatan Islam dan Pergulatan Kekuasaan di Indonesia: Sebelum dan Sesudah Runtuhnya Rezim Soeharto* (Yogyakarta: Pustaka Pelajar, 1999); M. Rusli Karim, *Negara dan Peming-*

giran Islam Politik (Yogyakarta: Tiara Wacana, 1999); O. Farouk Bajunid, "Islam and State in Southeast Asia," in *State and Islam,* ed. C. van Dijk and A. H. de Groot (Leiden: Research School CNWS, 1995).

33. See for example Ali Said Damanik, *Fenomena Partai Keadilan: Transformasi 20 Tahun Gerakan Tarbiyah di Indonesia* (Jakarta: Teraju, 2002); Irfan S. Awwas, ed., *Risalah Kongres Mujahidin I dan Penegakan Syari'ah Islam* (Yogyakarta: Wihdah Press, 2001); Habib M. Rizieq Syihab, *Dialog Piagam Jakarta: Kumpulan Jawaban* (Jakarta: Pustaka Ibnu Sidah, 2000); Khamami Zada, *Islam Radikal: Pergulatan Ormas-Ormas Islam Garis Keras di Indonesia* (Jakarta: Teraju, 2002); Michael Davis, "Laskar Jihad and the Political Position of Conservative Islam in Indonesia," *Contemporary Southeast Asia* 24 (April 2002); Noohaidi Hasan, "Faith and Politics: The Rise of the Laskar Jihad in the Era of Transition in Indonesia," *Indonesia* 73 (April 2002): pp. 145–170; "Mengenal Hizbut Tahrir: Partai Politik Islam Ideologis," official booklet (n.p., 2001); Majelis Mujahidin, "Undang-Undang Hukum Pidana Sesuai Syari'ah Islam" (Yogyakarta, Markaz Pusat Majelis Mujahidin, 2002).

34. "Kinikah Saatnya Negara Islam?" [Is it Time for an Islamic State?], *Sabili* 13 (6 January 1999); "Sebuah Ancaman dari Jalan Kanan" [A Threat from the Right Wing], *Adil* (14 September 2000); "Penerapan Syariat Islam di Negara Sekuler: Absah atau Bermasalah?" [The Application of *Shari'a* in a Secular State: Valid or Problematic?], *al-Wa'ie* 11 (July 2001); "Menggagas Negara Baru" [Proposing A New State], *al-Wa'ie* 13 (September 2001).

35. "Hidupkan Kembali Piagam Jakarta" [Revive the Jakarta Charter], *Sabili* 16 (24 February 1999); "Demi Tegaknya Hukum dan Keadilan Terapkan Syariat Islam" [For the Sake of Law and Justice, Apply *Shari'a*], *Sabili* 24 (17 May 2000).

36. Effendy, *Islam dan Negara,* p. 52.

37. Mir Zohair Husain, "The Ideologization of Islam: Meaning, Manifestations and Causes," in *Islam in a Changing World: Europe and the Middle East,* ed. Anders Jerichow and Jorgen Baek Simonsen, pp. 92–93 (Surrey: Curzon Press, 1997).

Chapter 6. Different Conception of Nationalism

1. William C. Smith, *Islam in Modern History* (Princeton, N.J.: Princeton University Press, 1957), p. 74.

2. George McTurnan Kahin, *Nationalism and Revolution in Indonesia, Studies on Southeast Asia; No. 35* (Ithaca, N.Y.: Southeast Asia Program Publications, Southeast Asia Program, Cornell University, 2003), p. 38. The other three factors were Malay as the national language, the existence of Volksraad, and press and radio as means of dissemination.

3. Deliar Noer, *Gerakan Modern Islam di Indonesia 1900–1942* (Jakarta: LP3ES, 1980), p. 260.

4. Kahin, *Nationalism,* pp. 70–76; Martin van Bruinessen, "Muslims of the Dutch East Indies and the Caliphate Question," *Studia Islamika* 2, no. 3 (1995): pp. 120–121; M. C.

Ricklefs, *History of Modern Indonesia since c. 1200* (Stanford, Calif.: Stanford University Press, 2001), p. 173.

5. See Noer, *Gerakan Modern,* p. 268.

6. Tjokroaminoto, *Islam dan Sosialisme,* as quoted in Hasnul Arifin Melayu, "Islam as an Ideology: The Political Thought of Tjokroaminoto," *Studia Islamika* 9, no. 3 (2002): p. 62.

7. Ricklefs, *History,* p. 190.

8. Bernhard Dahm, *Sukarno and the Struggle for Indonesian Independence* (Ithaca, N.Y.: Cornell University Press, 1969), p. 175.

9. Dahm, *Sukarno and the Struggle,* p. 175.

10. Soekarno, "Nasionalisme, Islamisme dan Marxisme," *Suluh Indonesia Muda,* 1926. Reproduced in Iman Toto K. Rahardjo and Herdianto WK, eds., *Bung Karno dan Wacana Islam* (Jakarta: Grasindo, 2001), pp. 7–12, henceforth referred to as *Bung Karno.*

11. Ricklefs, *History,* p. 183.

12. See Kahin, *Nationalism,* pp. 90–91.

13. Bruinessen, "Muslims of the Dutch East Indies," pp. 129–132.

14. Bruinessen, "Muslims of the Dutch East Indies," p. 135.

15. Noer, *Gerakan Modern,* p. 154. It is not clear why the word 'Sarekat' changed to the Arabic 'Sjarikat.' Perhaps this is simply the choice of the party's leaders, who preferred to spell the word as in its original language, which was Arabic.

16. Howard M. Federspiel, *Persatuan Islam: Islamic Reform in Twentieth Century Indonesia* (Ithaca, N.Y.: Modern Indonesia Project, Cornell University, 1970), p. 87.

17. Ricklefs, *History,* p. 190.

18. Federspiel, *Persatuan Islam,* pp. 87–89; Noer, *Gerakan Modern,* p. 281.

19. For instance, the Persatuan Muslim Indonesia (PERMI) was in doubt about the value of Pan-Islamism. Instead, from its inception in 1930, this Minangkabau-based Muslim organization attempted to unite Islam and nationalism. See Noer, *Gerakan Modern,* pp. 172–173; Ricklefs, *History,* p. 190.

20. As cited from *Pembela Islam* 36 (October 1931) in Noer, *Gerakan Modern,* p. 281.

21. Noer, *Gerakan Modern,* p. 299.

22. Noer, *Gerakan Modern,* p. 304; *Bung Karno,* pp. 112–113.

23. Noer, *Gerakan Modern,* p. 314.

24. Noer, *Gerakan Modern,* p. 315.

25. Noer, *Gerakan Modern,* p. 307.

26. Noer, *Gerakan Modern,* pp. 306–307.

27. See for example Robert Dahl, *Polyarchy; Participation and Opposition* (New Haven, Conn.: Yale University Press, 1971); Joseph Schumpeter, *Capitalism, Socialism, and Democracy.* Fifth Edition (London: Routledge, 1994).

28. Noer, *Gerakan Modern,* pp. 290–291. Ironically, the red and white with a crescent is now the flag of Singapore, where Muslims are a minority.

Chapter 7. Formation of the Indonesian State

1. See for instances, B. J. Boland, *The Struggle of Islam in Modern Indonesia* (The Hague: Martinus Nijhoff, 1982); Endang Saifuddin Anshari, *Piagam Jakarta: 22 Juni 1945* (Jakarta: Gema Insani Press, 1997).

2. What I mean by 'founding fathers' are those sixty-two members who were actively involved during the meetings of the Investigatory Committee of the Independence of Indonesia (BPUPKI) in mid-1945. For a full list of names of members, see *Risalah Sidang Badan Penyelidik Usaha-usaha Persiapan Kemerdekaan Indonesia (BPUPKI) Panitia Persiapan Kemerdekaan Indonesia (PPKI),* Third Edition (Jakarta: Sekretariat Negara Republik Indonesia, Ghalia Indonesia, 1995).

3. Muhammad Yamin, *Naskah Persiapan Undang-undang Dasar 1945,* vol. I (Yayasan Prapanca, 1959), p. 111.

4. For full description, see Harry J. Benda, *The Crescent and the Rising Sun: Indonesian Islam under the Japanese Occupation, 1942–1945* (The Hague-Bandung: Van Hoeve, 1958).

5. Benda, *The Crescent,* pp. 188–189.

6. See Prawoto Mangkusasmito, *Pertumbuhan Historis Rumusan Dasar Negara: Sebuah Proyeksi* (Jakarta: Hudaya, 1970).

7. Daniel S. Lev, *Islamic Courts in Indonesia: A Study in the Political Bases of Legal Institutions* (Berkeley: University of California Press, 1972), pp. 36–39.

8. Lev, *Islamic Courts,* p. 37.

9. Although Hatta was educated in the Netherlands, he was a devout Muslim from West Sumatra. He regarded Islam, however, as principally *din* (religion) in the sense of a personal religion, and not as an ideological system to be put into practice in the area of *dawla* (government or politics). On Hatta's biography, please see Deliar Noer, *Mohammad Hatta: Biografi Politik* (Jakarta: LP3ES, 1990).

10. Lev, *Islamic Courts,* p. 40.

11. Lev, *Islamic Courts,* p. 40.

12. M. C. Ricklefs, *History of Modern Indonesia since c. 1200* (Stanford, Calif.: Stanford University Press, 2001), p. 190.

13. Pancasila today consists of the following five principles, which are included in the preamble to the Indonesian constitution of 1945: (1) belief in one Almighty God, (2) a just and civilized humanitarianism, (3) national unity, (4) Indonesian democracy through consultation and consensus, and (5) social justice.

14. Yamin, *Naskah,* pp. 110–114.

15. Yamin, *Naskah,* pp. 114–115.

16. Yamin, *Naskah,* p. 115.

17. Yamin, *Naskah,* p. 117. This English translation is taken from Boland, *The Struggle,* p. 20.

18. Yamin, *Naskah,* p. 118; Cf. Boland, *The Struggle,* p. 21.

19. Yamin, *Naskah,* pp. 74–75. Cf. Boland, *The Struggle,* pp. 22–23.

20. See Ki Bagus Hadikusumo, *Islam Sebagai Dasar Negara dan Achlak Pemimpin* (Djo-gyakarta: Pustaka Rahaju, n.d.).

21. Hadikusumo, *Islam Sebagai,* as cited from Syaifullah, *Gerak Politik dalam Masyumi* (Jakarta: Pustaka Utama Grafiti, 1997), p. 101.

22. Hadikusumo, *Islam Sebagai,* as cited in Syaifullah, *Gerak Politik,* pp. 102–104.

23. Q. 3:103 and Q. 5:2.

24. As quoted in Syaifullah, *Gerak Politik,* p. 106.

25. See Boland, *The Struggle,* pp. 25–26; Anshari, *Piagam Jakarta,* p. 30.

26. See Boland, *The Struggle,* p. 27.

27. Boland, *The Struggle,* p. 27.

28. Boland, *The Struggle,* pp. 36–37.

29. Yamin, *Naskah,* p. 259. Translation is from Boland, *The Struggle,* pp. 28–29.

30. Yamin, *Naskah,* p. 259; Boland, *The Struggle,* p. 29.

31. Yamin, *Naskah,* pp. 278, 282–284; Boland, *The Struggle,* p. 31.

32. Yamin, *Naskah,* p. 373.

33. Boland, *The Struggle,* p. 31.

34. Yamin, *Naskah,* pp. 303–305.

35. Yamin, *Naskah,* pp. 371, 373–374.

36. Yamin, *Naskah,* pp. 261–262; Boland, *The Struggle,* p. 30.

37. Yamin, *Naskah,* pp. 262–263; Boland, *The Struggle,* p. 30.

38. Yamin, *Naskah,* p. 379.

39. Yamin, *Naskah,* p. 382.

40. Yamin, *Naskah,* p. 383.

41. Yamin, *Naskah,* pp. 386–387.

42. Anshari, *Piagam Jakarta,* pp. 54–56; Deliar Noer, *Partai Islam Di Pentas Nasional, 1945–1965* (Jakarta: Grafitipers, 1987), pp. 40–41.

43. Whether Wahid Hasjim was present at the meeting on 18 August 1945 is controversial. Hatta noted that he was present. Referring to firsthand oral information, Boland agrees. However, Prawoto has said otherwise. Prawoto's view was supported by the fact that during Ramadan, Hasjim was busy in his *pesantren* (Islamic school) in Jombang. On that day, according to Abdurrahman Wahid, Hasjim's first son, Hasjim was on the way to Jakarta. It is not clear how Hasjim was transported to Jakarta and arrived for the meeting only in the afternoon. On this account, see Syaifullah, *Gerak Politik,* p. 123.

44. Kasman Singodimedjo was a former chairman of Jong Islamiten Bond (JIB) and later became a Masyumi leader.

45. Boland, *The Struggle,* pp. 35–36.

Chapter 8. Reproducing the Millet System

1. Muhammad Yamin, *Naskah Persiapan Undang-undang Dasar 1945,* vol. I (n.p.: Yayasan Prapanca, 1959), pp. 457–462; B. J. Boland, *The Struggle of Islam in Modern Indonesia* (The Hague: Martinus Nijhoff, 1982), p. 37.

2. For a list of the work and scope of the MORA at its early establishment, please see Boland, *The Struggle,* pp. 108–109.

3. For a detailed description of *Het Kantoor voor Inlandsche zaken,* please see Aqib Suminto, *Politik Islam Hindia Belanda* (Jakarta: LP3ES, 1985); Harry J. Benda, "Christian Snouck Hurgronje and the Foundations of Dutch Islamic Policy in Indonesia," *The Journal of Modern History* 30 (December 1958).

4. Deliar Noer, *Administration of Islam in Indonesia* (Ithaca, N.Y.: Cornell Modern Indonesia Project, Southeast Asia Program, Cornell University, 1978), pp. 8–9, 13; Boland, *The Struggle,* p. 106.

5. Boland, *The Struggle,* p. 106.

6. Martin van Bruinessen, "State Islam Relations in Contemporary Indonesia; 1915–1990," in *State and Islam,* ed. C. van Dijk and A. H. de Groot, p. 102 (Leiden, The Netherlands: Research School CNWS, 1995).

7. C. Geertz, *The Religion of Java* (New York: The Free Press, 1960), p. 200; Cf. Boland, *The Struggle,* p. 106.

8. J. W. M. Bakker S.J. *De Godsdienstvrijheid in de Indonesische Grondwetten,* p. 215, as cited in Boland, *The Struggle,* p. 107.

9. The overall votes for by Islamic parties were no more than 45 percent. For details of the 1955 election, see Herbert Feith, *The Indonesian Elections of 1955* (Ithaca, N.Y.: Modern Indonesia Project, Southeast Asia Program, Cornell University, 1957).

10. See for example Boland, *The Struggle,* p. 107; Noer, *Administration,* pp. 8–23; C. A. O. van Nieuwenhuijze, *Aspects of Islam in Post-Colonial Indonesia: Five Essays* (The Hague: W. van Hoeve, 1958), pp. 217–243; Howard Federspiel, "Islamic Values, Law and Expectations in Contemporary Indonesia," in *Shari'a and Politics in Modern Indonesia,* ed. Arskal Salim and Azyumardi Azra, pp. 199–201 (Singapore: ISEAS, 2003); Moch. Nur Ichwan, "Official Reform of Islam: State Islam and the Ministry of Religious Affairs in Contemporary Indonesia 1966–2004" (PhD dissertation, Leiden University, 2006).

11. Bruinessen, "State Islam Relations," p. 102.

12. Daniel S. Lev, *Islamic Courts in Indonesia: A Study in the Political Bases of Legal Institutions* (Berkeley: University of California Press, 1972), pp. 44–45.

13. Lev, *Islamic Courts,* pp. 47, 58.

14. Lev, *Islamic Courts,* p. 58.

15. See C. Fasseur, "Cornerstone and Stumbling Block Racial Classification and the Late Colonial State in Indonesia," in *The Late Colonial State in Indonesia: Political and Eco-*

nomic Foundations of the Netherlands Indies 1880–1942, ed. Robert Cribb (Leiden: KITLV Press, 1994).

16. Joseph Schacht, "Problems of Modern Islamic Legislation," *Studia Islamica* 12 (1960): p. 99.

17. Lev, *Islamic Courts,* pp. 58–59.

18. Lev, *Islamic Courts,* pp. 75–76. A recent decree issued by President Megawati, no. 49/2002, modified this vertical structure of the MORA, limiting it to the regency or municipality level only.

19. Lev, *Islamic Courts,* pp. 53–54.

20. See Nur Ahmad Fadil Lubis, "The State's Legal Policy and the Development of Islamic Law in Indonesia's New Order," in *Shari'a and Politics in Modern Indonesia,* ed. Arskal Salim and Azyumardi Azra, pp. 56–57 (Singapore: ISEAS, 2003).

21. Munawir Sjadzali, "Landasan Pemikiran Politik Hukum Islam dalam Rangka Menentukan Peradilan Agama di Indonesia," in *Hukum Islam di Indonesia: Pemikiran dan Praktek,* ed. Eddi Rudiana Arief et al., p. 52 (Bandung: Rosda Karya, 1991).

22. Arskal Salim and Azyumardi Azra, "Introduction: The State and *Shari'a* in the Perspective of Indonesian Legal Politics," in *Shari'a and Politics in Modern Indonesia,* ed. Arskal Salim and Azyumardi Azra, p. 7 (Singapore: ISEAS, 2003).

Chapter 9. Constitutional Dissonance

1. Ann E. Mayer, "Conundrums in Constitutionalism: Islamic Monarchies in an Era of Transition," *UCLA Journal of Islamic and Near Eastern Law* (Spring/Summer 2002): p. 183.

2. See "The Religion-State Relationship and the Right to Freedom of Religion or Belief: A Comparative Textual Analysis of the Constitution of Predominantly Muslim Countries," United States Commission on International Religious Freedom, March 2005. http://www.uscirf.gov/countries/global/comparative_constitutions/03082005/Study0305.pdf (accessed 7 August 2005).

3. See "The Religion-State Relationship," p. 7.

4. Hasan Turabi, *Islam, Democracy, the State, and the West: A Round Table with Dr. Hasan Turabi,* ed. A. Lowrie (Tampa, Fla.: The World of Islam Studies Enterprise, 1993), p. 25.

5. Under the current Iraqi constitution, which was approved by October 2005, this provision is still maintained. Chapter One on Basic Principles reads, "The constitution is the highest law of the land. No law may be passed that contradicts the constitution, the undisputed laws of Islam, or the principles of democracy."

6. See "The Religion-State Relationship," pp. 29–52.

7. See Yash Ghai and Jill Cottrell, "A Note on Constitutions of Islamic States," p. 2. http://www.cic.nyu.edu/pdf/YashGhai%20AnoteonconstitutionsofIslamicstates.pdf (accessed 8 July 2004).

8. See, for instance, Carol Riphenburg, "Afghanistan's Constitution: Success or Sham?" *Middle East Policy* 12, no. 1 (2005): pp. 31–43; Hannibal Travis, "Freedom or Theocracy? Constitutionalism in Afghanistan and Iraq," *Northwestern University Journal of International Human Rights* 3, no. 4 (Spring 2005).

9. According to Jan-Erik Lane, these two issues are basic to constitutionalism. See his *Constitutions and Political Theory* (Manchester: Manchester University Press, 1996), pp. 25, 62.

10. Muslim thinkers who promoted this notion are, among others, al-Mawardi, al-Ghazali, and Ibn Taymiyya. For further detail, see for instance Anthony Black, *The History of Islamic Political Thought* (New York: Routledge, 2001).

11. Ann Elizabeth Mayer, *Islam and Human Rights.* 3rd ed. (Boulder, Colo.: Westview Press, 1999), p. 45.

12. See Ebrahim Moosa, "The Dilemma of Islamic Rights Schemes," *Journal of Law and Religion* 15 (2000–2001): p. 191.

13. Moosa, "The Dilemma," pp. 191–192; See also Maqbul Ilahi Malik, "The Concept of Human Rights in Islamic Jurisprudence," *Human Rights Quarterly* (1981): pp. 56–67; Riffat Hassan, "Religious Human Rights and the Qur'an," *Emory International Law Review* 10 (1996): pp. 85–96.

14. See Donna E. Artz, "The Application of International Human Rights in Islamic States," *Human Rights Quarterly* 12 (1990): p. 205.

15. See interview of Khaled Abou El-Fadl, "Hak Asasi Manusia di atas Hak Asasi Tuhan" [The rights of human beings are above the rights of God], at http://islamlib.com/id/index.php?page=article&id=864 (accessed on 25 August 2005); Cf. Khaled Abou El-Fadl, *Islam and the Challenge of Democracy* (Princeton, N.J.: Princeton University Press, 2004), pp. 27–28.

16. Moosa, "The Dilemma," p. 197.

17. Izhak Englard, "Constitutional Protection of Religious Minorities: The Tension Between Collective and Individual Religious Freedom," paper presented at Round Table Constitution and Religion, Athens, 22–26 May 2002, pp. 1–3.

18. Noel J. Coulson, "The State and the Individual in Islamic Law," *International and Comparative Law Quarterly* 6 (1957): p. 51.

19. Mayer, *Islam and Human Rights,* p. 81.

20. For a detailed discussion of the Ottoman millet system, see chapter 4.

21. See Englard, "Constitutional Protection," pp. 3–4.

22. The case of 109/35 *The Attorney General v. Sharif Shanti,* 8 Collection of Judgments 651, p. 656, as cited by Englard, "Constitutional Protection," pp. 5–6.

23. Englard, "Constitutional Protection," p. 6.

24. See Gary F. Bell, "Minority Rights and Regionalism in Indonesia – Will Constitutional Recognition Lead to Disintegration or Discrimination?" *Singapore Journal of International and Comparative Law* 5 (2001): p. 795.

25. For further discussion on minority rights, see for example Jennifer Jackson Preece, *Minority Rights: Between Diversity and Community* (Cambridge: Polity Press, 2005).

26. Cf. Bell, "Minority Rights."

Chapter 10. Bringing Back the 'Seven Words'

1. For a full account, see Adnan Buyung Nasution, *The Aspiration for Constitutional Government in Indonesia: A Socio-Legal Study of the Indonesian Konstituante 1956–1959* (Jakarta: Pustaka Sinar Harapan, 1992), pp. 51–129. For further discussion on Islam and Pancasila in Indonesian politics, see for example Douglas E. Ramage, *Politics in Indonesia: Democracy, Islam, and the Ideology of Tolerance* (London and New York: Routledge, 1997); Robert Cribb, ed., *Islam and the Pancasila.* South East Asian Monograph, no. 28 (Townsville, North Queensland, Australia: James Cook University of North Queensland, Centre for Southeast Asian Studies, 1991).

2. See B. J. Boland, *The Struggle of Islam in Modern Indonesia* (The Hague: Martinus Nijhoff, 1982), pp. 90–99.

3. See "Risalah Rapat Pleno ke-9 Panitia Ad Hoc I Badan Pekerja MPR," *Buku Kedua Jilid I: Risalah Rapat Panitia Ad Hoc I Badan Pekerja MPR RI ke-1 s.d 10 Tanggal 11 Januari 2002 s.d 5 Maret 2002* (Jakarta: Sekretariat Jenderal MPR RI, 2002), pp. 639–640.

4. See Endang Saefuddin Anshari, *Piagam Jakarta 22 Juni 1945* (Jakarta: Gema Insani Press, 1997), pp. 129–143; Yusril Ihza Mahendra, *Dinamika Tata Negara Indonesia* (Jakarta: Gema Insani Press, 1996), pp. 73–88.

5. See Andree Feillard, *NU vis-à-vis Negara: Pencarian Isi, Bentuk dan Makna,* transl. Lesmana (Yogjakarta: LKIS, 1995), pp. 120–141.

6. See Allan Samson, "Conception of Politics, Power, and Ideology in Contemporary Indonesia," in *Political Power and Communication in Indonesia,* ed. Karel D. Jackson and Lucian W. Pye, pp. 221–222 (Berkeley and Los Angeles: University of California Press, 1978).

7. For more details on Parmusi, please see Ken Ward, *The Foundation of The Partai Muslimin Indonesia* (Ithaca, N.Y.: Cornell Modern Indonesia Project, 1970).

8. Samson, "Conceptions of Politics," pp. 221–222.

9. See Boland, *The Struggle,* pp. 153, 159.

10. See for example R. William Liddle, *Leadership and Culture in Indonesian Politics* (Sydney: Allen and Unwin, 1996); Mahfud MD, *Politik Hukum di Indonesia* (Jakarta: LP3ES, 1998); Bahtiar Effendy, "Reformasi Konstitusi sebagai Prasyarat Demokratisasi: Pengalaman Indonesia," *Analisis CSIS* 4 (2000); Guy J. Pauker, "Policy Implication of Political

Institutionalization and Leadership Change in Southeast Asia," *Asian Affairs: An American Review* 13, no. 3 (1986).

11. The post–New Order Islamic parties are of two types. First are those parties that put Islam as their basis (PPP, PBB, PK, PNU, PKU, PSII, Partai Masyumi). Second are parties that have most of their constituents drawn from particular Muslim organizations, for example, PKB (NU) and PAN (Muhammadiyah). See Arskal Salim, *Partai Islam dan Relasi Agama Negara* (Jakarta: Puslit dan JPPR, 1999).

12. See Umar Basalim, *Pro-Kontra Piagam Jakarta Di Era Reformasi* (Jakarta: Pustaka Indonesia Satu, 2002); Denny Indrayana, "Indonesian Constitutional Reform 1999–2002: An Evaluation of Constitution-Making in Transition" (PhD thesis, the University of Melbourne, 2005).

13. See "Risalah Rapat Pleno ke-27 Panitia Ad Hoc I Badan Pekerja MPR," *Buku Kedua Jilid 3 Risalah Rapat Panitia Ad Hoc I Badan Pekerja MPR RI ke-21 s.d 30 tanggal 28 Maret 2002 s.d 19 Juni 2002 Masa Sidang Tahunan MPR RI tahun 2002* (Jakarta: Sekretariat Jenderal MPR RI, 2002), pp. 392, 397.

14. "Duet Mega-Hamzah Bisa Pecah Karena Piagam Jakarta," *Koran Tempo,* 21 September 2001; "Wapres: Piagam Jakarta Tak Akan Masuk dalam UUD 1945," *Suara Pembaruan,* 20 September 2001.

15. See "Risalah Rapat Pleno ke-3 Panitia Ad Hoc I Badan Pekerja MPR," *Buku Kedua Jilid 1 Risalah Rapat Panitia Ad Hoc I Badan Pekerja MPR RI ke-1 s.d 10 tanggal 11 Januari 2002 s.d 5 Maret 2002 Masa Sidang Tahunan MPR RI tahun 2002* (Jakarta: Sekretariat Jenderal MPR RI, 2002), p. 106.

16. See "Risalah Rapat Pleno ke-17 Panitia Ad Hoc I Badan Pekerja MPR," *Buku Kedua Jilid 2 Risalah Rapat Panitia Ad Hoc I Badan Pekerja MPR RI ke-11 s.d 20 tanggal 11 Maret 2002 s.d 27 Maret 2002 Masa Sidang Tahunan MPR RI tahun 2002* (Jakarta: Sekretariat Jenderal MPR RI, 2002), pp. 340, 343.

17. See "Risalah Rapat Pleno Perumusan Panitia Ad Hoc I," pp. 161–162, 181–182.

18. See "Risalah Rapat Pleno ke-27," pp. 405–406.

19. Cf. Tim Lindsey, "Indonesian Constitutional Reform: Muddling Towards Democracy," *Singapore Journal of International & Comparative Law* 6 (2002): p. 270.

20. Lukman Hakim Saifuddin, interview with the author, 13 February 2004.

21. See Nandang Burhanuddin, *Penegakan Syariat Islam menurut Partai Keadilan* (Jakarta: Al-Jannah, 2003), pp. 119–127.

22. See "Pendapat Akhir Fraksi Partai Bulan Bintang Terhadap Rancangan Putusan MPR RI Hasil Sidang Tahunan MPR RI 2001," in *Memperjuangkan Syariat Islam: Kumpulan Pidato Fraksi Partai Bulan Bintang Pada Sidang Tahunan Majelis Permusyawaratan Rakyat Republik Indonesia Tahun 2000–2002* (Jakarta: Sekretariat Fraksi PBB MPR RI, 2003), pp. 90–92.

23. Hamdan Zoelva, interview with the author, 16 February 2004. Cf. Aharon Layish,

"The Contribution of the Modernists to the Secularization of Islamic Law," *Middle Eastern Studies* 24 (1978): pp. 263–277.

24. Hamdan Zoelva, interview. Other proponents of *shariʻa* in Indonesia, such as Majelis Mujahidin Indonesia, Front Pembela Islam, Hizbut Tahrir, and Laskar Jihad, would vehemently disagree with Zoelva's statement. For more information on the *shariʻa* views of these Islamic groups, see for instance Jamhari and Jajang Jahroni, eds., *Gerakan Salafi Radikal di Indonesia* (Jakarta: Rajagrafindo Persada, 2004); Indonesian Centre for Islam and Pluralism, "Islam and Peace Building in Indonesia: The Analysis of Radical Movement and Their Implication for Security-Development Prospects" (Jakarta: ICIP-JICA, 2004); Khamami Zada, *Islam Radikal: Pergulatan Ormas-Ormas Islam Garis Keras di Indonesia* (Jakarta: Teraju, 2002).

25. See El-Fadl, *Islam and the Challenge,* p. 36; Cf. my working definition of *shariʻa* in chapter 1.

26. In a discussion held by the AsiaLink, the University of Melbourne, 15 February 2003, Hasyim Muzadi, chairman of NU, explained the stance of NU opposing the insertion of seven words into Article 29 of the constitution. He said that NU does not expect *shariʻa* to be codified as state law, but merely as communal directives for Muslims.

27. See "NU Tolak Piagam Jakarta," *Suara Pembaruan,* 12 September 2001; "Tiga Ormas Islam Tolak Piagam Jakarta," *Media Indonesia,* 30 May 2002; "Muhammadiyah Lega, Pasal 29 Tetap", *Media Indonesia,* 12 August 2002.

Chapter 11. The Failure of Amendment

1. "Risalah Rapat Pleno ke-44 Panitia Ad Hoc I Badan Pekerja MPR," *Buku Kedua Jilid 3C Risalah Rapat-Rapat Panitia Ad Hoc Badan Pekerja MPR* (Jakarta: Sekretariat Jenderal MPR RI, 2000), pp. 541–542.

2. "Risalah Rapat Pleno ke-17 Panitia Ad Hoc I Badan Pekerja MPR," *Buku Kedua Jilid 2 Risalah Rapat Panitia Ad Hoc I Badan Pekerja MPR RI ke-11 s.d 20 tanggal 11 Maret 2002 s.d 27 Maret 2002 Masa Sidang Tahunan MPR RI Tahun 2002* (Jakarta: Sekretariat Jenderal MPR RI, 2002), pp. 356–357.

3. "Risalah Rapat Pleno ke-27 Panitia Ad Hoc I Badan Pekerja MPR," *Buku Kedua Jilid 3 Risalah Rapat Panitia Ad Hoc I Badan Pekerja MPR RI ke-21 s.d 30 tanggal 28 Maret 2002 s.d 19 Juni 2002 Masa Sidang Tahunan MPR RI Tahun 2002* (Jakarta: Sekretariat Jenderal MPR RI, 2002), p. 393.

4. See "Pemandangan Umum Fraksi Partai Bulan Bintang MPR RI terhadap Hasil-Hasil Badan Pekerja Majelis dan Usul Pembentukan Komisi-Komisi Majelis pada Sidang Komisi A," in *Memperjuangkan Syariat Islam: Kumpulan Pidato Fraksi Partai Bulan Bintang Pada Sidang Tahunan Majelis Permusyawaratan Rakyat Republik Indonesia Tahun 2000–2002*

(Jakarta: Sekretariat Fraksi PBB MPR RI, 2003), pp. 17–18; Cf. also "Pendapat Akhir Fraksi Partai Bulan Bintang Majelis Permusyawaratan Rakyat Republik Indonesia Terhadap Hasil Sidang-Sidang Komisi Tahun 2000," in *Memperjuangkan Syariat Islam,* pp. 43–45.

5. See "Risalah Rapat Pleno ke-17," pp. 335–337.

6. See Q. 2:183 and Q. 2:178.

7. See "Risalah Rapat Perumusan Panitia Ad Hoc I Badan Pekerja MPR RI," *Buku Kes-atu Jilid I: Risalah Rapat Tertutup Risalah Rapat Perumusan Panitia Ad Hoc I Badan Pekerja MPR RI ke-1 s.d 4 tanggal 3 s.d 6 April 2002 Masa Sidang Tahunan MPR RI Tahun 2002* (Jakarta: Sekretariat Jenderal MPR RI, 2002), pp. 169–170.

8. For further details, please see Ibn Rushd, *Bidaya al-mujtahid wa-nihaya al-muqtasid* (Bayrut, Lubnan: Dar al-Ma'rifa, 1986).

9. For further discussion on *wasiyya* see for instance Abdulaziz Mohammed Zaid, *The Islamic Law of Bequest* (London: Scorpion, 1986).

10. "Risalah Rapat Pleno ke-27," pp. 411–412.

11. "Risalah Rapat Pleno ke-27," p. 427.

12. "Risalah Sinkronisasi ke-4 Panitia Ad Hoc I Badan Pekerja MPR RI," *Buku Kesatu Jilid 2 Risalah Rapat Sinkronisasi Panitia Ad Hoc I Badan Pekerja MPR RI* ke-1 s.d 8 tang-gal 27 s.d 30 Juni Masa Sidang Tahunan MPR RI Tahun 2002 (Jakarta: Sekretariat Jenderal MPR RI, 2002), p. 221.

13. See "Risalah Rapat Pleno ke-17," pp. 365–366.

14. See "Risalah Rapat Pleno ke-27," pp. 417–418; "Risalah Sinkronisasi ke-4," pp. 223–224.

15. See "Risalah Rapat Pleno ke-38 Panitia Ad Hoc I Badan Pekerja MPR RI," *Buku Kedua Jilid 4 Risalah Rapat Panitia Ad Hoc I Badan Pekerja MPR RI ke-31 s.d 38 Tanggal 20 Juni 2002 s.d 25 Juli 2002 Masa Sidang Tahunan MPR RI Tahun 2002* (Jakarta: Sekretariat Jenderal MPR RI, 2002), p. 535.

16. See "Risalah Rapat Paripurna ke-3 (Lanjutan) Sidang Tahunan MPR Tahun 2002," *Buku Keempat Risalah Rapat Paripurna MPR RI ke-1 s.d 7 Tanggal 1 s.d 11 Agustus 2002 Masa Sidang Tahunan MPR RI Tahun 2002* (Jakarta: Sekretariat Jenderal MPR RI, 2002), p. 297.

17. See "Risalah Rapat Komisi A ke-3 Sidang Tahunan MPR RI," *Buku Kelima Jilid I Risalah Rapat Komisi A MPR RI ke-1 s.d 5 Tanggal 4 s.d 8 Agustus 2002 Masa Sidang Tahu-nan MPR RI Tahun 2002* (Jakarta: Sekretariat Jenderal, 2002), p. 324; and "Risalah Rapat Paripurna ke-6 Sidang Tahunan MPR Tahun 2002," *Buku Kelima Jilid I Risalah Rapat Komisi A MPR RI ke-1 s.d 5 Tanggal 4 s.d 8 Agustus 2002 Masa Sidang Tahunan MPR RI Tahun 2002* (Jakarta: Sekretariat Jenderal MPR RI, 2002), p. 528.

18. Asnawi Latief, interview with the author, 18 February 2004.

19. For further information on activities of Hartono Mardjono and Abdul Qadir Djae-lani, see http://www.tokohindonesia.com/ensiklopedi/h/hartono-mardjono/index.shtml and www.pdat.co.id/hg/apasiapa/html/A/ads,20030617-29,A.html.

20. See "Risalah Rapat Pleno ke-27," p. 418.

21. Asnawi Latief, interview.

22. See "Risalah Rapat Pleno ke-44," p. 531.

23. See "Fraksi Reformasi Ajukan Konsep Baru Pasal 29," *Republika,* 5 November 2001.

24. For discussion on the Medina Charter and interpretation of it as the first constitution for multi-ethnic and religious groups, see W. Montgomery Watt, *Muhammad at Medina* (London: Oxford University Press, 1956).

25. See "Risalah Rapat Pleno ke-17," pp. 330–332.

26. See "Risalah Rapat Pleno ke-17," p. 369.

27. Mutammimul Ula, interview with the author, 17 February 2004.

28. A. M. Fatwa, public discussion, University of Melbourne, Australia, 26 July 2002.

29. See Nandang Burhanuddin, *Penegakan Syariat Islam menurut Partai Keadilan* (Jakarta: Al-Jannah, 2003); Untung Wahono, *Penegakan Syariat Islam dan Koalisi Partai* (Jakarta: Pustaka Tarbiatuna, 2003).

30. See his interview "Agama Perlu dalam Berpolitik," *Jawa Pos,* 4 November 2001; see also "PK: Piagam Madinah Solusi Amandemen," *Jawa Pos,* 5 November 2001; Cf. also Hidayat Nur Wahid, "Upaya Wujudkan Konstitusi yang Adil dan Demokratis: Kasus Amandemen Pasal 29 Ayat 1 UUD 1945," *Republika,* 29 June 2002; *Demokrasi Madinah: Model Demokrasi Cara Rasulullah* (Jakarta: Republika, 2003), pp. 83–92.

31. See Hidayat Nur Wahid's interview in Burhanuddin, *Penegakan Syariat,* p. 157.

32. Yusuf Muhammad, interview with the author, 28 February 2004.

33. See "Risalah Rapat Perumusan," p. 166.

34. "Risalah Rapat Pleno ke-27," p. 402.

35. See "Risalah Rapat Pleno ke-27," p. 428.

36. See "Risalah Rapat Pleno ke-27," p. 417.

37. See "Risalah Sinkronisasi ke-4," pp. 225–226.

38. "Risalah Sinkronisasi ke-4," p. 236.

39. "Risalah Sinkronisasi ke-4," p. 237.

40. "Risalah Sinkronisasi ke-4," pp. 237–238.

41. "Risalah Sinkronisasi ke-4," p. 240.

42. "Risalah Sinkronisasi ke-4," p. 242.

43. Zein Badjeber, interview with the author, 16 February 2004.

44. Gregorius Seto Harianto, interview with the author, 18 February 2004.

45. Cf. *Panduan Dalam Memasyarakatkan Undang-Undang Dasar Negara Republik Indonesia Tahun 1945: Latar Belakang, Proses dan Hasil Perubahan* (Jakarta: Sekretariat Jenderal MPR RI, 2003), p. 220.

46. For further details on this issue, see Muhammad Sirozi, "Secular-Religious Debates on the Indonesian National Education System: Colonial Legacy and a Search for National Identity in Education," *Intercultural Education* 15, no. 2 (June 2004): pp. 123–139.

47. "Risalah Rapat Paripurna ke-6 Lanjutan-2 Sidang Tahunan MPR Tahun 2002," *Buku Keempat Risalah Rapat Paripurna MPR RI ke-1 s.d 7 Tanggal 1 s.d 11 Agustus 2002 Masa Sidang Tahunan MPR RI Tahun 2002* (Jakarta: Sekretariat Jenderal MPR RI, 2002), p. 743.

48. "Risalah Rapat Paripurna ke-6 Lanjutan-2," p. 748.

49. "Risalah Rapat Paripurna ke-6 Lanjutan-2," p. 749. Seven members of PK were Mutammimul Ula, Mashadi, Syamsul Balda, Irwan Prayitno, Zirlyrosa Jamil, Abdul Roqib, and T. B. Soemandjaja. Later, Nurdiati Akma, a member from PAN (F-Reformasi), and Abduh Paddare from the F-PPP followed PK's stance.

50. The overall votes were around 11 percent: the PPP got 8.15 percent, while the PBB only tallied 2.62 percent. See "Rekapitulasi Perolehan Suara Sah Untuk DPR RI," at http://www.kpu.go.id/suara/hasilsuara_dpr_sah.php (accessed 8 December 2005).

Chapter 12. Limiting Human Rights

1. Tim Lindsey, "Indonesian Constitutional Reform: Muddling Towards Democracy," *Singapore Journal of International & Comparative Law* 6 (2002): p. 253.

2. See "Risalah Rapat Pleno ke-43 Panitia Ad Hoc I Badan Pekerja MPR," *Buku Kedua Jilid 3C Risalah Rapat-Rapat Panitia Ad Hoc Badan Pekerja MPR* (Jakarta: Sekretariat Jenderal MPR RI, 2000), pp. 7, 26. Additionally, Hamdan Zoelva of the F-PBB stated that constitutional provisions on human rights were enough and no further legislation on human rights were necessary since, according to him, lower-level regulations were often manipulated to control and to curb people's rights.

3. See "Risalah Rapat Pleno ke-43 Panitia Ad Hoc I Badan Pekerja MPR," pp. 5, 26.

4. Nadirsyah Hosen, "Syari'ah and Constitutional Reform in Indonesia (1999–2002)" (PhD dissertation, National University of Singapore, 2005), p. 191.

5. Hosen, "Syari'ah and Constitutional Reform," p. 191.

6. See "Risalah Rapat Komisi A ke-5 Sidang Tahunan MPR," *Risalah Persidangan Majelis Permusyawaratan Rakyat RI 2000* [CD] (Jakarta: Setjen MPR RI and the British Council, 2000), p. 16.

7. See Hosen, "Syari'ah and Constitutional Reform," p. 193.

8. See Hyung-Jun Kim, "The Changing Interpretation of Religious Freedom in Indonesia," *Journal of Southeast Asian Studies* 29, no. 2 (September 1998): pp. 357–370.

9. Cf. Ridarson Galingging, "MUI Fatwa Negates Freedom of Religion, Human Rights," *Jakarta Post,* 12 August 2005.

10. Yusman Roy finally was sentenced to two years in prison for inspiring hatred. He was acquitted of a more serious charge of despoiling religion (Article 156A of the Penal Law). An expert witness, Ulil Abshar Abdalla, who is also the coordinator of the Liberal Islam Network (JIL), appeared before the court to argue that Roy's practice did not deviate

from Islamic teaching. See "Prosecutor seeks three years for 'heretic' Muslim cleric," *The Jakarta Post*, 19 August, 2005; See also "Cleric sentenced to two years for sparking hatred," *The Jakarta Post*, 31 August 2005.

11. Imam Abu Hanifa (d. 765) was an important Islamic scholar and jurist and is considered the founder of the Hanafi *madhhab*, which is now largely subscribed to by Muslims in Turkey and South Asia.

12. A *fatwa* of the MUI that declared Ahmadiyya a heretical sect had already been issued earlier in the 1980s. For a recent study on these *fatwa*, see Piers Gillespie, "Current Issues in Indonesian Islam: Analyzing the 2005 Council of Indonesian Ulama Fatwa No. 7 Opposing Pluralism, Liberalism and Secularism," *Journal of Islamic Studies* 18, no. 3 (2007).

Chapter 13. The Institutionalization of *Zakat*

1. See Farishta G. de Zayas. *The Law and Philosophy of Zakat: The Islamic Social Welfare System* (Damascus: al-Jadidah Printing Press, 1960); Mahmoud Abu-Saud, *Fiqh Al-Zakat Al-Mu'asir* (East Burnham, Bucks, UK: Oxford Publishing, 1989).

2. Those entitled to receive *zakat* are listed in Q. 9:60. "The alms are only for the poor and the needy, and those who collect them, and those whose hearts are to be reconciled, and to free the captives and the debtors, and the cause of Allah, and (for) the wayfarers: a duty imposed by Allah. Allah is All-knowing, Wise."

3. For further details, see for example Abdul Rehman Ansari, *Zakaat, the Religious Tax of Islam* (Durban, South Africa: Premier Press, 1973).

4. See Jamal Malik, *Colonialization of Islam: Dissolution of Traditional Institutions in Pakistan* (New Delhi: Manohar, 1996), p. 85.

5. Timur Kuran, "Islamic Redistribution through Zakat: Historical Record and Modern Realities," in *Poverty and Charity in Middle Eastern Contexts,* ed. Michael Bonner, Mine Ener, and Amy Singer, p. 277 (Albany: State University of New York Press, 2003).

6. See A. T. Abu Kuraysha, *Al-Zaka wa al-Tanmiya* (Cairo, 1999), as quoted in A. Zysow, "Zakat," in *The Encyclopaedia of Islam,* New Edition, vol. XI (2002), p. 420.

7. Kuran, "Islamic Redistribution," pp. 275–276.

8. Q. 9:60. See note 2 above.

9. Q. 9:103. "Take alms of their wealth, wherewith you may purify them and may make them grow."

10. See Suliman Bashear, "On the Origins and Development of the Meaning of Zakat in Early Islam," *Arabica* 40 (1993): pp. 84–113.

11. See Jonathan Benthall, "Financial Worship: The Qur'anic Injunction to Almsgiving," *Journal of the Royal Anthropological Institute* 5 (March 1999): pp. 29–30; Zakiah Daradjat, *Zakat: Pembersih Harta Dan* (Jakarta: YPI Ruhana, 1991).

12. See Timur Kuran, "The Economic Impact of Islamic Fundamentalism," in *Funda-*

mentalisms and the State: Remaking Polities, Economies and Militance, ed. M. Marty and S. Appleby, p. 318 (Chicago: University of Chicago Press, 1993).

13. See Josep-Antoni Ybarra, "The Zaqat in Muslim Society: An Analysis of Islamic Economic Policy," *Social Science Information* 35 (1996): pp. 643–656; See also Safwan Idris, *Gerakan Zakat dalam Pemberdayaan Ekonomi Umat: Pendekatan Transformatif* (Jakarta: Cita Putra Bangsa, 1997).

14. See Benthall, "Financial Worship," p. 29; Zysow, "Zakat," p. 420.

15. Zysow, "Zakat," pp. 418–419.

16. Zysow, "Zakat," p. 419.

17. See for example Ann E. Mayer, "Islamization and Taxation in Pakistan," in *Islamic Reassertion in Pakistan: The Application of Islamic Laws in a Modern State,* ed. Anita M. Weiss, pp. 59–77 (New York: Syracuse University Press, 1986); Grace Clark, "Pakistan's Zakat and 'Ushr as a Welfare System," in *Islamic Reassertion in Pakistan: The Application of Islamic Laws in a Modern State,* ed. Anita M. Weiss, pp. 79–95 (Syracuse, N.Y.: Syracuse University Press, 1986); Dimitri B. Novossyolov, "The Islamization of Welfare in Pakistan," in *Russia's Muslim Frontiers: New Directions in Cross-Cultural Analysis,* ed. Dale F. Eickel-man, pp. 160–174 (Bloomington and Indianapolis: Indiana University Press, 1993); Malik, *Colonialization of Islam,* pp. 85–119; Gilles Kepel, *Jihad: The Trail of Political Islam,* trans. Anthony F. Roberts (Cambridge, Mass.: The Belknap Press of Harvard University, 2002), pp. 98–105.

18. It must be acknowledged that the practice of *zakat* in Pakistan has distributed resources from those better off to those worse off, and so has achieved some reduction in measured income inequality. However, the amount of change is generally small. See Geoffrey A. Jehle, "Zakat and Inequality: Some Evidence from Pakistan," *The Review of Income and Wealth* 40 (June 1994): pp. 205–216; Cf. Clark, "Pakistan's Zakat," pp. 93–94.

19. Kepel, *Jihad: The Trail,* p. 102.

20. Novossyolov, "The Islamization of Welfare," p. 160.

21. Mayer, Islamization and Taxation," pp. 71–72.

22. Mayer, Islamization and Taxation," p. 72.

23. Mayer, Islamization and Taxation," p. 72.

24. See Kepel, *Jihad: The Trail,* p. 102.

25. Mayer, "Islamization and Taxation," p. 73.

26. Mayer, "Islamization and Taxation," p. 62.

27. Mayer, "Islamization and Taxation," p. 64.

28. Mayer, "Islamization and Taxation," p. 71. *Zakat* evasion was also observable in Kedah, Malaysia, from 1968 to 1978. In this case, evasion was largely simple reluctance on the part of some farmers to pay *zakat,* for various reasons. For further details see James C. Scott, "Resistance without Protest and without Organization: Peasant Opposition to the Islamic Zakat and the Christian Tithe," *Comparative Studies in Society and History* 29 (July 1987): pp. 417–452.

29. Malik, *Colonialization of Islam,* p. 104–105.

30. Novossyolov, "The Islamization of Welfare," pp. 168–171.

Chapter 14. Managing the Collection of *Zakat*

1. See Christiaan Snouck Hurgronje, *Nasihat-Nasihat C. Snouck Hurgronje Semasa Kepegawaiannya kepada Pemerintah Hindia Belanda 1880–1936,* trans. Sukarsi, vol. VII (Jakarta: INIS, 1992), pp. 1323–1379. This hereafter will be referred to as *Nasihat-Nasihat* VII.

2. *Nasihat-Nasihat* VII, p. 1325.

3. G. P. Rouffaer, "Vorstenlanden," *Adatrechtbundels,* XXXIV: *Java en Madoera* ('s-Gravenhage: Martinus Nijhoff, 1931), p. 309. I thank Merle Ricklefs for pointing out to me this particular piece and translating it from Dutch.

4. These letters were compiled and edited by E. Gobee and C. Adriannse, *Ambtelijk Adviezen van C. Snouck Hurgronje 1889–1936* ('s-Gravenhage: Martinus Nijhoff, 1957) vol. II, chapter XXVIII on *djakat en pitrah.* I am referring here to its Indonesian version, *Nasihat-Nasihat* VII, pp. 1323–1379.

5. As an official advisor to the Office for Indigenous Affairs (Het Kantoor voor Inlandsche zaken), Snouck Hurgronje advised the government of Netherlands East Indies in various parts of Java on *zakat* from 1889 to 1906.

6. *Nasihat-Nasihat* VII, pp. 1364, 1376; Cf. Karel A. Steenbrink, *Beberapa Aspek Tentang Islam di Indonesia Abad ke-19* (Jakarta: Bulan Bintang, 1984), p. 230.

7. For general discussion on Snouck Hurgronje's influence over the colonial Islamic policy, please see Harry J. Benda, "Christian Snouck Hurgronje and the Foundations of Dutch Islamic Policy in Indonesia," *The Journal of Modern History* 30 (December 1958).

8. See *Nasihat-Nasihat* VII, p. 1348.

9. See *Nasihat-Nasihat* VII, p. 1377.

10. See *Nasihat-Nasihat* VII, p. 1351.

11. See *Nasihat-Nasihat* VII, pp. 1358–1359.

12. B. J. Boland, *The Struggle of Islam in Modern Indonesia* (The Hague: Martinus Nijhoff, 1982), pp. 9–10.

13. Andi Lolo Tonang, "Beberapa Pemikiran tentang Mekanisme Badan Amil Zakat," in *Zakat dan Pajak,* ed. B. Wiwoho, p. 262 (Jakarta: PT Bina Rena Pariwara, 1992).

14. Under the leadership of Mohammad Dachlan (1968–1971), the MORA set out to ground all its religious programs in the framework of the Jakarta Charter. See his speech delivered in the commemoration of the Jakarta Charter on 29 June 1968. This speech can be found at "Piagam Djakarta Sumber Hukum Mendjiwai U.U.D. 1945," *Kiblat,* no. 3–4/XVI.

15. See Tonang, "Beberapa Pemikiran," p. 264.

16. See Decree of Minister of Religion 4/1968 on the Establishment of Badan Amil Zakat (Zakat Agency) and his Decree 5/1968 on the Foundation of Baitul Mal (Islamic Treasury).

17. See his speech delivered at the Isra' Mi'raj (Prophet's Ascension) Celebration on 26 October 1968. The full text of Soeharto's speech can be found in *Pedoman Zakat* (Jakarta: Proyek Pembinaan Zakat dan Wakaf, 1992/1993), pp. 403–409.

18. Presidential Decree no. 07/PRIN/10/1968 dated 31 October 1968. The three military officers were Major-General Alamsyah, Colonel Azwar Hamid, and Colonel Ali Afandi. See Taufik Abdullah, "Zakat Collection and Distribution in Indonesia," in *The Islamic Voluntary Sector in Southeast Asia,* ed. Mohammed Ariff, p. 51 (Singapore: ISEAS, 1991).

19. Presidential letter no. B.133/Pres/11/1969 dated 28 November 1968.

20. See Ministerial Instruction of Minister of Religion no. 16/1968, dated 28 October 1968.

21. Abdullah, "Zakat Collection," p. 69.

22. *Sedekah* is a kind of Islamic alms. While *zakat* is obligatory, *sedekah* is voluntary.

23. Muslim civil servants in the Corps of Indonesian State Employees (KORPRI) were required to contribute almsgiving (*sedekah*) from fifty rupiahs to one thousand rupiahs per person depending on their employment strata. By 1991, YABMP had collected more than US$80 million and built more than four hundred mosques. See Bahtiar Effendy, *Islam dan Negara: Transformasi Pemikiran dan Praktik Politik Islam di Indonesia* (Jakarta: Paramadina, 1998), p. 305.

24. Abdullah, "Zakat Collection," p. 60.

25. Abdullah, "Zakat Collection," p. 61.

26. According to research conducted by the Public Interest Research and Advocacy Center (PIRAC) in eleven cities across Indonesia, 66 percent of Muslims in fact pay *zakat* to the local committee close to their home and 28 percent of them give *zakat* payment directly to eligible recipients. See *Pola Kecenderungan Masyarakat Berzakat* (Jakarta: PIRAC, 2002), pp. 17–18.

27. See Effendy, *Islam dan Negara,* p. 300.

28. It is worth noting here that on one occasion in 1991, Munawir Sjadzali (minister of religious affairs) and K. H. Hasan Basri (chairman of Indonesian Council of Ulama) consulted with President Soeharto. Both requested President Soeharto to issue either a presidential decree (*keppres*) or a presidential instruction (*inpres*) on *zakat* management and asked if Soeharto would be able to again act as an official national *amil.* Soeharto refused this request and said it would be better administered by the joint decree of two ministers. See *Pedoman Pembinaan BAZIS: Hasil Pertemuan Nasional I BAZIS se-Indonesia tanggal 3–4 Maret 1992* (Jakarta: Dirjen Bimas Islam Urusan Haji Departemen Agama, 1992), pp. 79, 83.

29. The full text of these joint ministerial decrees and ministerial instructions can be found in Cholid Fadlullah, *Mengenal Hukum ZIS dan Pengamalannya di DKI Jakarta* (Jakarta: BAZIS DKI, 1993), pp. 260–263, 316–323. Also see *Pedoman Pembinaan,* pp. 116–131.

30. Mukhtar Zarkasyi, interview with the author, 11 September 2003.

Chapter 15. Legislating Zakat Payment

1. No less than the minister of religion, Majelis Ulama Indonesia (MUI), and eleven provincial *zakat* agencies (West Java, North Sumatra, East Java, West Kalimantan, South Sulawesi, West Sumatra, East Kalimantan, Yogyakarta, Central Kalimantan, Central Java, and North Sulawesi) supported the idea of National Zakat Board. See *Pedoman Pembinaan BAZIS: Hasil Pertemuan Nasional I BAZIS se-Indonesia tanggal 3–4 Maret 1992* (Jakarta: Dirjen Bimas Islam Urusan Haji Departemen Agama, 1992), pp. 90–104.

2. See Rudini's remark delivered at the opening ceremony of the national meeting of BAZIS, Jakarta, 3 March 1992, in *Pedoman Pembinaan,* p. 87.

3. They were Dompet Dhuafa Republika, BAZIS DKI Jakarta, Baitul Mal PT Pupuk Kujang, Baitul Mal PT Pupuk Kaltim, Baitul Mal Pertamina, Telkom Jakarta, Bapekis Bank Bumi Daya, LKS-Bank Muamalat Indonesia, Baperohis Hotel Indonesia, PT. Internusa Hasta Buana, and Sekolah Tinggi Ekonomi Indonesia (STEI) Jakarta.

4. See *Direktori Organisasi Pengelola Zakat di Indonesia* (Jakarta: FOZ, 2001), p. xi.

5. The bill had been drafted in February 1999 by a team formed by the MORA, which included representatives and figures from various institutions: Department of Justice, Department of Finance, MUI, universities, the FOZ, and several legislative members. Mukhtar Zarkasyi, interview with the author, 11 September 2003; Miftahul Munir, interview with the author, 27 August 2003.

6. Mukhtar Zarkasyi, interview.

7. These reasons are extracted from Remarks of the Minister of Religion at the Plenary Session of DPR on the Bill of Zakat Administration, Jakarta, 26 July 1999, and from recommendations made in the First Congress of the FOZ in Jakarta, 7–9 January 1999.

8. Mukhtar Zarkasyi, interview.

9. Mukhtar Zarkasyi, interview; Isbir Fadly, interview with the author, 3 September 2003.

10. "Risalah Rapat Jum'at 3 September 1999," *Pembicaraan Tingkat III Pembahasan RUU tentang Pengelolaan Zakat* (Jakarta: Sekretariat Komisi VII Sekjen DPR RI, 1999), pp. 20–25.

11. "Risalah Rapat Jum'at 3 September 1999," pp. 26–27.

12. Some *zakat* agencies, such as Dompet Dhuafa, BAZIS DKI Jakarta, and PKPU, have organized activities intended to raise Muslims' awareness of *zakat* payment to the agencies and to inform Muslims about where the benefits of *zakat* go. For further details, visit their websites: www.dompetdhuafa.org, www.bazisdki.go.id, and www.pkpu.or.id.

13. The authority of the president to settle disputes between ministries is based on Presidential Decree no. 188/1998.

14. "Risalah Rapat Jum'at 3 September 1999."

15. Mukhtar Zarkasyi, interview.

16. See records made by the FOZ on the meeting between the FOZ and the DPR on 28 January 2002. A copy of these records is available with the author.

17. Ismail Yusanto, interview with the author, 27 August 2003.

18. This information was obtained from "Presentations of FOZ in the Meeting between FOZ and the Commission Six of DPR," Jakarta, 28 January 2002. A copy of this presentation is available with the author.

19. For further details, please see *Hasil Rumusan Musyawarah Nasional III Forum Zakat* (Jakarta: FOZ, 2003).

20. See Jamal Do'a and Sunarsip presentations, "Urgensi Amandemen Undang-Undang nomor 38/1999 tentang Pengelolaan Zakat dalam Konteks Pengentasan Kemiskinan." in *Hasil Rumusan Musyawarah Nasional III Forum Zakat* (Jakarta: FOZ, 2003), pp. 75–83.

21. See papers presented by Tulus, director of *zakat* and *wakaf* at the Ministry of Religious Affairs, and by Wahiduddin Adam, director of harmonization of regulations at the Ministry of Justice, in *Hasil Rumusan Musyawarah Nasional III Forum Zakat* (Jakarta: FOZ, 2003), pp. 75–83.

22. See research findings reported by Murasa Sarkaniputra et al., "Respon Institusi Pengelola Zakat terhadap Efektivitas Undang-Undang no. 38 tahun 1999" (Jakarta: Lembaga Penelitian UIN Syarif Hidayatullah, 2002/2003).

Chapter 16. Overlapping *Zakat* and Taxation

1. B. Wiwoho, ed., *Zakat dan Pajak* (Jakarta: PT Bina Rena Pariwara, 1992), pp. 277–292.

2. Masdar F. Mas'udi, *Agama Keadilan: Risalah Zakat (Pajak) dalam Islam* (Jakarta: P3M, 1991), p. xiii.

3. Mas'udi, *Agama Keadilan,* pp. 113–125.

4. Masdar F. Mas'udi, "Zakat: An Ethical Concept of Taxation and State: A Reinterpretation of Third Pillar of Islam" (unpublished paper), pp. 19–20.

5. Cf. my working definition of Islamic state in chapter 5.

6. Masdar F. Mas'udi, interview with the author, 25 August 2003.

7. See Mas'udi, "Zakat: An Ethical Concept," p. 20.

8. See Mas'udi, "Zakat: An Ethical Concept," p. 18.

9. See Mas'udi, "Zakat: An Ethical Concept," p. 21.

10. Mas'udi, interview.

11. Dawam Rahardjo, "Manajemen Zakat," in *Pedoman Pembinaan BAZIS: Hasil Pertemuan Nasional I BAZIS Se-Indonesia tanggal 3–4 Maret 1992* (Jakarta: Bimas Islam dan Urusan Haji, 1992), p. 25.

12. Rahardjo, "Manajemen Zakat," p. 25; Also Dawam Rahardjo, interview with the author, 28 August 2003.

13. See Ministerial Decree no. KEP.650/MK/11/5/1976 issued by minister of finance, Ali Wardhana, and a circular letter no. SE-11/PJ.62/1979 signed by general director of taxation, Sutadi Sukarya.

14. It is stated that "*zakat* that has been paid to the official agency is deducted from the rest of taxable profit or income of the tax payer according to applicable regulations."

15. It says, "In order to estimate the amount of taxable income of resident taxpayers or enterprises, it is not allowed to deduct . . . except *zakat* on income that is correctly paid by Muslim individuals or indigenous companies owned by Muslims to the official *zakat* agencies."

16. For a general overview of the F-Reformasi faction and government replies during the amendment to the laws of taxation, please see *Pembahasan Lima Rancangan Undang-Undang tentang Perubahan UU di Bidang Perpajakan (Buku 1B)* (Jakarta: Sekjend DPR RI, PPPI, 2000).

17. "Pelaksanaan UU Zakat Belum Bisa Diterapkan Masyarakat," *Media Indonesia,* 4 April 2002.

18. Didin Hafiduddin, interview with the author, 30 August 2003.

19. See the Decree of the General Directorate of Taxation number KEP-163/PJ/2003 on "Perlakuan Zakat atas Penghasilan dalam Penghitungan Penghasilan Kena Pajak Pajak Penghasilan."

20. M. Ikhsan, "Tithe and Tax Reduction," *The Jakarta Post,* 5 December 2001.

21. See for instance Eri Sudewo, "Mengkritisi UU Zakat," *Republika,* 23 May 2003; see also the decision made by the B Commission at the Third National Congress of the FOZ, *Hasil Rumusan Musyawarah Nasional III Forum Zakat* (Jakarta: FOZ, 2003), p. 4.

22. "*Zakat* Plan Questioned," *The Jakarta Post,* 1 December 2001.

23. "Tax Deduction of Zakat Must Apply to Non-Muslims," *The Jakarta Post,* 29 November 2001.

24. "Govt Wants to Focus on Zakat First: Minister," *The Jakarta Post,* 3 December 2001.

25. Isbir Fadly, interview with the author, 3 September 2003; Jamil, interview with the author, 18 October 2004.

26. See Didin Hafiduddin, *Zakat dalam Perekonomian Modern* (Jakarta: Gema Insani Press, 2002), p. 58.

Chapter 17. Formalizing *Shari'a* Locally Through *Ulama*

1. Harry J. Benda, "South-East Asian Islam in the Twentieth Century," in *The Cambridge History of Islam,* vol. 2, ed. P. M. Holt, Ann K. S. Lambton, and Bernard Lewis (Cambridge and New York: Cambridge University Press, 1970).

2. For further discussion on the *ulama* vs. the *uleëbalang,* please see Eugene E. Morris, "Islam and Politics in Aceh: A Study of Center-Periphery Relations in Indonesia" (PhD dissertation, Cornell University, 1983); Nazaruddin Sjamsuddin, *The Republican Revolt: A Study of the Acehnese Rebellion* (Singapore: Institute of Southeast Asian Studies, 1985).

3. Sjamsuddin, *The Republican Revolt,* p. 111.

4. On this particular account, please see M. N. El-Ibrahimy, *Peranan Tgk. M. Daud Beureu-eh dalam Pergolakan Aceh,* Revised Edition (Jakarta: Media Dakwah, 2001).

5. C. van Dijk, *Rebellion under the Banner of Islam: The Darul Islam in Indonesia* (The Hague: Martinus Nijhoff, 1981), pp. 288–289.

6. See Arskal Salim, "Shari'a From Below in Aceh (1930s–1960s): Islamic Identity and the Right to Self Determination with Comparative Reference to the Moro Islamic Liberation Front (MILF)," *Indonesia and Malay World* 32 (March 2004): p. 89.

7. For a full account of the relationship between both movements of Darul Islam in West Java and Aceh during the 1950s to early 1960s, see Sjamsuddin, *The Republican Revolt;* see also van Dijk, *Rebellion.*

8. Morris, "Islam and Politics," pp. 245–246.

9. They were Tgk. H. Abdullah Ujung Rimba (chief of the provincial Syariah Court); Tgk. H. Hasan (chief of the Provincial Office of Religious Affairs); and Drs. Tgk. H. Ismail Muhammad Syah (rector of the State Institute of Islamic Studies (IAIN) at Banda Aceh.

10. See Ismuha, *Sejarah Singkat Majelis Ulama Propinsi Daerah Istimewa Aceh* (Banda Aceh: Sekretariat Majelis *Ulama* Propinsi Daerah Istimewa Aceh, 1983), pp. 1–7. The participants of the conference are listed in the appendix (pp. 76–78).

11. See Ismuha, *Sejarah Singkat,* pp. 11–12.

12. Ismuha, *Sejarah Singkat,* p. 9.

13. The selected five members were Tgk. H. Abdullah Ujung Rimba; Tgk. H. Hasan; Drs. H. Ismail Muhammad Syah aka Ismuha; Ibrahim Husein, MA; and M. Yasin. These five figures were chosen because they lived in Banda Aceh and could meet regularly. The other two presidium members lived outside Banda Aceh: Tapak Tuan (Tgk. Zamzami Yahya) and Takengon (Tgk. Abdul Jalil).

14. Ismuha, *Sejarah Singkat,* Appendix VII, p. 104.

15. The *ulama* who joined this team were Tgk. H. Abdullah Ujung Rimba; Tgk. H. Hasan; Drs. H. Ismail Muhammad Syah; and Tgk. Hamzah Yunus, while the rest of the team comprised four military officers, a provincial legislative member, a local police official, and a local public prosecutor. See appendix IX in Ismuha, *Sejarah Singkat,* p. 112.

16. M. C. Ricklefs, *History of Modern Indonesia since c. 1200.* Third Edition (Stanford, Calif.: Stanford University Press, 2001), p. 389.

17. For details of the structure of the council of *ulama* in each regency, see *Tata Tertib/ Tata Laksana Madjlis Ulama dalam Propinsi Daerah Istimewa Atjeh dan Peraturan2 Lainnya* (Banda Aceh: Sekretariat Madjlis Ulama Propinsi Daerah Istimewa Atjeh, 1970).

18. Prior to his chairmanship of the *ulama* council, Rimba had served as a religious judge of the Syariah High Court since 1946, and this status continued until he retired in 1971. This means he had a double function for five years (1966–1971) as the chairman of *ulama* council (MPU) as well as chief of the Syariah High Court (Mahkamah Tinggi Syariah). Additionally, Rimba was appointed in 1968 as a member of the Supreme Advisory Council (DPA), and later, from 1977 to 1982, he was a Golkar representative for the People's Consultative Assembly (MPR). See Misri A. Muchsin, "Tasawwuf di Aceh dalam Abad XX: Studi Pemikiran Teungku Haji Abdullah Ujong Rimba (1907–1983)" (PhD thesis, IAIN Sunan Kalijaga Yogyakarta, 2003), pp. 136–138.

19. Before taking over the leadership of MUI of Aceh in 1982, Hasjmy was a rector of IAIN Al-Raniry Banda Aceh (1977–1982). Earlier, he was active as a government official at the provincial office of the Social Ministry from 1946 to 1956. Indeed, he was the first governor of the special territory of Aceh (1957–1964). See Sirajuddin, "Konsepsi Kenegaraan dalam Pemikiran A. Hasjmy" (MA thesis, IAIN Ar-Raniry Banda Aceh, 1999).

20. For a study of *fatwa* in Indonesia, see Atho Mudzhar, *Fatwa-fatwa Majelis Ulama Indonesia: sebuah Studi tentang Pemikiran Hukum Islam di Indonesia, 1975–1988* (Jakarta: INIS, 1993); M. B. Hooker, *Indonesian Islam: Social Change through Contemporary Fatawa* (Honolulu: University of Hawai'i Press, 2003).

21. See Badruzzaman Ismail and Yusny Saby, *Majelis Ulama Indonesia dalam Pembangunan* (Banda Aceh: MUI Propinsi DI Aceh, 1995); Majelis Permusyawaratan *Ulama, Kumpulan Fatwa-Fatwa Majelis Ulama Daerah Istimewa Aceh* (Banda Aceh: 2003).

22. See Kaoy Syah and Lukman Hakim, *Keistimewaan Aceh dalam Lintasan Sejarah: Proses Pembentukan UU no. 44/1999* (Jakarta: PB Al-Washliyyah, 2000), pp. 36–37.

23. B. J. Boland, *The Struggle of Islam in Modern Indonesia* (The Hague: Martinus Nijhoff, 1982), p. 185; Morris, "Islam and Politics," p. 285.

24. Morris, "Islam and Politics," p. 260.

25. Rodd McGibbon, "Local Politics and Leadership: Islam, Democracy and the Transformation of the Acehnese Elite," paper presented at the Conference on the Historical Background of the Aceh Problem, Singapore, 28–29 May 2004, p. 8.

26. McGibbon, "Local Politics," p. 9.

27. McGibbon, "Local Politics," p. 8.

28. *Meunasah* is a multipurpose building set up in every village in Aceh that serves not only as a center of worship but also as a meeting place for the local community.

29. See Syah and Hakim, *Keistimewaan Aceh,* pp. 49–50.

30. Tim Kell, *The Roots of Acehnese Rebellion, 1989–1992* (Ithaca, N.Y.: Cornell Modern Indonesia Project, 1995), p. 48.

31. Kell, *The Roots,* p. 45.

32. Kaoy Syah, interview with the author, 30 July 2004; Cf. McGibbon, "Local Politics," p. 13.

33. Morris, "Islam and Politics," p. 284; McGibbon, "Local Politics," p. 13.

34. See Morris, "Islam and Politics," p. 286; McGibbon, "Local Politics," p. 7.

35. See Yusny Saby, "The Ulama in Aceh: A Brief Historical Survey," *Studia Islamika Indonesian Journal for Islamic Studies* 9, no. 1 (2001): p. 21; Martin van Bruinessen, "Indonesia's *Ulama* and Politics: Caught Between Legitimising the Status Quo and Searching for Alternatives," *Prisma The Indonesian Indicator* 49 (1990): p. 52.

36. Rusjdi Ali Muhammad, *Revitalisasi Syari'at Islam di Aceh: Problem, Solusi dan Implementasi* (Jakarta: Logos, 2003), p. 79.

37. McGibbon, "Local Politics," p. 12.

38. See Karim D. Crow, "Aceh—The 'Special Territory' in North Sumatra: A Self-Fulfilling Promise?" *Journal of Muslim Minority Affairs* 20, no. 1 (2000): pp. 91–99.

39. International Crisis Group, "Aceh: Can Autonomy Stem the Conflict?" ICG Asia Report no. 18, 27 June 2001, p. 14.

40. The first study that focused on this organization was Mahmuddin, "Melacak Peran Gerakan Sipil di Aceh: Studi Gerakan Thaliban Aceh" (MA thesis, Universitas Gadjah Mada Yogyakarta, 2001). Parts of this thesis can be found in Soraya Devy et al., *Politik dan Pencerahan Peradaban* (Banda Aceh: Ar-Raniry Press, 2004), pp. 137–208.

41. See Devy, *Politik dan Pencerahan,* pp. 180–182.

42. "*Ulama* Tuntut Referendum," *Serambi Indonesia,* 16 September 1999.

43. See Devy, *Politik dan Pencerahan,* p. 181.

44. This is not to say, however, that the idea of referendum was completely ignored by every individual within the *ulama* council of Aceh. Mahmuddin, interview with the author, 28 August 2004.

45. See "Usman Hasan: Soal Penyelesaian Aceh Tegaskan Berlakunya Syariat Islam," *Kompas,* 25 July 1999.

46. McGibbon, "Local Politics," p. 18.

47. See Article 9 of Law no. 44/1999 and its elucidation. The role of *ulama* in Aceh has been further regulated in three *perdas:* (1) Perda 3/2000 on the Foundation and the Organization of the Ulama Consultative Council of the Special Province of Aceh; (2) Perda 43/2001 on the First Amendment over Perda 3/2000 on the Foundation and the Organization of the Ulama Consultative Council of the Special Province of Aceh; and (3) Qanun 9/2003 on the Functional Relationship between the Ulama Consultative Council (MPU) and the Executive, the Legislative and other Institutions.

48. For a detailed discussion on this subject, see Amirul Hadi, *Islam and State in Sumatra: A Study of Seventeenth-Century Aceh* (Leiden: Brill, 2004).

49. Mukhtar Aziz, interview with the author, 28 July 2004.

50. Muslim Ibrahim, interview with the author, 15 July 2004; Al Yasa' Abubakar, interview with the author, 30 October 2004.

51. Since 2000, the executive branch of the provincial government has issued at least ten decrees or instructions to support the implementation of *shari'a* in Aceh. For details,

see *Himpunan Undang-Undang,Keputusan Presiden, Peraturan Daerah/Qanun, Instruksi Gubernur, Edaran Gubernur Berkaitan Pelaksanaan Syariat Islam* (Banda Aceh: Dinas Syariat Islam, 2004).

52. Al Yasa' Abubakar, interview; see *Laporan Evaluasi Pelaksanaan Syariat Islam Tahun 2003* (Banda Aceh: Dinas Syariat Islam, 2003).

53. Yusni Sabi, interview with the author, 31 October 2004.

Chapter 18. *Ulama* and *Qanun* Lawmaking

1. For instance, the term *ulama* as defined in Perda 3/2000 on the Establishment and the Organization of the Ulama Consultative Council (MPU) refers first to those (rural) *ulama* who have *pesantren* or *dayah,* while the Muslim intellectual or urban *ulama* comes under the second category of *ulama.*

2. See Muslim Ibrahim, "Rekonstruksi Peran *Ulama* Aceh Masa Depan," in *Syariat di Wilayah Syariat,* ed. Fairus M. Nur, p. 249 (Banda Aceh: Dinas Syariat Islam NAD, 2002).

3. Dr. Muslim Ibrahim completed his tertiary studies mostly at Middle Eastern universities. He is currently a lecturer at IAIN Ar-Raniry of Banda Aceh and has no *dayah.* Despite this, he cannot be considered an urban *ulama* as most of his opinions reflect the traditional interpretation of Islam, the main characteristic of the rural *ulama.* His opinions can be found regularly in the local newspaper *Serambi Indonesia* under *Konsultasi Agama Islam* [Answers and Questions on Islamic Issues].

4. Daud Zamzami is the *ulama* who leads the *dayah* of Riyadus Shalihin in Aceh Besar. He also serves as chairman of the Advisory Board of the United Development Party (PPP) of Aceh.

5. Azhari Basyar, interview with the author, 14 July 2004.

6. See Article 14 of Qanun 3/2000.

7. See Article 14 of Qanun 3/2000.

8. Muslim Ibrahim, interview with the author, 15 July 2004; Fachry Anshary, interview with the author, 14 July 2004.

9. See descriptions in Article 16B of Perda 43/2001 on the First Amendment compared with Perda 3/2000 on the Foundation and the Organization of the MPU.

10. Kaoy Syah, interview with the author, 31 July 2004.

11. See Article 16A of Perda 43/2001.

12. See Article 3 of Perda 3/2000.

13. See Articles 3 through 15 of Qanun 9/2003 on the Functional Relationship between the Ulama Consultative Council (MPU) and the Executive, the Legislative and other Institutions.

14. Muslim Ibrahim, interview.

15. For further information on *ta'zir*, see Mohammed El-Awa, "*Ta'zir* in the Islamic Penal System," *Journal of Islamic and Comparative Law* 6 (1976).

16. For details on this issue, see Muhammad El-Awa, *Punishment in Islamic Law* (Indianapolis: American Trust Publishers, 1980).

17. "Caning comes into effect in Aceh on 1st day of Ramadhan," *The Jakarta Post,* 28 October 2002.

18. Hamid Sarong, interview with the author, 12 July 2004.

19. Hamid Sarong, interview.

20. See Article 1 (on General Terms) of Perda 11/2002.

21. Azhari Basyar, interview.

22. They were, among others, Teuku Safir Iskandar Wijaya, Yusni Saby, and Daniel Djuned.

23. Azhari Basyar, interview.

24. Hamid Sarong, interview.

25. On this constitutional provision, see the discussion in chapter 12.

26. Muslim Ibrahim, interview.

27. Hamid Sarong, interview.

Chapter 19. After the Tsunami

1. "15 Penjudi Dicambuk," *Serambi Indonesia,* 25 June 2005.

2. Hamid Sarong, interview with the author, 14 June 2005; Safir Wijaya, interview with the author, 17 June 2005.

3. Alyasa Abubakar, interview with the author, 18 June 2005.

4. Azwar Abubakar, in fact, issued a Governor's Decree (Peraturan Gubernur Provinsi Nanggroe Aceh Darussalam nomor 10 tahun 2005 on Petunjuk Teknis Pelaksanaan Uqubat Cambuk or the Technical Guidance of the Implementation of Caning) to signify his approval. A copy of this regulation is held by the author.

5. Among those who attended the meeting with the attorney general were Soufyan Saleh, chairman of the Provincial Mahkamah Syar'iyyah; Muslim Ibrahim, chairman of the Ulama Consultative Assembly; Badruzzaman Ismail, chairman of Aceh Adat Council; Al Yasa' Abubakar, chairman of Provincial Office of Islamic Shari'a; and the chairman of Commission E of the Provincial Legislature. Cf. "Jaksa Agung Dukung Pelaksanaan Hukuman Cambuk di Aceh," *Kompas,* 6 June 2005.

6. Muslim Ibrahim, interview with the author, 17 June 2005. See also "Jaksa Agung Dukung Hukuman Cambuk di NAD," *Republika,* 6 June 2005.

7. "Mahkamah Syar'iyah Kerja Tanpa Dana Operasional," *Serambi Indonesia,* 14 June 2005.

8. "HM Saleh Puteh: Pasca Tsunami, Mahkamah Syariah Kebanjiran Perkara Waris" at http://www.hukumonline.com/detail.asp?id=13866&cl=Wawancara (accessed on 5 December 2005).

9. See "Fatwa tentang Perlindungan Hak Atas Tanah, Hak Nasab bagi Anak Yatim, Hak Isteri dan Ahli Waris Mafqud Akibat Gempa dan Gelombang Tsunami," Appendix One of the Decree of the Ulama Consultative Assembly (MPU) number 3/2005. A copy of this *fatwa* is held by the author.

10. Soufyan Saleh, interview with the author, 15 June 2005.

11. Muslim Ibrahim, interview; Yusny Saby, interview with the author, 16 June 2005; Soufyan Saleh, interview.

12. "*Ulama* Aceh Temui Wapres Bahas Pembangunan Aceh, http://www.detiknews .com/index. php/detik.read/tahun/2005/bulan/01tgl/26; "*Ulama* Minta Dilibatkan dalam Perencanaan Aceh," http://www.hidayatullah.com/index.php?option=com_content&task =view&id=1693&Itemid=2 (accessed on 22 April 2005).

13. The full text of the blueprint on the aspects of religion, social culture, and human resources can be found in Appendix Eight of the Presidential Regulation (Peraturan Presiden) 30/2005 on *Rencana Induk Rehabilitasi dan Rekonstruksi Wilayah dan Kehidupan Masyarakat Provinsi Nanggroe Aceh Darussalam dan Kepulauan Nias Provinsi Sumatera Utara*. It can be accessed at http://www.acehmediacenter.or.id/?dir=data&file=detail&id=135.

14. "Taushiyah Silaturrahmi *Ulama-ulama* Dayah Se-Nanggroe Aceh Darussalam 8–9 April 2005," a press release issued in Banda Aceh, 10 April 2005, by Persatuan Dayah Inshafuddin, Himpunan *Ulama* Dayah Aceh and Rabithah Thaliban Aceh. A copy of this press release is held by the author.

15. "Ulama Aceh: Blue Print NAD belum Miliki 'Roh'," *Republika*, 12 April 2005.

16. Kuntoro Mangkusubroto (Javanese) currently is the chairman. Muslim Ibrahim says that although his personal nominee (whose name I have been asked not to disclose) was non-Acehnese as well, he had a good understanding of Aceh and the Acehnese. In addition, the appointment of Fuad Mardatillah, a lecturer of IAIN Banda Aceh who received his masters degree from McGill University in Canada, as deputy executive chairman on the aspects of religion and social culture was contrary to *ulama*'s wishes. Muslim Ibrahim, interview; Fuad Mardatillah, interview with the author, 16 June 2005. Moreover, the appointment of Safir Wijaya, an intellectual of IAIN who in late 2006 replaced Fuad Mardatillah, did not meet the expectation of *ulama* as well.

17. Muslim Ibrahim, interview.

Conclusion

1. Cf. Lucinda Peach, *Legislating Morality: Pluralism and Religious Identity in Lawmaking* (Oxford: Oxford University Press, 2002), p. 7.

2. Specifically, Article 28I (2) of the 1945 constitution reads: "Each person has the right to be free from discriminatory treatment in order to gain the same opportunities and benefits in the attainment of equality and justice."

3. See Rudolph Peters, "From Jurist's Law to Statute Law or What Happens When the Shari'a is Codified," in *Shaping the Current Islamic Reformation*, ed. B. A. Roberson (London: Frank Cass, 2003).

4. Sami Zubaida, *Law and Power in the Islamic World* (London and New York: IB Tauris, 2003), p. 221.

5. See B. J. Boland, *The Struggle of Islam in Modern Indonesia* (The Hague: Martinus Nijhoff, 1982), p. 189.

6. See Perda 33/2001 on the Formation, Structure and Job Description of Dinas Syariat Islam.

7. See *Laporan Evaluasi Pelaksanaan Syariat Islam Tahun 2003* (Banda Aceh: Dinas Syariat Islam, 2003).

8. See Gregory C. Kozlowski, "When the 'Way' Becomes the 'Law': Modern States and the Transformation of *Halakhah* and *Shari'a*," in *Studies in Islamic and Judaic Traditions II*, ed. William M. Brinner and Stephen D. Ricks, p. 106 (Atlanta, Ga.: Scholars Press, 1989); Cf. M. B. Hooker, "Introduction: Islamic Law in South-east Asia," *The Australian Journal of Asian Law* 4, no. 3 (2002): pp. 217–218; also cf. Ahmad Baso, *Islam Pasca-kolonial: Perselingkuhan Agama, Kolonialisme dan Liberalisme* (Bandung: Mizan, 2005).

9. See Arskal Salim, "The Influential Legacy of Dutch Islamic Policy on the Formation of Zakat (Alms) Law in Modern Indonesia," *Pacific Rim Law and Policy Journal* 15, no. 3 (2006).

10. See *Kompas*, 7 August 2002.

11. See Hidayat Nur Wahid's interview at http://www.tokohindonesia.com/ensiklopedi/h/hidayat-nur-wahid/wawancara.shtml.

12. Hamdan Zoelva, interview with the author, 16 February 2004.

13. J. Isawa Elaigwu, "The Shadow of Shari'a over Nigerian Federalism," *The Journal of Federalism* 33, no. 3 (Summer 2003): pp. 123–144. See also "Political Shari'a'?: Human Rights and Islamic Law in Northern Nigeria," *Human Rights Watch* 16, no. 9 (September 2004); Vincent O. Nmehielle, "Sharia Law in the Northern States of Nigeria: To Implement or Not to Implement, the Constitutionality Is the Question," *Human Rights Quarterly* 26 (2004): pp. 730–759.

14. See William Miles, "Muslim Ethnopolitics and Presidential Elections in Nigeria," *Journal of Muslim Minority Affairs* 20, no. 2 (2000): pp. 229–241.

15. For details on this issue, see Rose Ismail, ed., *Hudud in Malaysia: The Issues at Stake* (Kuala Lumpur: SIS Forum, 1995); Muhammad Hashim Kamali, "Punishment in Islamic Law: A Critique of the *Hudud* Bill of Kelantan, Malaysia," *Arab Law Quarterly* (1998): pp. 203–234; M. B. Hooker, "Submission to Allah: The Kelantan Syariah Criminal Code (II),

1993," in *Malaysia Islam, Society and Politics: Essays in Honour of Clive S. Kessler* (Singapore: ISEAS, 2003), pp. 80–98.

16. See *shariʻa*-related provisions in this law, such as on the application of Islamic *shariʻa* (Articles 125–127), the *shariʻa* court (Articles 128–137), the MPU or *ulama* council (Articles 138–140), the police force (Articles 207 (1 and 4)), the public prosecutor (Articles 208 (2) and 210), and human rights (Article 227 (1c)).

Glossary

Ahl al-dhimma   the people of the covenant; Jews, Christians, and others accepted as subjects under Muslim rule and entitled to legal protection in return for payment of taxes.

Ahlussunnah wal Jama'ah   derived from Arabic term (*ahl al-sunna wa al-jama'a*). Widely understood as Sunni, this term literally means 'the people of the traditional way and of the congregation of believers.' It is often described technically as 'the people who follow the Prophetic Sunna and adhere to the largest mass of the Muslims beginning with the congregation of the Companions of the Prophet Muhammad.'

Akidah   from Arabic term (*aqida*), meaning 'Islamic creeds.'

Alternative One   the original text of Article 29 of the 1945 Constitution.

Alternative Two   the proposed amendment draft to insert the 'seven words' into Article 29, making it as follow: 'the state is based on belief in One God *with the obligation to carry out Islamic shari'a for its adherents.*'

Alternative Three   another proposed amendment draft to Article 29, which states: 'the state is based on belief in One God *with the obligation to carry out religious teachings for respective believers.*'

Amil   an executing person or institution that manages the collection and distribution of zakat.

Amr ma'ruf nahy munkar   promote the good and prohibit the evil.

Baitul Mal   Islamic Treasury.

Bhinneka Tunggal Ika   a Sanskrit phrase that means 'Unity in Diversity.'

Bid'a   innovation; deviation from Islamic tradition; distinct from custom and law prescribed by the *shari'a*.

Dar al-Harb   the land of war, territory not under Islamic law and subject to conquest by Muslims.

Dar al-Islam   'abode of peace'; Islamic territory, where Islamic law is in force.

Dayah   Islamic boarding schools in Aceh; in Java, it is known as *pesantren*.

Dhimmis   'protected' or covenanted people; non-Muslim citizen afforded security of life and property in *Dar al-Islam* on payment of a poll tax (*jizya*).

Fatawa   plural of fatwa, which means 'legal opinions.'

Fatwa   religious opinion issued by a competent scholar of Islamic law.

Fiqh   Islamic jurisprudence. Literally means 'understanding.'

Fukaha (Fuqaha)   Plural of *faqih*, which means legal expert; scholar of Islamic law, jurist.

Gampong   literally means village. It is a legal community unit, which is the lowest government organization in Aceh, led by a head of village called *Keuchik*.

Hadith   Prophet's saying; collected traditions, teachings, and stories of the prophet
Muhammad, accepted as a source of Islamic doctrine and law second only to the
Qur'an.

Hajj   The pilgrimage to Mecca

Halal   permitted, lawful activities particularly foods which comply with Islamic dietary
rules.

Haqq Allah   the right of God.

Haqq al-Insan   the right of human being.

Hudud   fixed punishments for certain crimes such as adultery or fornication and theft.

'idda   legally prescribed period during which a woman may not remarry after having been
widowed or divorced.

Islamic parties   those parties based on Islamic ideology or because their constituents
mostly come from members of Muslim organizations (e.g. Muhammadiyah and
Nahdlatul Ulama).

Islamic Faction   a group of factions that proposed and supported the amendment of Article 29 in various ways. They include the F-PPP, the F-PBB, the F-PDU, the F-Reformasi, and the F-PKB.

Jakarta Charter   See 'Piagam Jakarta.'

Khalifa (Caliphate)   a Qur'anic word that refers to the vicegerency of man as the trustee of
Allah on earth. Historically it referred to political leadership in Islam.

Khalwat (*khalwa*)   a close proximity between a male and female who have no marriage or
kin relationship, in a place or situation where intimate contact is possible.

Khulafa al-rashidun   The first four caliphs who were immediate successors to the Prophet
Muhammad. They were Abu Bakr, 'Umar b. Khattab, 'Uthman b. 'Affan, and 'Ali b.
Abu Talib. The period of rule of these four caliphs lasted almost thirty years, from
632 to 661 CE.

Madhhab   Muslim schools of law such as Hanafi, Maliki, Shafi'i, and Hanbali. These
schools of law refer to their founding fathers respectively: Abu Hanifa (d. 767), Anas
b. Malik (d. 795), Muhammad Idris al-Shafi'i (d. 820), and Ahmad b. Hanbal (d.
855).

Madrasa   Islamic school.

Mahkamah Syar'iyyah   derived from Arabic (*'al-mahkama al-shar'iyya'*). It became the
name for *shari'a* court in Aceh.

Medina Charter   the covenant between Prophet Muhammad and other non-Muslim
believers in Medina. It was considered 'the first constitution' that laid down the plural policy, which fully recognized the co-existence of religious, ethnic, linguistic, and
tribal diversities within the society of Medina.

Meunasah a multipurpose building set up in almost every village in Aceh, which serves not only as a center of worship, but also a meeting place for the local community.

Mihna An inquisition undertaken by the Abbasid caliph, al-Ma'mun in particular, to force government officials and religious leaders to accept his religious views (such as the 'createdness' of the Qur'an) and his authority in matters of religious ritual and doctrine.

Millet distinctive social system to organize and regulate religious diversity of people during the Ottoman era.

Muhammadiyah the second largest Muslim association in Indonesia, after NU. It was established in 1912 and generally advocates reinterpretations of established religious practices and the heritage of Salafiya modernist movement.

Mukim a legal community unit of a number of *gampong* in Aceh headed by a leader called *Imum Mukim.*

muzakki zakat payers

Nahdlatul Ulama (NU) the largest association of Indonesian Muslims. It was founded in 1926 and has strong membership in Java. It follows mostly the Shafi'i *madhhab.*

Nationalist faction a group of factions that rejects the idea of constitutional amendment of Article 29 on Religion. It consisted of the F-PDIP, the F-PG, the F-KKI, the F-PDKB, and the F-TNI/POLRI.

nisab a certain minimum amount required for zakat payment.

Ottomanism the idea of regarding all individuals living in the Ottoman territories as equal subjects, regardless of their faith and language.

Pancasila literally means 'five principles.' It is found in the preamble to the 1945 Indonesian constitution and included (1) belief in One Almighty God, (2) a just and civilized humanitarianism, (3) national unity, (4) Indonesian democracy through consultation and consensus, and (5) social justice.

Pedoman Dasar Basic Guidance.

Pesantren a boarding school for Muslim students.

Piagam Jakarta literally means Jakarta Charter. It was actually the first draft of the preamble to the Indonesian constitution and it contained what has since become a well-known phrase in Indonesia, consisting of 'seven words': *dengan kewajiban menjalankan syariat Islam bagi pemeluknya* [with the obligation of carrying out Islamic shari'a for its adherents]. See also 'Alternative Two.'

Piagam Madinah in the Indonesian political context, it refers to the proposed amendment to Article 29 on Religion that required the state to oblige each religious adherent to perform religious duties; see also 'Alternative Three.'

Qanun exclusively refers to Regional Regulations produced by the legislature of Aceh from the year 2002 onwards, whether or not relating to Islamic norms.

Qisas just retaliation, which is mostly applied for the punishment of murder or injuries.

Santri   practicing Muslim. An Indonesian social group which devoutly practices Islamic doctrines, as opposed to the *Abangan* group, whose practice is less devout.

Sedekah   a kind of Islamic alms, which is voluntary in nature.

Seven Words   see *'Piagam Jakarta'* and 'Alternative Two.'

Shaykh al-Islam   a chief of mufti; the head of the religious establishment in the Ottoman Empire.

Siyasa al-shar'iyya   a doctrine that allows Muslim rulers to take any acts, including legislating to supplement the *shari'a* and creating new courts which are necessary for the public good, provided that the *shari'a* is not infringed or as long as the *shari'a* does not prohibit the acts.

Sunna   way or practice of the Prophet. It became one of the basic sources of Islamic law, based on Muhammad's words and deeds as recorded in the Hadith. The Sunna complements and often explains the Qur'an.

Sunni   the largest group of Muslims, which believes in the traditions of the Sunna and accepts the first four caliphs as rightful successors to Prophet Muhammad.

Shi'i   a group of Muslims who consider Ali, the cousin of Muhammad, and his descendants as Prophet Muhammad's true successors.

Ta'zir   a discretionary punishment for committing the prohibited acts or for omitting the obligatory acts. Although the legal texts of Qur'an and Sunna mention both prohibited and obligatory acts, there is no punishment specified therein. The punishment of *ta'zir* is left to the discretion of the ruler.

Tanzimat   literally means 'reorganizations.' This was a program for Ottoman governmental reforms, which was undertaken from 1839 to 1876, largely during the reign of Sultan Abd al-Madjid.

Tawhid   God's oneness.

Ulama   religious scholars.

(rural) *Ulama*   loosely analytical category in an Aceh context for those who preferred not to pursue their tertiary education to Islamic higher institution such IAIN, but were usually satisfied with *dayah* level education. They are also often identified as 'traditional *ulama*.'

(urban) *Ulama*   loosely analytical category in an Aceh context for those who pursued their Islamic education to the university (IAIN) level after completing their study in *dayah*. They are mostly considered Muslim intellectuals or 'modern *ulama*.'

Uleëbalang   aristocrats or self-governing rulers in Aceh during Dutch colonial times.

Umara   plural of *amir*, which means commander or ruler.

Umma/Umat   community, group of people; Muslim community as identified by the integration of its ideology, religion, law, mission and purpose of life, group consciousness, and ethics and mores, irrespective of their differences in origin, region, color, language, and so on.

Wakaf (*Waqf*)   religious endowments; a charitable trust dedicated to some pious or socially beneficial purposes.

Wawasan nusantara   a doctrine that emphasizes that the whole archipelago should be an integrated, compact unity of fatherland; it describes society, nation, mainland, ocean, and air as a union which cannot be separated. It is involved in political union, legal union, cultural and social union, economic union, and secure defensive union.

Wilaya al-faqih   rule by Islamic jurists or 'Mandate of the Jurist,' which requires the religious elites to play a major role in governance.

Wilayatul Hisbah   derived from Arabic *wilaya al-hisba*. It was an early Islamic institution that organized public administrative functions of both moral/normative and administrative/technical sorts. In the context of Aceh, it is defined as an institution whose task is to monitor and to advocate the application of *qanun* for the sake of promoting good and prohibiting evil (*amar ma'ruf nahy munkar*). It is sometimes inaccurately referred to as '*shari'a* police.'

Zakat   religious taxation or Islamic alms; an obligation on every Muslim to purify his earnings and possessions by giving away a portion to the poor and the needy on the basis of one's wealth.

zakat *profesi*   a religious tax paid by the professionals such as civil servants, lawyers, doctors, lecturers, and others.

References

Abdullah, Taufik. "Zakat Collection and Distribution in Indonesia." In *The Islamic Voluntary Sector in Southeast Asia,* edited by Mohammed Ariff. Singapore: ISEAS, 1991.

Abubakar, Al Yasa'. *Tanya Jawab Pelaksanaan Syariat Islam di Provinsi Nanggroe Aceh Darussalam.* Banda Aceh: Dinas Syariat Islam, 2003.

Abu-Rabi', Ibrahim M. *Intellectual Origins of Islamic Resurgence in the Modern Arab World.* New York: State University of New York Press, 1996.

Abu-Saud, Mahmoud. *Fiqh Al-Zakat Al-Mu'asir,* East Burnham, Bucks, UK: Oxford Publishing, 1989.

Ahmad, Feroz. "Unionist Relations with the Greek, Armenian, and Jewish Communities of the Ottoman Empire, 1908–1914." In *Christian and Jews in the Ottoman Empire: The Functioning of a Plural Society,* vol. I., edited by Benyamin Braude and Bernard Lewis. New York and London: Holmes & Meier Publishers, 1982.

al-Ahsan, Abdullah. *Ummah or Nation? Identity Crisis in Contemporary Muslim Society.* London: The Islamic Foundation, 1992.

Alfian. "The *Ulama* in Acehnese Society." In *Readings on Islam in Southeast Asia,* edited by Ahmad Ibrahim, Sharon Siddique, and Yasmin Hussain. Singapore: ISEAS, 1985.

Ali, Muhamad. "The Concept of Umma and the Reality of the Nation-State: A Western and Muslim Discourse. *Kultur* 2, no. 1 (2002).

Aminuddin. *Kekuatan Islam dan Pergulatan Kekuasaan di Indonesia: Sebelum dan Sesudah Runtuhnya Rezim Soeharto.* Yogyakarta: Pustaka Pelajar, 1999.

Amiruddin, Hasbi. *Perjuangan Ulama Aceh di Tengah Konflik.* Yogyakarta: Ceninnets Press, 2004.

Anderson, Benedict G. *Imagined Communities: Reflections on the Origin and Spread of Nationalism.* London: Verso, 1983.

———. "Indonesian Nationalism Today and in the Future," *Indonesia* 67 (1999).

Anderson, J. N. D. *Islamic Law in the Modern World.* London: Stevens & Sons Limited, 1959.

Ansari, Abdul Rehman. *Zakaat, the Religious Tax of Islam.* Durban, South Africa: Premier Press, 1973.

Anshari, Endang Saefuddin. *Piagam Jakarta: 22 Juni 1945.* Jakarta: Gema Insani Press, 1997.

Antoun, Richard T., and Mary Elaine Hegland, eds. *Religious Resurgence: Contemporary Cases in Islam, Christianity and Judaism.* New York: Syracuse University Press, 1987.

Arabi, Oussama. *Studies in Modern Islamic Law and Jurisprudence.* The Hague, London, New York: Kluwer Law International, 2001.

Ariel, Rav Yaacov, and Rosh Yeshiva-Yamit. "Secular Courts in the State of Israel." *Jewish Law: Examining Halacha, Jewish Issues and Secular Law.* http://www.jlaw.com/Articles/SecularCourts.html. Accessed 8 August 2002.

Arjomand, Said Amir. "Constitution-Making in Islamic Iran: The Impact of Theocracy on the Legal Order of a Nation-State." In *History and Power in the Study of Law: New Directions in Legal Anthropology,* edited by June Starr and Jane F. Collier. Ithaca, N.Y., and London: Cornell University Press, 1989.

———. "Shi'ite Jurisprudence and Constitution Making in the Islamic Republic of Iran." In *Fundamentalism and The State: Remaking Polities, Economies and Militance,* edited by Martin E. Marty and R. Scott Appleby. Chicago and London: The University of Chicago Press, 1993.

———. *The Turban for the Crown: The Islamic Revolution in Iran.* New York: Oxford University Press, 1988.

Armstrong, Karen. *The Battle for God: Fundamentalism in Judaism, Christianity and Islam.* New York: Alfred A. Knopf, 2000.

Artz, Donna E. "The Application of International Human Rights in Islamic States." *Human Rights Quarterly* 12 (1990): pp. 202–230.

Ashmawi, Muhammad S. *Against Islamic Extremism.* Translated and edited by C. Fluehr-Lobban. Gainesville: University Press of Florida, 1998.

Aspinall, Edward. "Sovereignty, the Successor State, and Universal Human Rights: History and the International Structuring of Acehnese Nationalism." *Indonesia* 73 (2002).

al-Attas, S. M. N. *Preliminary Statement on a General Theory of Islamization of the Malay-Indonesian Archipelago.* Kuala Lumpur: Dewan Bahasa dan Pustaka, 1969.

el-Awa, Muhammad. *Punishment in Islamic Law.* Indianapolis, Ind.: American Trust Publishers, 1980.

———. "Ta'zir in the Islamic Penal System." *Journal of Islamic and Comparative Law* 6 (1976).

Awwas, Irfan S., ed. *Risalah Kongres Mujahidin I dan Penegakan Syari'ah Islam.* Yogyakarta: Wihdah Press, 2001.

Ayubi, Nazih. *Political Islam: Religion and Politics in the Arab World.* London and New York: Routledge, 1991.

Azra, Azyumardi. "The Indonesian Marriage Law of 1974: An Institutionalisation of the Shari'a for Social Change." In *Shari'a and Politics in Modern Indonesia,* edited by Arskal Salim and Azyumardi Azra. Singapore: ISEAS, 2003.

———. *Jaringan Ulama Timur Tengah dan Kepulauan Nusantara Abad XVII dan XVIII: Melacak Akar-Akar Pembaruan Pemikiran Islam di Indonesia.* Bandung: Mizan, 1994.

————. *Renaisans Islam Asia Tenggara: Sejarah Wacana dan Kekuasaan.* Bandung: Remaja Rosdakarya, 1999.

Azra, Azyumardi, and Saiful Umam, eds. *Menteri-Menteri Agama RI: Biografi Sosial Politik.* Jakarta: INIS-PPIM-Balitbang Depag RI, 1998.

Bajunid, O. Farouk. "Islam and State in Southeast Asia." In *State and Islam,* edited by C. van Dijk and A. H. de Groot. Leiden: Research School CNWS, 1995.

Bakti, Andi Faisal. *Islam and Nation Formation in Indonesia: From Communitarian to Organizational Communications.* Jakarta: Logos, 2000.

Basalim, Umar. *Pro-Kontra Piagam Jakarta Di Era Reformasi.* Jakarta: Pustaka Indonesia Satu, 2002.

Bashear, Suliman. "On the Origins and Development of the Meaning of Zakat in Early Islam." *Arabica* 40 (1993): pp. 84–113.

Baso, Ahmad. *Islam Pasca-kolonial: Perselingkuhan Agama, Kolonialisme dan Liberalisme.* Bandung: Mizan, 2005.

Bell, Gary F. "Minority Rights and Regionalism in Indonesia – Will Constitutional Recognition Lead to Disintegration or Discrimination?" *Singapore Journal of International and Comparative Law* 5 (2001): pp. 784–806.

Benda, Harry J. "Christian Snouck Hurgronje and the Foundations of Dutch Islamic Policy in Indonesia." *The Journal of Modern History* 30 (December 1958).

————. *The Crescent and the Rising Sun: Indonesia Under the Japanese Occupation 1942–1945.* The Hague-Bandung: Van Hoeve, 1958.

————. "South-East Asian Islam in the Twentieth Century." In *The Cambridge History of Islam,* vol. 2., edited by P. M. Holt, Ann K. S. Lambton, and Bernard Lewis. Cambridge and New York: Cambridge University Press, 1970.

Benthall, Jonathan. "Financial Worship: The Qur'anic Injunction to Almsgiving." *Journal of the Royal Anthropological Institute* 5 (March 1999).

Birai, Umar M. "Islamic Tajdid and the Political Process in Nigeria." In *Fundamentalism and The State: Remaking Polities, Economies and Militance,* edited by Martin E. Marty and R. Scott Appleby. Chicago and London: the University of Chicago Press, 1993.

Black, Anthony. *The History of Islamic Political Thought.* New York: Routledge, 2001.

Boland, B. J. *The Struggle of Islam in Modern Indonesia.* The Hague: Martinus Nijhoff, 1982.

Bowen, John. *Islam, Law and Equality in Indonesia: An Anthropology of Public Reasoning.* Cambridge: Cambridge University Press, 2003.

Braten, Eldar. "To Colour, Not Oppose: Spreading Islam in Rural Java." In *Muslim Diversity: Local Islam in Global Context,* edited by Leif Manger. Surrey: Curzon Press, 1999.

Braude, Benyamin. "Foundation Myths of the Millet System." In *Christian and Jews in the Ottoman Empire: The Functioning of a Plural Society,* vol. I., edited by Benyamin Braude and Bernard Lewis. New York and London: Holmes & Meier Publishers, 1982.

Braude, Benyamin, and Bernard Lewis, eds. *Christian and Jews in the Ottoman Empire: The Functioning of a Plural Society,* vol. I. New York and London: Holmes & Meier Publishers, 1982.

Brown, Nathan J. "Shari'a and State in the Modern Muslim Middle East." *International Journal of Middle East* 29 (1997).

Bruinessen, Martin Van. "Genealogies of Islamic Radicalism in Post-Suharto Indonesia." *South East Asia Research* 10, no. 2. (2002): pp. 117–154.

———. "Indonesia's *Ulama* and Politics: Caught Between Legitimising the Status Quo and Searching for Alternatives." *Prisma The Indonesian Indicator* 49 (1990).

———. "Muslims of the Dutch East Indies and the Caliphate Question." *Studia Islamika* 2, no. 3 (1995).

———. "Shari'a Court, Tarekat and Pesantren: Religious Administration in the Banten Sultanate." *Archipel* 50 (1995): pp. 166–199.

———. "State Islam Relations in Contemporary Indonesia 1915–1990." In *State and Islam,* edited by C. Van Dijk and A. H. de Groot. Leiden, The Netherlands: Research School CNWS, 1995.

Burhanuddin, Nandang. *Penegakan Syariat Islam menurut Partai Keadilan.* Jakarta: Al-Jannah, 2003.

Cammack, Mark. "Islam, Nationalism, and the State in Suharto's Indonesia." *Wisconsin International Law Journal* 17, no. 1 (1999).

Chomsky, Noam. *Media Control: The Spectacular Achievements of Propaganda.* 2nd ed. New York: Seven Stories Press, 2002.

Clark, Grace. "Pakistan's Zakat and 'Ushr as a Welfare System." In *Islamic Reassertion in Pakistan: The Application of Islamic Laws in a Modern State,* edited by Anita M. Weiss. New York: Syracuse University Press, 1986.

"Consonance and Dissonance." http://www.answers.com/topic/consonance-and-dissonance. Accessed 28 December 2005.

Coulson, Noel J. *Conflicts and Tensions in Islamic Jurisprudence.* Chicago and London: The University of Chicago Press, 1969.

———. *History of Islamic Law.* Edinburgh: Edinburgh University Press, 1964.

———. "The State and the Individual in Islamic Law." *International and Comparative Law Quarterly* 6 (1957).

Creveld, Martin van. *The Rise and Decline of the State.* Cambridge: Cambridge University Press, 1999.

Cribb, Robert, ed. *Islam and the Pancasila.* South East Asian Monograph, no. 28. Townsville, North Queensland, Australia: James Cook University of North Queensland, Centre for Southeast Asian Studies, 1991.

Crow, Karim D. "Aceh—The 'Special Territory' in North Sumatra: A Self-Fulfilling Promise?" *Journal of Muslim Minority Affairs* 20, no. 1 (2000): pp. 91–99.

Cummings, W. "Scripting Islamization: Arabic Texts in Early Modern Makassar." *Ethnohistory* 48, no. 4 (2001): pp. 559–586.

Dahl, Robert. *Polyarchy Participation and Opposition*. New Haven, Conn.: Yale University Press, 1971.

Dahlan, Muhammad. "Piagam Djakarta Sumber Hukum Mendjiwai U.U.D. 1945." *Kiblat*, 3–4/XVI.

Dahm, Bernhard. *Sukarno and the Struggle for Indonesian Independence*. Ithaca, N.Y.: Cornell University Press, 1969.

Damanik, Ali Said. *Fenomena Partai Keadilan: Transformasi 20 Tahun Gerakan Tarbiyah di Indonesia*. Jakarta: Teraju, 2002.

Daradjat, Zakiah, *Zakat: Pembersih Harta Dan Jiwa*. Jakarta: YPI Ruhana, 1991.

Davis, Michael. "Laskar Jihad and the Political Position of Conservative Islam in Indonesia." *Contemporary Southeast Asia* 24 (April 2002).

Davison, Roderick H. *Reform in the Ottoman Empire, 1856–1876*. Princeton, N.J.: Princeton University Press, 1963.

Demokrasi Madinah: Model Demokrasi Cara Rasulullah. Jakarta: Republika, 2003.

Denny, Frederick. "The Meaning of Ummah in the Qur'an." *History of Religions* 15, no. 1 (1975).

———. "Ummah in the Constitution of Medina." *Journal of Near Eastern Studies* 36 (1977).

Devy, Soraya, et al. *Politik dan Pencerahan Peradaban*. Banda Aceh: Ar-Raniry Press, 2004.

Dijk, C. van. *Rebellion under the Banner of Islam: The Darul Islam in Indonesia*. The Hague: Martinus Nijhoff, 1981.

Direktori Organisasi Pengelola Zakat di Indonesia. Jakarta: FOZ, 2001.

Drewes, G. W. J. *An Early Javanese Code of Muslim Ethics*. The Hague: Martinus Nijhoff, 1978.

———. "New Light on the Coming of Islam to Indonesia?" *Bijdragen tot de Taal-, Land-en Volkenkunde* 124 (1968).

Effendy, Bahtiar. *Islam dan Negara: Transformasi Pemikiran dan Praktik Politik Islam di Indonesia*. Jakarta: Paramadina, 1998.

———. "Reformasi Konstitusi sebagai Prasyarat Demokratisasi: Pengalaman Indonesia." *Analisis CSIS* 4 (2000).

Elaigwu, J. Isawa. "The Shadow of Shari'a over Nigerian Federalism." *The Journal of Federalism* 33, no. 3 (Summer 2003): pp. 123–144.

Enayat, Hamid. "Iran: Khumayni's Concept of the Guardianship of the Jurisconsult." In *Islam in the Political Process*, edited by James P. Piscatori. Cambridge: Cambridge University Press, 1993.

Englard, Izhak. "Constitutional Protection of Religious Minorities: The Tension Between Collective and Individual Religious Freedom." Paper presented at Round Table Constitution and Religion, Athens, 22–26 May 2002.

————. "Law and Cultural Heritage in Multicultural Societies." In *Law and Multicultural Societies: Proceedings of the IALL Meeting,* edited by E. I. Cuomo. Jerusalem, International Association of Law Libraries, 1989.

————. *Religious Law in the Israel Legal System.* Jerusalem: Harry Sacher Institute for Legislative Research and Comparative Law, 1975.

Esposito, John. *Islam and Politics,* Revised 2nd ed. New York: Syracuse University Press, 1987.

El-Fadl, Khaled Abou. "Hak Asasi Manusia di atas Hak Asasi Tuhan" [The right of human beings are above the right of God], http://islamlib.com/id/index.php?page =article&id=864. Accessed 25 August 2005.

————. *Islam and the Challenge of Democracy.* Princeton, N.J.: Princeton University Press, 2004.

Fadlullah, Cholid. *Mengenal Hukum ZIS dan Pengamalannya di DKI Jakarta.* Jakarta: BAZIS DKI, 1993.

Fasseur, C. "Cornerstone and Stumbling Block Racial Classification and the Late Colonial State in Indonesia." In *The Late Colonial State in Indonesia: Political and Economic Foundations of the Netherlands Indies 1880–1942,* edited by Robert Cribb. Leiden: KITLV Press, 1994.

Federspiel, Howard. "Islamic Values, Law and Expectations in Contemporary Indonesia." In *Shari'a and Politics in Modern Indonesia,* edited by Arskal Salim and Azyumardi Azra. Singapore: ISEAS, 2003.

————. *Persatuan Islam: Islamic Reform in Twentieth Century Indonesia.* Ithaca, N.Y.: Modern Indonesia Project, Cornell University, 1970.

Feillard, Andree. *NU vis-à-vis Negara: Pencarian Isi, Bentuk dan Makna.* Translated by Lesmana. Yogjakarta: LKIS, 1995.

Feith, Herbert. *The Indonesian Elections of 1955.* Ithaca, N.Y.: Modern Indonesia Project, Southeast Asia Program, Cornell University, 1957.

Findley, Carter V. *Bureaucratic Reform in the Ottoman Empire: The Sublime Porte, 1789–1922, Princeton Studies on the Near East.* Princeton, N.J.: Princeton University Press, 1980.

Firmage, Edwin B., et al., eds. "Editors' Introduction." In *Religion and Law: Biblical Judaic and Islamic Perspectives.* Winona Lake, Ind.: Eisenbrauns, 1990.

Fyzee, Asaf A. A. *A Modern Approach to Islam.* Bombay: Asia Publishing House, 1963.

Geertz, Clifford. *Islam Observed: Religious Development in Morocco and Indonesia.* Chicago: The University of Chicago Press, 1968.

————. *The Religion of Java,* New York: The Free Press, 1960.

Gellner, Ernest. *Nation and Nationalism.* Oxford: Basil Blackwell, 1983.

Gerber, Haim. *Islamic Law and Culture 1600–1840.* Leiden, Boston, and Köln: Brill, 1999.

Ghai, Yash, and Jill Cottrell. "A Note on Constitutions of Islamic States." http://www.cic

.nyu.edu/pdf/YashGhai%20AnoteonconstitutionsofIslamicstates.pdf. Accessed 8 July 2004.

Giddens, Anthony. *The Nation-State and Violence.* Cambridge: Polity Press, 1985.

Gillespie, Piers. "Current Issues in Indonesian Islam: Analyzing the 2005 Council of Indonesian Ulama Fatwa No. 7 Opposing Pluralism, Liberalism and Secularism." *Journal of Islamic Studies* 18, no. 3 (2007).

Guibernau, Montserrat. *The Nation-State and Nationalism in the Twentieth Century.* Cambridge: Polity Press, 1996.

Hadi, Amirul. *Islam and State in Sumatra: A Study of Seventeenth-Century Aceh.* Leiden: Brill, 2004.

Hadikusumo, Ki Bagus. *Islam Sebagai Dasar Negara dan Achlak Pemimpin.* Djogyakarta: Pustaka Rahaju, n.d.

Hafiduddin, Didin. *Zakat dalam Perekonomian Modern.* Jakarta: Gema Insani Press, 2002.

Hallaq, Wael B. "Juristic Authority vs. State Power: The Legal Crises of Modern Islam." *Journal of Law and Religion* 19 (2003–2004).

Hamayotsu, Kikue. "Politics of Syariah Reform: The Making of the State Religio-Legal Apparatus." *Malaysia Islam, Society and Politics: Essays in Honour of Clive S. Kessler.* Singapore: ISEAS, 2003.

Hasan, Noorhaidi. "Faith and Politics: The Rise of the Laskar Jihad in the Era of Transition in Indonesia." *Indonesia* 73 (April 2002): pp. 145–170.

Hasil Rumusan Musyawarah Nasional III Forum Zakat. Jakarta: FOZ, 2003.

Hassan, Riaz. *Faithlines: Muslim Conceptions of Islam and Society.* Oxford: Oxford University Press, 2002.

Hassan, Riffat. "Religious Human Rights and the Qur'an." *Emory International Law Review* 10 (1996): pp. 85–96.

Hefner, Robert W. "Islamizing Capitalism: On the Founding of Indonesia's First Islamic Bank." In *Towards a New Paradigm: Recent Developments in Indonesian Islamic Thought,* edited by Mark Woodward and J. Rush. Tempe: Arizona State University Program of Southeast Asian Studies, 1995.

———. "Islamizing Java? Religion and Politics in Rural East Java." *The Journal of Asian Studies* 46, no. 3 (1987): pp. 533–554.

———. "The Political Economy of Islamic Conversion in Modern East Java." In *Islam and the Political Economy of Meaning: Comparative Studies of Muslim Discourse,* edited by William R. Roff. Berkeley: University of California Press, 1987.

Herman, Edward S., and Noam Chomsky. *Manufacturing Consent: The Political Economy of the Mass Media.* New York: Pantheon Books, 2002.

Himpunan Undang-Undang, Keputusan Presiden, Peraturan Daerah/Qanun, Instruksi Gubernur, Edaran Gubernur Berkaitan Pelaksanaan Syariat Islam. Banda Aceh: Dinas Syariat Islam, 2004.

Hisyam, Muhammad. *Caught Between Three Fires: The Javanese Pangulu Under the Dutch Colonial Administration 1882–1942.* Jakarta: INIS, 2001.

Hooker, M. B. *Indonesian Islam: Social Change through Contemporary Fatawa,* Honolulu: University of Hawai'i Press, 2003.

———. "Introduction: Islamic Law in South-east Asia." *The Australian Journal of Asian Law* 4, no. 3 (2002): pp. 213–231.

———. *Islamic Law in South-East Asia.* Kuala Lumpur: Oxford University Press, 1984.

———. "Submission to Allah: The Kelantan Syariah Criminal Code (II), 1993." In *Malaysia Islam, Society and Politics: Essays in Honour of Clive S. Kessler.* Singapore: ISEAS, 2003.

———. "The Translation of Islam into South-East Asia." In *Islam in South-East Asia,* edited by M. B. Hooker. Leiden: E. J. Brill, 1983.

Hosen, Ibrahim. *Bunga Rampai dari Percikan Filsafat Hukum Islam.* Jakarta: YIIQ, 1997.

Hosen, Nadirsyah. "Fatwa and Politics in Indonesia." In *Shari'a and Politics in Modern Indonesia,* edited by Arskal Salim and Azyumardi Azra. Singapore: ISEAS, 2003.

———. "Syari'ah and Constitutional Reform in Indonesia (1999–2002)." PhD diss., National University of Singapore, 2005.

Hourani, Albert H. "The Changing Face of the Fertile Crescent in the XVIIIth Century." *Studia Islamica* 8 (1957): pp. 89–122.

———. *A Vision of History: Near Eastern and Other Essays.* Beirut: Khayats, 1961.

Howell, Julia D. "Sufism and the Indonesian Islamic Revival." *Journal of Asian Studies* 60, no. 3 (2001): pp. 701–729.

Howell, Julia D., M. A. Subandi, and Peter L. Nelson. "Indonesian Sufism: Signs of Resurgence." In *New Trends and Development in the World of Islam,* edited by Peter B. Clarke. London: Luzac Oriental, 1997.

Hurgronje, Christiaan Snouck. *Nasihat-Nasihat C. Snouck Hurgronje Semasa Kepegawaiannya kepada Pemerintah Hindia Belanda 1880–1936,* vol. VII. Translated by Sukarsi. Jakarta: INIS, 1992.

Husain, Mir Zohair. "The Ideologization of Islam: Meaning, Manifestations and Causes." In *Islam in a Changing World: Europe and the Middle East,* edited by Anders Jerichow and Jorgen Baek Simonsen. Surrey: Curzon Press, 1997.

Ibn Majah, Muhammad ibn Yazid. *Sahih Sunan ibn Majah.* al-Riyad: Maktaba al-Ma'arif li al-Nashr wa-al-Tawzi', 1417 [1997].

Ibn Rushd. *Bidaya al-mujtahid wa-nihaya al-muqtasid.* Bayrut, Lubnan: Dar al-Ma'rifa, 1986.

Ibn Taymiyya. *al-Hisba fi al-Islam aw Wazifa al-Hukuma al-Islamiyya.* Egypt: Dar al-Katib al-'Arabi, n.d.

———. *al-Siyasa al-Shar'iyya fi Islah al-Ra'i wa al-Ra'iyya.* Egypt: Dar al-Katib al-'Arabi, 1969.

Ibrahim, Muslim. "Rekonstruksi Peran *Ulama* Aceh Masa Depan." In *Syariat di Wilayah Syariat,* edited by Fairus M Nur. Banda Aceh: Dinas Syariat Islam NAD, 2002.

El-Ibrahimy, M. N. *Peranan Tgk. M. Daud Beureu-eh dalam Pergolakan Aceh.* Revised Edition. Jakarta: Media Dakwah, 2001.

Ichwan, Moch. Nur. "Official Reform of Islam: State Islam and the Ministry of Religious Affairs in Contemporary Indonesia 1966–2004." PhD diss., Leiden University, 2006.

Idris, Ja'far Sheikh. *The Process of Islamization.* The Muslim Students' Association of the US and Canada, 1977, 4th Printing January 1983.

Idris, Safwan. *Gerakan Zakat dalam Pemberdayaan Ekonomi Umat: Pendekatan Transformatif.* Jakarta: Cita Putra Bangsa, 1997.

Indrayana, Denny. "Indonesian Constitutional Reform 1999–2002: An Evaluation of Constitution-Making in Transition." PhD diss., University of Melbourne, 2005.

International Crisis Group. "Aceh: Can Autonomy Stem the Conflict?" ICG Asia Report no. 18, 27 June 2001.

"Islam and Peace Building in Indonesia: The Analysis of Radical Movement and Their Implication for Security-Development Prospects." Jakarta: ICIP-JICA, 2004.

Ismail, Badruzzaman, and Yusny Saby. *Majelis Ulama Indonesia dalam Pembangunan.* Banda Aceh: MUI Propinsi DI Aceh, 1995.

Ismail, Rose, ed. *Hudud in Malaysia: The Issues at Stake.* Kuala Lumpur: SIS Forum, 1995.

Ismuha. *Sejarah Singkat Majelis Ulama Propinsi Daerah Istimewa Aceh.* Banda Aceh: Sekretariat Majelis *Ulama* Propinsi Daerah Istimewa Aceh, 1983.

Jackson, Sherman. *Islamic Law and the State: The Constitutional Jurisprudence of Shihab al-Din Qarafi.* Leiden: Brill, 1996.

Jamhari and Jajang Jahroni, eds. *Gerakan Salafi Radikal di Indonesia.* Jakarta: Rajagrafindo Persada, 2004.

al-Jawziyya, Ibn Qayyim. *al-Turuq al-Hukmiyya fi al-Siyasa al-Shar'iyya aw al-Firasat al-Mardiyya fi Ahkam al-Siyasa al-Shar'iyya.* Bayrut: Dar al-Kutub al-'Ilmiyya, 1995.

Jehle, Geoffrey A. "Zakat and Inequality: Some Evidence from Pakistan." *The Review of Income and Wealth* 40 (June 1994): pp. 205–216.

Kahin, George McTurnan. *Nationalism and Revolution in Indonesia, Studies on Southeast Asia No. 35.* Ithaca, N.Y.: Southeast Asia Program Publications, Southeast Asia Program, Cornell University, 2003.

Kamali, Muhammad Hashim. "The Islamic State and its Constitution." In *Shari'a Law and the Modern Nation-State,* edited by Norani Othman, pp. 45–66. Kuala Lumpur: Sisters in Islam, 1994.

———. "Law and Society: The Interplay of Revelation and Reason in the Shariah." In *The Oxford History of Islam,* edited by John L. Esposito. Oxford: Oxford University Press, 1999.

———. "Punishment in Islamic Law: A Critique of the *Hudud* Bill of Kelantan, Malaysia." *Arab Law Quarterly* (1998): pp. 203–234.

Karim, M. Rusli. *Negara dan Peminggiran Islam Politik.* Yogyakarta: Tiara Wacana, 1999.

Karpat, Kemal H. "Millets and Nationality: The Roots of the Incongruity of Nation and State in the Post-Ottoman Era." In *Christian and Jews in the Ottoman Empire: The Functioning of a Plural Society,* vol. I, edited by Benyamin Braude and Bernard Lewis. New York and London: Holmes & Meier Publishers, 1982.

———. *The Politicization of Islam: Reconstructing Identity, State, Faith, and Community in the Late Ottoman State, Studies in Middle Eastern History.* New York: Oxford University Press, 2000.

Kechichian, Joseph A. "The Role of the Ulama in the Politics of an Islamic State: The Case of Saudi Arabia." *International Journal of Middle East Studies* 18 (1986).

Keddie, Nikki R. "Iran: Change in Islam: Islam and Change." *International Journal of Middle Eastern Studies* 11 (1980).

Kell, Tim. *The Roots of Acehnese Rebellion, 1989–1992.* Ithaca, N.Y.: Cornell Modern Indonesia Project, 1995.

Kepel, Gilles. *Jihad: The Trail of Political Islam.* Translated by Anthony F. Roberts. Cambridge, Mass.: The Belknap Press of Harvard University, 2002.

Khadduri, Majid. "Islam and the Modern Law of Nations." *American Journal of International Law* 50, no. 2 (April 1956).

Kim, Hyung-Jun. "The Changing Interpretation of Religious Freedom in Indonesia." *Journal of Southeast Asian Studies* 29, no. 2 (September 1998): pp. 357–370.

King, Michael. "Religion into Law, Law into Religion: The Construction of a Secular Identity for Islam." In *Nationalism, Racism and the Rule of Law,* edited by Peter Fitzpatrick. Aldershot: Dartmouth, 1995.

Kozlowski, Gregory C. "When the 'Way' Becomes the 'Law': Modern States and the Transformation of *Halakhah* and *Shari'a.*" In *Studies in Islamic and Judaic Traditions II,* edited by William M. Brinner and Stephen D. Ricks. Atlanta, Ga.: Scholars Press, 1989.

Krämer, Gudrun. "Techniques and Values: Contemporary Muslim Debates on Islam and Democracy." In *Islam, Modernism and the West: Cultural and Political Relations at the End of the Millennium,* edited by Gema Martin Munoz. London and New York: IB Tauris, 1999.

Kumar, Krishna. "Religious Fundamentalism in India and Beyond." *Parameters* 32 (2002).

Kuran, Timur. "The Economic Impact of Islamic Fundamentalism." In *Fundamentalisms and the State: Remaking Polities, Economies and Militance.* Chicago: University of Chicago Press, 1993.

———. "Islamic Redistribution through Zakat: Historical Record and Modern Realities." In *Poverty and Charity in Middle Eastern Contexts,* edited by Michael Bonner, Mine Ener, and Amy Singer. Albany: State University of New York Press, 2003.

Kuraysha, A. T. Abu. *Al-Zaka wa al-Tanmiya.* Cairo, 1999.

Lane, Jan-Erik. *Constitutions and Political Theory*. Manchester: Manchester University Press, 1996.

Lapidus, Ira M. "The Separation of State and Religion in the Development of Early Islamic Society." *International Journal of Middle East Studies* 6 (1975).

———. "State and Religion in Islamic Societies." *Past and Present* 151 (May 1996).

Laporan Evaluasi Pelaksanaan Syariat Islam Tahun 2003. Banda Aceh: Dinas Syariat Islam, 2003.

Latif, Hamdiah A. "Persatuan *Ulama* Seluruh Aceh (PUSA): Its Contribution to Educational Reforms in Aceh." MA thesis, McGill University, 1992.

Layish, Aharon. "The Contribution of the Modernists to the Secularization of Islamic Law." *Middle Eastern Studies* 24 (1978): pp. 263–277.

Lawrence, Bruce B. *Defenders of God: The Fundamentalist Revolt Against the Modern Age*. New York: Harper and Row, 1989.

Lev, Daniel S. *Islamic Courts in Indonesia: A Study in the Political Bases of Legal Institutions*. Berkeley: University of California Press, 1972.

Liddle, R. William. *Leadership and Culture in Indonesian Politics*. Sydney: Allen and Unwin, 1996.

Liebman, Charles S. "Jewish Fundamentalism and the Israeli Polity." In *Fundamentalism and The State: Remaking Polities, Economies and Militance,* edited by Martin E. Marty and R. Scott Appleby. Chicago and London: The University of Chicago Press, 1993.

Lindsey, Tim. "Indonesian Constitutional Reform: Muddling Towards Democracy." *Singapore Journal of International & Comparative Law* 6 (2002): pp. 244–301.

Lubis, Nur Ahmad Fadhil. "The State's Legal Policy and the Development of Islamic Law in Indonesia's New Order." In *Shari'a and Politics in Modern Indonesia,* edited by Arskal Salim and Azyumardi Azra. Singapore: ISEAS, 2003.

Ma'arif, Syafi'i. *Islam dan Masalah Kenegaraan: Studi Tentang Percaturan dalam Konstituante*. Jakarta: LP3ES, 1985.

Mahendra, Yusril Ihza. *Dinamika Tata Negara Indonesia*. Jakarta: Gema Insani Press, 1996.

Mahmood, Tahir. "Law in the Qur'an—A Draft Code." *Islamic and Comparative Law Quarterly* 7, no. 1 (1987).

Mahmuddin. "Melacak Peran Gerakan Sipil di Aceh: Studi Gerakan Thaliban Aceh." MA thesis, Universitas Gadjah Mada Yogyakarta, 2001.

Maila, Joseph. "The Arab Christians: From the Eastern Question to the Recent Political Situation of the Minorities." In *Christian Communities in the Arab Middle East,* edited by Andrea Pacini. Oxford: Clarendon Press, 1998.

Majelis Mujahidin. *Undang-Undang Hukum Pidana Sesuai Syari'ah Islam*. Yogyakarta, Markaz Pusat Majelis Mujahidin, 2002.

Majelis Permusyawaratan Ulama. *Kumpulan Fatwa-Fatwa Majelis Ulama Daerah Istimewa Aceh*. Banda Aceh: Majelis Ulama, 2003.

Malik, Jamal. *Colonialization of Islam: Dissolution of Traditional Institutions in Pakistan.* New Delhi: Manohar, 1996.

Malik, Maqbul Ilahi. "The Concept of Human Rights in Islamic Jurisprudence." *Human Rights Quarterly* (1981): pp. 56–67.

Mangkusasmito, Prawoto. *Pertumbuhan Historis Rumusan Dasar Negara: Sebuah Proyeksi.* Jakarta: Hudaya, 1970.

Mantran, Robert. "Foreign Merchants and the Minorities in Istanbul during the Sixteenth and Seventeenth Centuries." In *Christian and Jews in the Ottoman Empire: The Functioning of a Plural Society,* vol. I., edited by Benyamin Braude and Bernard Lewis. New York and London: Holmes & Meier Publishers, 1982.

Mas'udi, Masdar F. *Agama Keadilan: Risalah Zakat (Pajak) dalam Islam.* Jakarta: P3M, 1991.

———. "Zakat: An Ethical Concept of Taxation and State: A Reinterpretation of Third Pillar of Islam." Unpublished paper.

Masters, Bruce. "Ottoman Policies Toward Syria in the 17th and 18th Centuries." In *The Syrian Land in the 18th and 19th Century,* edited by Thomas Philip. Stuttgart: Franz Steiner Verlag, 1992.

al-Mawardi. *al-Ahkam al-Sultaniyya.* Bayrut: al-Maktab al-Islami, 1996.

al-Mawdudi, Abu al-A'la. *The Islamic Law and Constitution.* Translated and edited by Khursyid Ahmad. Lahore: Islamic Publications, 1977.

Mayer, Ann E. "Conundrums in Constitutionalism: Islamic Monarchies in an Era of Transition." *UCLA Journal of Islamic and Near Eastern Law* (Spring/Summer 2002).

———. "The Fundamentalist Impact on Law, Politics and Constitutions in Iran, Pakistan and the Sudan." In *Fundamentalism and The State: Remaking Polities, Economies and Militance,* edited by Martin E. Marty and R. Scott Appleby. Chicago and London: The University of Chicago Press, 1993.

———. *Islam and Human Rights.* 3rd ed. Boulder, Colo.: Westview Press, 1999.

———. "Islam and the State: Religious Law and Legal Pluralism." *Cardozo Law Review* (February/March 1991).

———. "Islamization and Taxation in Pakistan." In *Islamic Reassertion in Pakistan: The Application of Islamic Laws in a Modern State,* edited by Anita M. Weiss, pp. 59–77. New York: Syracuse University Press, 1986.

———. "Law and Religion in Muslim Middle East." *The American Journal of Comparative Law* 35 (1987).

———. "Religious Law and Legal Pluralism: Islam and the State." *Cardozo Law Review* 4 (February/March 1991): pp. 1015–1056.

McGibbon, Rodd. "Local Politics and Leadership: Islam, Democracy and the Transformation of the Acehnese Elite." Paper presented at the Conference on the Historical Background of the Aceh Problem, Singapore, 28–29 May 2004.

MD, Mahfud. *Politik Hukum di Indonesia.* Jakarta: LP3ES, 1998.

Melayu, Hasnul Arifin. "Islam as an Ideology: The Political Thought of Tjokroaminoto." *Studia Islamika* 9, no. 3 (2002).

Memperjuangkan Syariat Islam: Kumpulan Pidato Fraksi Partai Bulan Bintang Pada Sidang Tahunan Majelis Permusyawaratan Rakyat Republik Indonesia Tahun 2000–2002. Jakarta: Sekretariat Fraksi PBB MPR RI, 2003.

"Mengenal Hizbut Tahrir: Partai Politik Islam Ideologis." Official booklet. N.p.: 2001.

Milani, Mohsen M. "The Transformation of the Velayat-e Faqih Institution: From Khomeini to Khamenei." *The Muslim World* 82 (July–October 1991) : pp. 175–190.

Miles, William. "Muslim Ethnopolitics and Presidential Elections in Nigeria." *Journal of Muslim Minority Affairs* 20, no. 2 (2000): pp. 229–241.

Milner, A. C. "Islam and the Muslim State." In *Islam in South-East Asia,* edited by M. B. Hooker. Leiden: E. J. Brill, 1983.

Moosa, Ebrahim. "The Dilemma of Islamic Rights Schemes." *Journal of Law and Religion* 15 (2000–2001): pp. 185–215.

Morris, E. "Aceh: Social Revolution and the Islamic Vision." In *Regional Dynamics of the Indonesian Revolution: Unity from Diversity,* edited by Audrey R. Kahin. Honolulu: University of Hawai'i Press, 1985.

Morris, Eugene E. "Islam and Politics in Aceh: A Study of Center-Periphery Relations in Indonesia." PhD diss., Cornell University, 1983.

Mozaffari, Mehdi. *Authority in Islam: From Muhammad to Khomeini.* London: M. E. Sharpe, 1987.

Muchsin, Misri A. "Tasawwuf di Aceh dalam Abad XX: Studi Pemikiran Teungku Haji Abdullah Ujong Rimba (1907–1983)." PhD diss., IAIN Sunan Kalijaga Yogyakarta, 2003.

Mudzhar, Atho. *Fatwa-fatwa Majelis Ulama Indonesia: Sebuah Studi tentang Pemikiran Hukum Islam di Indonesia, 1975–1988.* Jakarta: INIS, 1993.

Muhammad, Rusjdi Ali. *Revitalisasi Syari'at Islam di Aceh: Problem, Solusi dan Implementasi.* Jakarta: Logos, 2003.

Muzaffar, Chandra. "Islamisation of State and Society: Some Further Critical Remarks." In *Shari'a Law and the Modern Nation-State,* edited by Norani Othman. Kuala Lumpur: Sisters in Islam, 1994.

an-Na'im, Abdullahi Ahmed. "Political Islam in National Politics and International Relations." In *The Desecularization of the World: Resurgent Religion and World Politics,* edited by Peter L. Berger. Washington, D.C.: Ethics and Public Policy Center, 1999.

Nasution, Adnan Buyung. *The Aspiration for Constitutional Government in Indonesia: A Socio-Legal Study of the Indonesian Konstituante 1956–1959.* Jakarta: Pustaka Sinar Harapan, 1992.

Nielsen, Jorgen S. *Towards a European Islam.* London: Macmillan Press Ltd., 1999.

Nieuwenhuijze, C. A. O., van. *Aspects of Islam in Post-Colonial Indonesia: Five Essays.* The Hague: W. van Hoeve, 1958.

Nmehielle, Vincent O. "Sharia Law in the Northern States of Nigeria: To Implement or Not to Implement, the Constitutionality Is the Question." *Human Rights Quarterly* 26 (2004): pp. 730–759.

Noer, Deliar. *Administration of Islam in Indonesia.* Ithaca, N.Y.: Cornell Modern Indonesia Project, Southeast Asia Program, Cornell University, 1978.

———. *Gerakan Modern Islam di Indonesia 1900–1942.* Jakarta, LP3ES, 1980.

———. *Mohammad Hatta: Biografi Politik.* Jakarta: LP3ES, 1990.

———. *Partai Islam Di Pentas Nasional, 1945–1965.* Jakarta: Grafitipers, 1987.

Noori, A. Y., and S. H. Amin. *Legal and Political Structure of an Islamic State: The Implication for Iran and Pakistan.* Glasgow: Royson Limited, 1987.

Noorduyn, J. "Makasar and the Islamization of Bima." *Bijdragen tot de Taal-, Land-en Volkenkunde* 143 (1987): pp. 312–342.

Novossyolov, Dimitri B. "The Islamization of Welfare in Pakistan." In *Russia's Muslim Frontiers: New Directions in Cross-Cultural Analysis,* edited by Dale F. Eickelman. Bloomington and Indianapolis: Indiana University Press, 1993.

Nur, Fairus M., ed. *Syariat di Wilayah Syariat: Pernik-Pernik Islam di Nanggroe Aceh Darussalam.* Banda Aceh: Dinas Syariat Islam, 2002.

Panduan Dalam Memasyarakatkan Undang-Undang Dasar Negara Republik Indonesia Tahun 1945: Latar Belakang, Proses dan Hasil Perubahan. Jakarta: Sekretariat Jenderal MPR RI, 2003.

Pauker, Guy J. "Policy Implication of Political Institutionalization and Leadership Change in Southeast Asia." *Asian Affairs: An American Review* 13, no. 3 (1986).

Peach, Lucinda. *Legislating Morality: Pluralism and Religious Identity in Lawmaking.* Oxford: Oxford University Press, 2002.

Peacock, J. L. *Purifying the Faith: The Muhammadiyah Movement in Indonesian Islam.* San Francisco: Cummings Publishing Company, 1978.

Pedoman Pembinaan BAZIS: Hasil Pertemuan Nasional I BAZIS se-Indonesia tanggal 3–4 Maret 1992. Jakarta: Dirjen Bimas Islam Urusan Haji Departemen Agama, 1992.

Pedoman Zakat. Jakarta: Proyek Pembinaan Zakat dan Wakaf, 1992/1993.

Pelras, Christian. "Religion, Tradition and the Dynamics of Islamization in South Sulawesi." *Archipel* 29, no. 1 (1985): pp. 107–135.

"Pemandangan Umum Fraksi Partai Bulan Bintang MPR RI terhadap Hasil-Hasil Badan Pekerja Majelis dan Usul Pembentukan Komisi-Komisi Majelis pada Sidang Komisi A." In *Memperjuangkan Syariat Islam: Kumpulan Pidato Fraksi Partai Bulan Bintang Pada Sidang Tahunan Majelis Permusyawaratan Rakyat Republik Indonesia Tahun 2000–2002.* Jakarta: Sekretariat Fraksi PBB MPR RI, 2003.

Pembahasan Lima Rancangan Undang-Undang tentang Perubahan UU di Bidang Perpajakan (Buku 1B). Jakarta: Sekjend DPR RI, PPPI, 2000.

"Pendapat Akhir Fraksi Partai Bulan Bintang Terhadap Rancangan Putusan MPR RI Hasil Sidang Tahunan MPR RI 2001." In *Memperjuangkan Syariat Islam: Kumpulan Pidato*

Fraksi Partai Bulan Bintang Pada Sidang Tahunan Majelis Permusyawaratan Rakyat Republik Indonesia Tahun 2000–2002. Jakarta: Sekretariat Fraksi PBB MPR RI, 2003.

Peraturan Perundang-Undangan Pengelolaan Zakat. Jakarta: Departemen Agama RI, 2003.

Peters, Rudolph. "From Jurist's Law to Statute Law or What Happens When the Shari'a is Codified." In *Shaping the Current Islamic Reformation,* edited by B. A. Roberson. London: Frank Cass, 2003.

Pipes, Daniel. "Oil Wealth and Islamic Resurgence." In *Islamic Resurgence in the Arab World,* edited by Ali E. Hillal Dessouki. New York: Praeger, 1982.

Piscatori, James P. *Islam in a World of Nation-States.* Cambridge: Cambridge University Press, 1986.

Pixley, Michael M. "The Development and Role of the Seyhulislam in Early Ottoman History." *Journal of the American Oriental Society* 96 (1976).

Pola Kecenderungan Masyarakat Berzakat. Jakarta: PIRAC, 2002.

"Political Shari'a'?: Human Rights and Islamic Law in Northern Nigeria." *Human Rights Watch* 16, no. 9 (September 2004).

Preece, Jennifer Jackson. *Minority Rights: Between Diversity and Community.* Cambridge: Polity Press, 2005.

Purwoko, Dwi, et al. *Negara Islam: Percikan Pemikiran H. Agus Salim, K.H. Mas Mansyur, K.H. Hasyim Asy'ari, dan Mohammad Natsir.* Jakarta: Permata Artistika Kreasi, 2001.

al-Qaradawi, Yusuf. *Madkhal Li Dirasah al-Shari'a al-Islamiyya.* N.p., n.d.

al-Qattan, Manna' Khalil. *Wujub Tahkim al-Shari'a al-Islamiyya.* Cairo: Dar al-Tawzi' wa al-Nashr al-Islamiyya, 1987.

Quataert, Donald. *The Ottoman Empire, 1700–1922, New Approaches to European History.* Cambridge: Cambridge University Press, 2000.

Qutb, Muhammad. *Hawla Tatbiq al-Shari'a.* N.p.: Maktaba al-Sunna, n.d.

Rahardjo, Dawam. "Manajemen Zakat." In *Pedoman Pembinaan BAZIS: Hasil Pertemuan Nasional I BAZIS Se-Indonesia tanggal 3-4 Maret 1992.* Jakarta: Bimas Islam dan Urusan Haji, 1992.

Rakover, N. "Jewish Law and the State of Israel: Jewish Elements in Israeli Legislation." In *Law in Multicultural Societies: Proceedings of the IALL Meeting,* edited by E. I. Cuomo. Jerusalem: International Association of Law Libraries, 1989.

Ramadan, Abdel Azim. "Fundamentalist Influence in Egypt: The Strategies of the Muslim Brotherhood and the Takfir Groups." In *Fundamentalism and The State: Remaking Polities, Economies and Militance,* edited by Martin E. Marty and R. Scott Appleby. Chicago and London: the University of Chicago Press, 1993.

Ramage, Douglas E. *Politics in Indonesia: Democracy, Islam, and the Ideology of Tolerance.* London and New York: Routledge, 1997.

"Rekapitulasi Perolehan Suara Sah Untuk DPR RI." At http://www.kpu.go.id/suara/hasilsuara_dpr_sah.php. Accessed 8 December 2005.

Ricklefs, M. C. *History of Modern Indonesia since c. 1200,* 3rd ed. Stanford, Calif.: Stanford University Press, 2001.

———. *Mystic Synthesis in Java: A History of Islamization from the Fourteenth to the Early Nineteenth Centuries.* Norwalk: Eastbridge, 2006.

———. *Polarising Javanese Society: Islamic and Other Visions c. 1830–1930.* Singapore: Singapore University Press; Honolulu: University of Hawai'i Press; Leiden: KITLV Press, 2007.

———. "Religion, Politics and Social Dynamics in Java: Historical and Contemporary Rhymes." Paper presented at the 2007 Indonesia Update Conference, Canberra, 7 September 2007.

———. "Six Centuries of Islamization in Java." In *Conversion to Islam,* edited by N. Levtzion. New York: Holmes & Meier Publishers, 1979.

Riphenburg, Carol. "Afghanistan's Constitution: Success or Sham?" *Middle East Policy* 12, no. 1 (2005): pp. 31–43.

"Risalah Rapat Jum'at 3 September 1999." *Pembicaraan Tingkat III Pembahasan RUU tentang Pengelolaan Zakat.* Jakarta: Sekretariat Komisi VII Sekjen DPR RI, 1999.

"Risalah Rapat Komisi A ke-3 Sidang Tahunan MPR RI." *Buku Kelima Jilid I Risalah Rapat Komisi A MPR RI ke-1 s.d 5 Tanggal 4 s.d 8 Agustus 2002 Masa Sidang Tahunan MPR RI Tahun 2002.* Jakarta: Sekretariat Jenderal MPR RI, 2002.

"Risalah Rapat Paripurna ke-3 (Lanjutan) Sidang Tahunan MPR Tahun 2002." *Buku Keempat Risalah Rapat Paripurna MPR RI ke-1 s.d 7 Tanggal 1 s.d 11 Agustus 2002 Masa Sidang Tahunan MPR RI Tahun 2002.* Jakarta: Sekretariat Jenderal MPR RI, 2002.

"Risalah Rapat Paripurna ke-6 Lanjutan-2 Sidang Tahunan MPR Tahun 2002." *Buku Keempat. Risalah Rapat Paripurna MPR RI ke-1 s.d 7 Tanggal 1 s.d 11 Agustus 2002 Masa Sidang Tahunan MPR RI Tahun 2002.* Jakarta: Sekretariat Jenderal MPR RI, 2002.

"Risalah Rapat Paripurna ke-6 Sidang Tahunan MPR Tahun 2002." *Buku Kelima Jilid I Risalah Rapat Komisi A MPR RI ke-1 s.d 5 Tanggal 4 s.d 8 Agustus 2002 Masa Sidang Tahunan MPR RI Tahun 2002.* Jakarta: Sekretariat Jenderal MPR RI, 2002.

"Risalah Rapat Perumusan Panitia Ad Hoc I Badan Pekerja MPR RI." *Buku Kesatu Jilid I: Risalah Rapat Tertutup Risalah Rapat Perumusan Panitia Ad Hoc I Badan Pekerja MPR RI ke-1 s.d 4 tanggal 3 s.d 6 April 2002 Masa Sidang Tahunan MPR RI Tahun 2002.* Jakarta: Sekretariat Jenderal MPR RI, 2002.

"Risalah Rapat Pleno ke-3 Panitia Ad Hoc I Badan Pekerja MPR." *Buku Kedua Jilid 1 Risalah Rapat Panitia Ad Hoc I Badan Pekerja MPR RI ke-1 s.d 10 tanggal 11 Januari 2002 s.d 5 Maret 2002 Masa Sidang Tahunan MPR RI tahun 2002.* Jakarta: Sekretariat Jenderal MPR RI, 2002.

"Risalah Rapat Pleno ke-9 Panitia Ad Hoc I Badan Pekerja MPR." *Buku Kedua Jilid I: Risalah Rapat Panitia Ad Hoc I Badan Pekerja MPR RI ke-1 s.d 10 Tanggal 11 Januari 2002 s.d 5 Maret 2002 Masa Sidang Tahunan MPR RI tahun 2002.* Jakarta: Sekretariat Jenderal MPR RI, 2002.

"Risalah Rapat Pleno ke-17 Panitia Ad Hoc I Badan Pekerja MPR." *Buku Kedua Jilid 2 Risalah Rapat Panitia Ad Hoc I Badan Pekerja MPR RI ke-11 s.d 20 tanggal 11 Maret 2002 s.d 27 Maret 2002 Masa Sidang Tahunan MPR RI tahun 2002.* Jakarta: Sekretariat Jenderal MPR RI, 2002.

"Risalah Rapat Pleno ke-27 Panitia Ad Hoc I Badan Pekerja MPR." *Buku Kedua Jilid 3 Risalah Rapat Panitia Ad Hoc I Badan Pekerja MPR RI. ke-21 s.d 30 tanggal 28 Maret 2002 s.d 19 Juni 2002 Masa Sidang Tahunan MPR RI tahun 2002.* Jakarta: Sekretariat Jenderal MPR RI, 2002.

"Risalah Rapat Pleno ke-38 Panitia Ad Hoc I Badan Pekerja MPR RI." *Buku Kedua Jilid 4 Risalah Rapat Panitia Ad Hoc I Badan Pekerja MPR RI ke-31 s.d 38 Tanggal 20 Juni 2002 s.d 25 Juli 2002 Masa Sidang Tahunan MPR RI Tahun 2002.* Jakarta: Sekretariat Jenderal MPR RI, 2002.

"Risalah Rapat Pleno ke-44 Panitia Ad Hoc I Badan Pekerja MPR." *Buku Kedua Jilid 3C Risalah Rapat-Rapat Panitia Ad Hoc Badan Pekerja MPR.* Jakarta: Sekretariat Jenderal MPR RI, 2000.

Risalah Sidang Badan Penyelidik Usaha-usaha Persiapan Kemerdekaan Indonesia (BPUPKI) Panitia Persiapan Kemerdekaan Indonesia (PPKI), 3 ed. Jakarta: Sekretariat Negara Republik Indonesia, Ghalia Indonesia, 1995.

"Risalah Sinkronisasi ke-4 Panitia Ad Hoc I Badan Pekerja MPR RI." *Buku Kesatu Jilid 2 Risalah Rapat Sinkronisasi Panitia Ad Hoc I Badan Pekerja MPR RI ke-1 s.d 8 tanggal 27 s.d 30 Juni Masa Sidang Tahunan MPR RI Tahun 2002.* Jakarta: Sekretariat Jenderal MPR RI, 2002.

Rose, Gregory. "*Velayat e-Faqih* and the Recovery of Islamic Identity in the Thought of Ayatollah Khomeini." In *Religion and Politics in Iran,* edited by Nikki R. Keddie. New Haven, Conn.: Yale University Press, 1983.

Rosenthal, Erwin I. J. *Islam in the Modern National State.* Cambridge: Cambridge University Press, 1965.

Rossler, Martin. "Islamization and the Reshaping of Identities in Rural South Sulawesi." In *Islam in an Era of Nation-States: Politics and Religious Renewal in Muslim Southeast Asia,* edited by Robert W. Hefner and Patricia Horvatich. Honolulu: University of Hawai'i Press, 1997.

Rouffaer, G. P. "Vorstenlanden." *Adatrechtbundels,* XXXIV: *Java en Madoera.* 's-Gravenhage: Martinus Nijhoff, 1931.

Saby, Yusny. "The Ulama in Aceh: A Brief Historical Survey." *Studia Islamika Indonesian Journal for Islamic Studies* 9, no. 1 (2001): pp. 1–54.

Safwat, Safiya. "Islamic Laws in the Sudan." In *Islamic Law: Social and Historical Contexts,* edited by Aziz al-Azmeh. London & New York: Routledge, 1988.

Sahliyeh, Emile, ed. *Religious Resurgence and Politics in the Contemporary World.* Albany: State University of New York Press, 1990.

Salim, Arskal. *Etika Intervensi Negara: Perspektif Etika Politik Ibnu Taimiyah.* Jakarta: Logos, 1998.

———. "The Influential Legacy of the Dutch Islamic Policy on the Formation of Zakat (Alms) Policy in Modern Indonesia." *The Pacific Rim Law and Policy Journal* 15, no. 3 (2006): pp. 683–701.

———. *Partai Islam dan Relasi Agama Negara.* Jakarta: Puslit dan JPPR, 1999.

———. "Shari'a from Below in Aceh (1930s–1960s): Islamic Identity and the Right to Self Determination with Comparative Reference to the Moro Islamic Liberation Front (MILF)." *Indonesia and Malay World* 32 (March 2004): pp. 80–99.

———. "Shari'a in Indonesia's Current Transition: An Update." In *Shari'a and Politics of Modern Indonesia,* edited by Arskal Salim and Azyumardi Azra. Singapore: ISEAS, 2003.

———. "Zakat Administration in Politics of Indonesian New Order." In *Shari'a and Politics of Modern Indonesia,* edited by Arskal Salim and Azyumardi Azra. Singapore: ISEAS, 2003.

Salim, Arskal, and Azyumardi Azra "Introduction: The State and *Shari'a* in the Perspective of Indonesian Legal Politics." In *Shari'a and Politics in Modern Indonesia,* edited by Arskal Salim and Azyumardi Azra. Singapore: ISEAS, 2003.

Salleh, Muhammad Syukri. "Islamization of State and Society: A Critical Comment." In *Shari'a Law and the Modern Nation-State,* edited by Norani Othman. Kuala Lumpur: Sisters in Islam, 1994.

Samson, Allan. "Conception of Politics, Power, and Ideology in Contemporary Indonesia." In *Political Power and Communication in Indonesia,* edited by Karel D. Jackson and Lucian W. Pye. Berkeley and Los Angeles: University of California Press, 1978.

Sankari, Farouk A. "Islam and Politics in Saudi Arabia." In *Islamic Resurgence in the Arab World,* edited by Ali E. Hillal Dessouki. New York: Praeger, 1982.

Santos, Soliman M. *The Moro Islamic Challenge: Constitutional Rethinking for the Mindanao Peace Process.* Quezon: University of the Philippines Press, 2001.

Sarkaniputra, Murasa, et al. "Respon Institusi Pengelola Zakat terhadap Efektivitas Undang-Undang no. 38 tahun 1999." Jakarta: Lembaga Penelitian UIN Syarif Hidayatullah, 2002/2003.

Sarong, Hamid, "Mahkamah Syar'iyah dan Kewenangannya di Nanggroe Aceh Darussalam." In *Syariat di Wilayah Syariat: Pernik-Pernik Islam di Nanggroe Aceh Darussalam,* edited by Fairus M. Nur. Banda Aceh: Dinas Syariat Islam, 2002.

Schacht, Joseph. *Introduction to the Islamic Law.* Oxford: Clarendon Press, 1964.

———. "Problems of Modern Islamic Legislation." *Studia Islamica* 12 (1960).

Shochetman, Eliav. "Israeli Law and Jewish Law—Interaction and Independence: A Commentary." *Israel Law Review* 24, no. 3–4 (1990).

Schumpeter, Joseph. *Capitalism, Socialism, and Democracy.* 5th ed. London: Routledge, 1994.

Scott, James C. "Resistance without Protest and without Organization: Peasant Opposition to the Islamic Zakat and the Christian Tithe." *Comparative Studies in Society and History* 29 (July 1987): pp. 417–452.

Shaw, Stanford J. *History of the Ottoman Empire and Modern Turkey,* vol. I. Cambridge and New York: Cambridge University Press, 1976.

———. *The Jews of the Ottoman Empire and the Turkish Republic.* London: Macmillan, 1991.

Sidahmed, Abdel Salam. *Politics and Islam in Contemporary Sudan.* New York: St. Martin Press, 1996.

Siegel, J. T. *The Rope of God.* Berkeley and Los Angeles: University of California Press, 1969.

Sirajuddin. "Konsepsi Kenegaraan dalam Pemikiran A. Hasjmy." MA thesis, IAIN Ar-Raniry Banda Aceh, 1999.

Sirozi, Muhammad. "Secular-Religious Debates on the Indonesian National Education System: Colonial legacy and a Search for National Identity in Education." *Intercultural Education* 15, no. 2 (June 2004): pp. 123–139.

Sivan, Emmanuel, and Menachem Friedman, eds. *Religious Radicalism and Politics in the Middle East.* Albany: State University of New York Press, 1990.

Sjadzali, Munawir. *Islam dan Tata Negara: Ajaran Sejarah dan Pemikiran.* Jakarta: UI Press, 1993.

———. "Landasan Pemikiran Politik Hukum Islam dalam Rangka Menentukan Peradilan Agama di Indonesia." In *Hukum Islam di Indonesia: Pemikiran dan Praktek,* edited by Eddi Rudiana Arief et al. Bandung: Rosda Karya, 1991.

Skocpol, Theda. "Bringing the State Back In: Strategies of Analysis in Current Research." In *Bringing the State Back In,* edited by Peter B. Evans, Dietrich Rueschemeyer, and Theda Skocpol. Cambridge: Cambridge University Press, 1985.

Smart, Ninian. "Three Forms of Religious Convergence." In *Religious Resurgence: Contemporary Cases in Islam, Christianity and Judaism,* edited by Richard T. Antoun and Mary Elaine Hegland. New York: Syracuse University Press, 1987.

Smith, Anthony. *National Identity.* London: Penguin Books, 1991.

Smith, William C. *Islam in Modern History.* Princeton, N.J.: Princeton University Press, 1957.

Soekarno. "Nasionalisme, Islamisme dan Marxisme" In *Bung Karno dan Wacana Islam,* edited by Iman Toto K. Rahardjo and Herdianto WK. Jakarta: Grasindo, 2001.

Steenbrink, Karel A. *Beberapa Aspek Tentang Islam di Indonesia Abad ke-19.* Jakarta: Bulan Bintang, 1984.

Suminto, Aqib. *Politik Islam Hindia Belanda.* Jakarta: LP3ES, 1985.

Syah, Kaoy, and Lukman Hakim. *Keistimewaan Aceh dalam Lintasan Sejarah: Proses Pembentukan UU no. 44/1999.* Jakarta: PB Al-Washliyyah, 2000.

Syaifullah. *Gerak Politik dalam Masyumi.* Jakarta: Pustaka Utama Grafiti, 1997.

Syamsuddin, M. Din. "Usaha Pencarian Konsep Negara dalam Sejarah Pemikiran Politik Islam." *Jurnal Ulumul Qur'an* 4, no. 2 (1993).

Syamsuddin, Nazaruddin. *The Republican Revolt: A Study of the Acehnese Rebellion.* Singapore: Institute of Southeast Asian Studies, 1985.

Syihab, Habib M. Rizieq. *Dialog Piagam Jakarta: Kumpulan Jawaban.* Jakarta: Pustaka Ibnu Sidah, 2000.

Taji-Farouki, Suha. *A Fundamental Quest: Hizb al-Tahrir and the Search for the Islamic Caliphate.* London: Grey Seal, 1996.

———. "Islamic State Theories and Contemporary Realities." In *Islamic Fundamentalism,* edited by A. S. Sidahmed and A. Ehteshani. Boulder, Colo.: Westview Press, 1996.

Tamadonfar, Mehran. "Islam, Law, and Political Control in Contemporary Iran." *Journal for the Scientific Study of Religion* 40, no. 2 (2001).

———. *The Islamic Polity and Political Leadership, Fundamentalism, Sectarianism and Pragmatism.* Boulder, Colo.: Westview Press, 1989.

Tata Tertib/Tata Laksana Madjlis Ulama dalam Propinsi Daerah Istimewa Atjeh dan Peraturan2 Lainnya. Banda Aceh: Sekretariat Madjlis Ulama Propinsi Daerah Istimewa Atjeh, 1970.

Tessler, Mark. "Religion and Politics in the Jewish State of Israel." In *Religious Resurgence and Politics in the Contemporary World,* edited by Emile Sahliyeh. Albany: State University of New York Press, 1990.

"The Religion-State Relationship and the Right to Freedom of Religion or Belief: A Comparative Textual Analysis of the Constitution of Predominantly Muslim Countries." http://www.uscirf.gov/countries/global/comparative_constitutions/03082005/Study0305.pdf. Accessed 7 August 2005.

Tibi, Bassam. *Arab Nationalism: Between Islam and the Nation-State,* 3rd ed. New York: St. Martin's Press, 1997.

———. *Islam Between Culture and Politics.* New York: Palgrave, 2001.

Tonang, Andi Lolo. "Beberapa Pemikiran tentang Mekanisme Badan Amil Zakat." In *Zakat dan Pajak,* edited by B. Wiwoho. Jakarta: PT Bina Rena Pariwara, 1992.

Travis, Hannibal. "Freedom or Theocracy? Constitutionalism in Afghanistan and Iraq." *Northwestern University Journal of International Human Rights* 3, no. 4 (Spring 2005).

Turabi, Hasan. *Islam, Democracy, the State, and the West: A Round Table with Dr. Hasan Turabi.* Edited by A. Lowrie. Tampa, Fla.: The World of Islam Studies Enterprise, 1993.

Vatikiotis, P. J. *Islam and the State.* London, New York, and Sydney: Croom Helm, 1987.

Vikør, Knut S. "The Shariʿa and the Nation State: Who Can Codify the Divine Law?" In *The Middle East in a Globalized World,* edited by Bjørn Olav Utvik and Knut S. Vikør. Bergen: Nordic Society for Middle Eastern Studies, 2000.

Vogel, Frank E. "Islamic Governance in the Gulf: A Framework for Analysis, Comparison, and Prediction." In *The Persian Gulf at The Millennium: Essays in Politics, Economy, Security, and Religion,* edited by Gary G. Sick and Lawrence G. Potter. New York: St. Martin's Press, 1997.

———. *Islamic Law and Legal System: Studies of Saudi Arabia.* Leiden, Boston, and Köln: Brill, 2000.

Voll, John. "Old Ulama Families and Ottoman Influence in Eighteenth Century Damascus." *American Journal of Arabic Studies* 3 (1975).

Wahono, Untung. *Penegakan Syariat Islam dan Koalisi Partai.* Jakarta: Pustaka Tarbiatuna, 2003.

Ward, Ken. *The Foundation of the Partai Muslimin Indonesia.* Ithaca, N.Y.: Cornell Modern Indonesia Project, 1970.

Watt, W. Montgomery. *Muhammad at Medina.* London: Oxford University Press, 1956.

———. *Muhammad: Prophet and Statesman.* London and New York: Oxford University Press, 1974.

Weiss, Anita M., ed. *Islamic Reassertion in Pakistan: The Application of Islamic Laws in a Modern State.* New York: Syracuse University Press, 1986.

Wertheim, W. F. "Religious Reform Movements in South and South-East Asia." *Archives de Sociologie des Religions* 12 (1961): pp. 53–62.

Wiwoho, B., ed., *Zakat dan Pajak.* Jakarta: PT Bina Rena Pariwara, 1992.

Woodward, Mark R. *Islam in Java: Normative Piety and Mysticism in Sultanate of Yogyakarta.* Tucson: The University of Arizona Press, 1989.

Yamin, Muhammad. *Naskah Persiapan Undang-undang Dasar 1945,* vol. I. N.p.: Yayasan Prapanca, 1959.

al-Yassini, Ayman. *Religion and State in the Kingdom of Saudi Arabia.* Boulder, Colo., and London: Westview Press, 1985.

Ybarra, Josep-Antoni. "The Zaqat in Muslim Society: An Analysis of Islamic Economic Policy." *Social Science Information* 35 (1996).

Zada, Khamami. *Islam Radikal: Pergulatan Ormas-Ormas Islam Garis Keras di Indonesia.* Jakarta: Teraju, 2002.

Zaid, Abdulaziz Mohammed. *The Islamic Law of Bequest.* London: Scorpion, 1986.

Zallum, Abdul Qadim. *al-Afkar al-Siyasiyya.* Beirut: Dar al-Ummah, 1994.

Zayas, Farishta G de. *The Law and Philosophy of Zakat: The Islamic Social Welfare System.* Damascus: al-Jadidah Printing Press, 1960.

Zubaida, Sami. *Islam, the People and the State: Essays on Political Ideas and Movements in the Middle East.* London and New York: Routledge, 1989.

———. *Law and Power in the Islamic World.* London and New York: I. B. Tauris, 2003.

Zysow, A. "Zakat." In *The Encylopaedia of Islam,* vol XI. New Edition, 2002.

Index